Where the Eagle Landed

Where the Eagle Landed

The Mystery of the German Invasion of Britain, 1940

PETER HAINING

ROBSON BOOKS

First published in Great Britain in 2004 by Robson Books, The Chrysalis Building, Bramley Road, London W10 6SP

An imprint of Chrysalis Books Group plc

British Library Cataloguing in Publication Data
A catalogue record for this title is available from the British Library.

ISBN 1 86105 750 4

Typeset by SX Composing DTP, Rayleigh, Essex
Printed by Creative Print & Design (Wales), Ebbw Vale

This book is dedicated to the memory of
DENNIS WHEATLEY
who inspired my interest in
an intriguing episode of history

'What next, then, if the British and French armies either surrender or are annihilated, as the Germans say they will be? The first invasion of England since 1066? England's bases on the Continent, barring a last-minute miracle, are gone. The lowlands just across the Channel and the narrow southern part of the North Sea, which it has always been a cardinal part of British policy to defend, are in enemy hands. And the French Channel ports which linked Britain with its French ally are lost. Most people here think Hitler will try now to conquer England.'

William Shirer
Berlin Diary, 29 May 1940

Contents

Foreword

In July 1940, the all-conquering forces of Nazi Germany stood on the coast of France with England, the greatest prize in their Führer's vast campaign of empire-building, literally in sight across the sullen waters of the English Channel. For years, Hitler had admired his adversary's inherent strengths and sense of destiny, which he believed to be similar to that of his own *Herrenvolk*. But now the defiance and belligerence of the English towards him – in particular that of their prime minister, Winston Churchill – were forcing him and a number of his cohorts towards an inevitable decision: an invasion and conquest of the embattled little island had become necessary.

That summer, when the likelihood of an invasion was a daily threat to the people of England, one of the most intriguing and persistent legends of World War Two was born – that German troops *did* land on the coast of East Anglia in a prelude to the invasion that was then only weeks, perhaps even days, away. It is a legend that has inspired writers such as Graham Greene (*The Lieutenant Died Last*), the filmmaker Alberto Cavalcanti (*Went The Day Well?*) and, of course, Jack Higgins, whose 1975 novel *The Eagle Has Landed* was an international bestseller and became a very popular film. But all of these stories are *fiction*.

There are, however, people in East Anglia who believe that the Nazi jackboot *was* planted on English soil – just as surely, though by no means for as prolonged a time, as it was on the

Channel Islands – and this book is their story told through personal narratives, contemporary reports, newspaper and magazine accounts, as well as a number of recently declassified documents from the National Archives, formerly the Public Record Office, based at Kew.

Where the Eagle Landed recounts the determined and often desperate measures of the people of eastern England – in company with the local authorities and the army, navy and air forces – to keep the invaders out of this vulnerable part of the country, and it tells how – and where – some of Hitler's men did make a landing. It also reveals the truth about the rumours that the bodies of scores of badly burned and scorched Germans were found washed up on the east coast and were spirited away by the military under a veil of secrecy. And it investigates the claims that these corpses may not have been German at all – but the bodies of British troops dressed in Nazi uniforms for a practice invasion that went disastrously wrong.

Further, the book examines the mysterious events that occurred at the isolated little Suffolk coastal village of Shingle Street, which had been evacuated of every man, woman and child earlier in the spring of 1940. Here, it was rumoured, tests were carried out on weapons of mass destruction – facts that have been kept secret for over half a century.

The mystery of where the German eagle landed has constantly fascinated me during the many years I have lived in East Anglia. It has several times been discussed in the media, including television, and is an enduring topic of local gossip. Yet now it is possible to unravel the facts, thanks to two eyewitness reports and the dogged research of my late friend, W O G Lofts, who bequeathed to me his files of information on the subject when he died in 1997. In the intervening years, I have retrodden the path he explored and broadened his research in order to write this book.

In particular, I have gathered information about East Anglia's centuries-old tradition as an 'Invasion Coast' and come to appreciate just why the region was such a focus of interest when the Germans were first formulating their invasion plan codenamed 'Operation Sea Lion'. My enquiries have also brought to light facts about the remarkable group of men who sought to keep England safe from a landing by devising a mind-boggling variety of ingenious inventions and schemes that formed what Churchill colourfully referred to as 'The Wizard War'.

Involved in this story, too, are the fighter pilots of the RAF and the Luftwaffe who battled for supremacy over the east coast; the soldiers who formed the pioneer British special operations force and the first German *kommandos*, who, in their different ways, sought to gain a foothold on the coasts of France and England; and, in particular, the seamen who crewed the English motor torpedo boats (MTBs) and German torpedo craft, the *Schnellboots* (fast boats) known as E-boats ('E' standing for 'Enemy'), and who, night after night throughout that long hot summer of 1940, regularly came within firing range of one another on the dangerous waters of the North Sea. Together, their stories finally resolve another great Second World War mystery.

Chapter 1

The Enemy in Sight

The North Sea was, for once, almost completely still, the normally heaving grey waters shimmering in the early-morning sun as they broke gently along the shore of the east coast in Suffolk. Against the sweep of blue horizon, a number of dark oblong shapes could be seen passing by: merchant ships moving in an endless procession to the south and the comparative safety of the Thames Estuary.

It was a perfect late July morning in 1940 – a day when the war seemed as far away as the ships, which, in fact, was not that far from the truth. For everyone living in East Anglia knew that the enemy was now only a few miles away on the coast of France and the Low Countries.

To the young man walking on the headland towards a beach such thoughts had no place in his mind, although the rolls of barbed wire and steel and concrete defences all along the seashore were a constant reminder that these were dangerous times. A German invasion was believed to be inevitable – even imminent.

Jeff Fisher, though, was intent on some sunbathing and perhaps a swim in the sea – although he knew it was unwise to go out any distance because of the hidden mines, both English and German. Like other young men and women living on this part of the coast, he had found out that there were always gaps in the defences that could be squeezed through, and more often than not the patrolling soldiers would turn a blind eye to a bit of harmless fun. Especially, of course, where the girls were concerned. Not that the army men looked away when they turned up in one-piece bathing suits or thin summer frocks tucked into their knickers to let their legs get brown.

The thoughts that were preoccupying Jeff concerned the job he was hoping to get the following day. Too young to be called up into the services, he had applied for an apprenticeship in the local engineering company where his father worked. It would be hard work, he knew, but a lot better than school.

Even though he was still in his teens, Jeff was not immune to the war. He had seen several attacks on the coastal shipping – the roar of explosions and the sight of flames leaping into the sky carrying across the bay. He had also seen several dogfights between British fighters and the Luftwaffe and the memory of one plane plunging into the sea, its engine screaming and on fire, was still very vivid.

This day, however, would prove to be one of the most memorable of his life. For he had walked only a short distance on the sands before he came across a small pile of objects that immediately excited his interest. Some were clearly pieces of wrapping paper, scraps of food and cigarette butts. The other, more distinctive item, was a cap – an unfamiliar cap with a golden-eagle badge on the front. One glance and he knew it must be a *German* officer's cap.

But what was it doing here? A little shiver ran down Jeff's spine as an idea flashed through his mind. If it was German, had there been a landing? And, if so, what had happened to the men involved? The answers to these questions would take years to resolve.

In fact, only now is it possible to reveal Jeff Fisher's 'find' as a most significant clue in helping to solve one of World War Two's most enduring mysteries – not *if* the German eagle landed on English soil, but *when* and *where*.

*

Almost as soon as the war with Germany was declared on 3 September 1939, East Anglia became a focus of enemy attacks. First, the heaving North Sea shipping lanes along the coast were targeted by German aircraft, followed not long afterwards by air raids on the busy ports and harbours along the east coast. Later it was the turn of the aerodromes, military installations and towns of Norfolk, Suffolk and Essex to be bombed and machine-gunned. The area became, in a sentence, Britain's first battlefront of the war.

Ever since 1936, when Hitler's march into the Rhineland had made war seem inevitable to the British Chiefs of Staff, there were also a number of military figures, politicians and even civilians who were convinced that the Nazis viewed East Anglia as a prime target for invasion. This conviction would harden in the following years, inspiring the minds and energies of a wide range of people in all walks of life. It would not finally disappear until Hitler's much-vaunted Third Reich was on the verge of collapse.

The threat was to hang like the Sword of Damocles over the people of the east coast. For many months they saw better than anyone else the attacks on the shipping lanes and the aerial battles above their heads and never doubted for a moment the observation of people like the bestselling novelist Nevil Shute – who would play a significant role in creating defence systems for the east coast – writing in 1956: 'The war seemed to me, in June 1940, to be desperately serious, and England in imminent peril of invasion.'

Most historians of World War Two describe the ten-month period between September 1939 and the opening of the Battle of Britain in July 1940 as the 'Phoney War', because, while the major conflict raged in Europe, there was apparently little action in this country. That, though, was not at all the case in East Anglia.

The shipping lanes that ran from rugged Cromer Knoll in Norfolk to the Thames Estuary were regarded as probably the most dangerous waters around the British Isles, continually heaving with mountainous waves and lashed by gale-force winds. Yet this was the route that convoys of vessels bringing vital supplies from across the Atlantic and the north of England had to sail – sometimes as many as three hundred of them at a time – all making their way cautiously through the minefields laid to *protect* them by the Royal Navy and those planted by the Germans to *destroy* them.

Rarely were these lanes wide enough for the merchantmen to sail more than two abreast. Just to add to the dangers, the Luftwaffe rarely let a day pass without appearing to bomb them. In the main unarmed, they had to rely on the protection of the Royal Navy's cruisers, minesweepers and occasional motor torpedo boats.

Even though the Navy had bases at Yarmouth, Lowestoft, Brightlingsea and Harwich, their resources were invariably stretched to the limit by the sheer numbers of merchantmen and their vulnerability – spread out as they were across mile after mile of the turbulent North Sea. A few of the ships did try to protect themselves with bizarre devices: wires attached to rockets, which they fired across the path of enemy aircraft; kites and balloons to try to distract the pilots; and even fireworks that were actually quite harmless!

The RAF flew daily patrols along the coast doing their best to protect the ships. Unfortunately, Fighter Command could answer calls only from convoys actually under attack, and their fighters too often arrived on the scene after the enemy had carried out his raid and disappeared into the lowering winter clouds.

For those people who lived on the east coast, the roar of attacking aircraft, the thump of exploding bombs and the telltale columns of smoke rising on the horizon soon became almost everyday events. Some of these incidents were more terrible than others. On 8 January 1940, for example, the London steamer, *Upminster*, was attacked off Lowestoft by two low-flying German aircraft, which dropped several bombs, machine-gunned the vessel and killed the captain and two crewmembers. Even the ten men who managed to escape in a small boat had to run the gauntlet of another attack before they were picked up. Two days later, a second steamer, the 5,123-ton *Traviata*, struck a mine, burst into flames amidships and sank.

In the last week of that month, a number of merchant ships in the vicinity of Yarmouth were subjected to repeat attacks by German aircraft that released dozens of bombs, which were so powerful they even shook buildings on land. Reporting these raids, the *East Anglian Daily Times* informed its readers, 'For the first time Yarmouth has been witness to aerial activity of a kind that it has been anxious not to have connected with its name.'

On the morning of 30 January it was the turn of the people of Southwold to see bombing at first hand, when the SS *Royal Crown* was set on fire. After fifteen members of the crew had rowed ashore – the local lifeboat rescued another ten – the ruined vessel drifted into shore and beached itself at Covehithe. For several hours, the Auxiliary Fire Service used a longshore boat as a fire float to battle the flames, only to be subjected at one stage to a machine-gun attack from another lurking German raider.

Trawlers, in particular, suffered from the Germans' war of attrition off the east coast. Several unexpectedly caught mines in their trawls, which exploded as they were being drawn in, causing havoc on board. Others were frequently strafed and bombed while trying to land precious catches of fish.

Skipper Arthur Moore of the Lowestoft trawler, *Celita*, was just one among many seamen to be on the end of an attack that winter. Thankfully, he and his crew survived the terrifying ordeal so that he could recount his experiences:

The German plane circled and, coming down only a few yards above our mast, he loosed off at us with a machine-gun. All the crew were grouped on the foredeck gutting the fish we'd just taken out of the net and if the gunner's aim had been more accurate we should have been in a bad spot. As it was, the bullets only went through the funnel or glanced off the rails.

Cargo ships, too, were treated to similar violence, as were several of the lightships anchored off the coast between the Wash and the River Thames. As sitting targets with no real means of defence, these vessels suffered horrendous losses in the early months of 1940, with crewmen killed on board or alternately when trying desperately to reach the shore.

During the month of January alone, a total of eleven ships were sunk off the east coast in the 'North Sea War'. In the weeks that followed, the Admiralty at last began to catch up with arming the merchant ships with machine guns from the Home Fleet. By April, the situation had improved somewhat, thanks to the recruitment of navy gunners who were transferred from ship to ship for voyages along the dangerous coast.

In the interim the enemy had grown bolder, though, and a report to the Admiralty in February stated that during one night alone a total of 110 mines had been laid in the Orford Ness–Shipwash Bank area off Harwich 'without interference'. Because clearing mines was such a painstaking and dangerous business, it was decided to supply the trawlers with a new sweeping device that had been designed to deal more effectively with any magnetic mines that might be swept into their nets.

However, no sooner had the captains mastered this piece of equipment than they found themselves having to cope with the menace of U-boats. The enemy submarines were prowling the North Sea shipping lanes at night and rising unexpectedly to the surface to fire their torpedoes. Two incidents off the coast of Suffolk will serve for many more to illustrate this grim time when explosions would rend the darkened skies, emphasising to those on land just how close the enemy was.

On the night of 28 February, a huge ball of smoke and flames fourteen miles out to sea signalled the torpedoing of the 4,350-ton *Mirella*, which sank in less than two minutes. Only sixteen members of her crew were able to scramble into the lifeboats and beach at Aldeburgh at first light the following day. That same day another ship, the *Marie Rose*, was torpedoed even closer to land. Ten crewmembers lost their lives this time, but two groups of men were able to reach the safety of land. According to an *East Anglian Daily Times* report, 'Nine members of the *Marie Rose*'s crew were found on the shore at Haven House suffering from exposure; and a further seven were rescued from a small boat off Sizewell.'

The sinking of the *Marie Rose* was an event that left quite an impression on one young man. Jeff Fisher heard all about the bedraggled seamen being brought into his hometown and the incident was never far from his thoughts when he later came to appreciate the significance of the German mementoes he discovered.

During this period of raids on the east coast shipping lines, the Luftwaffe occasionally crossed the coast, but rarely took any action. On 3 February, for instance, a pair of enemy bombers flew over Southwold Pier and headed north. Although there was no time for the alarm to be sounded, some local residents walking along the seafront did wonder whether this intrusion might mark a new phase in the war. They were right to be apprehensive – although their answer was a little while in coming.

In fact, it would be several months before the German campaign of attacks switched to mainland England on Thursday, 11 July – inaugurating the period known famously in history as 'the Battle of Britain' and bringing the attacks right to the front doors of East Anglians.

Dawn had only just broken on that July morning when a lone Dornier 17M, the black-and-white cross emblems unmistakable on its fuselage and wings, flew in across the North Sea towards Lowestoft. Any thoughts that it might be on a mission to attack the shipping lanes were quickly dispelled.

The aircraft was, it later transpired, carrying out the first raid of Germany's operation codenamed '*Kanalkampf*', directed against the ports of the east coast as part of a plan to destroy Britain's naval strength. This was, though, to be only the prelude to the Luftwaffe's major offensive against the nation's aerodromes, radar installations and aircraft factories. These two phases would then be followed by invasion, it was said, *when* the Führer deemed the time was right.

The mission of the Dornier from the Holzhammer Squadron based in Arras was to commence a *blitzkrieg* against Britain similar to that which had enabled German forces to overrun much of Europe with such terrifying speed. The day was cloudy and overcast with heavy rain falling as the invader circled Lowestoft harbour and dropped ten 110lb bombs over the cluster of ships.

Just as the Dornier was turning for home, however, a lone Hurricane swept in from the southwest, its eight Browning machine guns blazing. At the controls sat Squadron Leader Peter Townsend, the commander of 85 Squadron based at Martlesham near Ipswich, a man later to become famous for his love affair with the king's younger daughter, Princess Margaret. After an early radar warning, Townsend had decided to take on the lone German raider himself – but so heavy was the rain as he crossed the coast at Southwold that he had to slide open his cockpit cover to be sure of his enemy's position before opening fire.

Although the Hurricane put more than two hundred bullets into the fuselage of the Dornier – all striking the raider with what Townsend would recall as 'small dancing yellow flames' – the German managed to escape into the heavy clouds and return safely to base. By so doing, the pilot denied Townsend the first 'kill' of this new phase of the war.

That honour would, though, fall later that same morning to another pilot who now enjoys almost mythic status in the wartime history of the RAF, Squadron Leader Douglas Bader. Bader had lost both legs in a peacetime flying accident, yet managed through a mixture of skill and cussedness to qualify as a fighter pilot. He had not long been appointed squadron leader of 242 Squadron, based at the newly commissioned aerodrome of Coltishall near Norwich, and was now at the controls of a Hurricane in pursuit of a second Dornier 17M that had been spotted crossing the coast.

Low cloud was still hampering flying and had enabled the Dornier's gunner to beat off two Spitfires near Yarmouth only minutes before Bader appeared. The legless air ace had just enough time to let off two bursts before the enemy disappeared into the murk.

When Bader returned to base he felt sure the German must have escaped him. But within the hour the station received a report that a Dornier had, in fact, been seen crashing into the North Sea just after the squadron leader's engagement, leaving three crewmembers to swim for their lives. For perhaps the first – and last – time in the war, Bader was truly modest about his achievement. 'It was a lucky shot for a new CO,' he said.

Before the day was over, the area was attacked again by four German aircraft that emerged out of the clouds above Martlesham and dropped a total of eighteen high-explosive bombs on the airfield. Fortunately, their aim was impaired by the driving rain and the bombs all fell on the perimeter without causing any casualties and doing very little actual damage to buildings. Other 'terror attacks' – as they were referred to in the media – in the following days targeted Lowestoft, Felixstowe and Ipswich.

Stories of these raids on the mainland were soon filling the regional newspapers, BBC radio bulletins and the conversations of local people. Their reactions varied from a resigned acceptance to outrage, such as that of an unnamed farm labourer living at Eyke, a little village near Hollesley Bay on the Suffolk coast. He was interviewed by a representative of the

Mass Observation Unit who made visits to communities all over the region throughout the war scrupulously noting down the minutiae and talk of everyday life. Copies of their invaluable notes are still kept in the group's archives at Sussex University. The man from Eyke did not beat about the bush in his views:

> They never ought to have been invented, them bloody things. If everyone stayed in their own country, there'd be none of this trouble. There must be an awful lot of dead people out there, piles of them, German or British, it don't make no difference. There's one thing which ought to happen and stop all this. There ought to be an earthquake in France and swallow the whole bloody lot up, guns, men, tanks and all. That's the only way to stop war. There'll never be no end till they stop having armies. No one wants to fight. They all have to go now. We all ought to stay at home and do nothing. That'd stop it.

There was also an understandable concern among people living on the east coast to be able to identify the different types of aircraft – friend and foe – that were now filling their skies with sound and fury. Such details as were known – or could be published – began to appear in the national press as well as specialist magazines such as *Flight* and *Aeroplane*. They were required reading for every small boy.

Most numerous among the planes was the single-seater Hawker Hurricane that had been developed in the thirties and constituted two-thirds of the RAF strength at the outbreak of war. Its compatriot, the Spitfire, had not become operational until 1938, but its greater speed and manoeuvrability soon made it popular with pilots, not to mention a legend with the public that summer. There was a special affection locally for the Spitfire as its creator, Reginald J Mitchell, had carried out many of his high-speed trial flights from Felixstowe inspiring rumours about a new plane 'jist about too fast ter see', according to one early eyewitness walking his dog in Hollesley Bay.

The Dornier DM17s with their 2,200lb bomb loads were to prove the most persistent raiders, followed by the Messerschmidt 110 fighter-bombers, whose main purpose was to cut through the British defences to open a path for the heavy bombers. Both were often to be seen during the early days of the Luftwaffe's campaign, making many lightning hit-and-run raids on targets all over Suffolk and Norfolk.

The Heinkel 111 and the twin-engined Junkers 88 fighter-bombers were used mostly on bombing operations as well as for laying mines off the coast. Notable by its absence was the Messerschmidt 109 fighter, which was known to match the Spitfire in performance, but was limited in range. Equally, the fearsome Junkers 87 'Stuka' dive-bomber, which had been such a success in the European theatre of war, but proved no match for the RAF's Hurricanes and Spitfires.

In between the appearance of the lone Dornier and the beginning of the Battle of Britain, there was one particular tragedy that gave the clearest possible indication of the nature of the German threat to the east coast and its people. On 30 April, the resort town of Clacton was the scene of the first civilian casualties inflicted by the Luftwaffe.

The tragedy followed hard on an impudent raid in broad daylight the previous week, when a German seaplane had landed just two miles off the coast of nearby Felixstowe and begun laying mines. Even when the guns on the nearby foreshore had opened up, the raider leisurely completed its mission before taking to the skies. It left eyewitnesses dumbfounded – and provoked feverish speculation all along the coast.

Then, on 30 April, a Heinkel 111 was also spotted laying mines off Harwich. An AA battery on the shore opened fire and managed to damage the aircraft's tail. As the German flew, wavering, across the sky, he turned first out to sea and then switched direction and began a descent towards Clacton.

As the Heinkel plunged towards the ground, it just missed a recreation ground and ploughed instead into a row of houses. The mines it was still carrying exploded thunderously, damaging fifty dwellings and blowing the windows out of every building within half a mile. The four crewmembers were killed instantly along with two local residents. A total of 132 men, women and children required treatment for their injuries.

Although the crash was reported both on the radio and in the papers, rumours offered several wildly differing versions of the event that provide another indication of the mood of the times when gathered by the Mass Observation Unit. According to one account by a woman from Felixstowe, 'My sister said she thought the plane crashed on purpose. The Germans knew they had to come down, so they thought they would do some damage.' Another story by a Chelmsford man claimed that the plane had crashed near Clacton Station. 'It was full of mines and damaged two rows of houses,' he maintained, 'and killed 100 people, mostly children.'

It was just such a mixture of fact and fiction that also fuelled the rumours that an invasion was imminent on the east coast that summer of 1940.

Although the people of East Anglia were soon able to recognise the aircraft battling in the skies above them, they knew little about the sophisticated defence system of fighter groups that had been set up across the countryside to counter the German aerial threat. Nor did they know about the rapidly developing radar system with its string of listening stations along the coast – although the purpose of the tall masts on Bawdsey Point, at Hopton, Dunwich and other locations was the subject of much speculation.

They were ignorant, too, of the fact that discussions about the possibility of invasion had been a regular topic among the inner circles of government and the Chiefs of Staff in Whitehall since the previous year. Indeed, General Sir Walter Kirke, commander-in-chief of the Home Forces, had been ordered to set in motion a plan to prepare for just such a threat – codenamed 'Julius Caesar' – and he had quickly identified what he believed to be a particularly vulnerable area. As a result, the general issued instructions that 'a suitable proportion of troops who would normally be at home should be disposed within easy reach of the east coast'.

It was a fact that, by January 1940, all the professional soldiers of the East Anglian regiments were serving abroad and their places would have to be taken by Territorials or recent recruits. To this end, several army infantry divisions that were not fully equipped, or had not completed sufficient training to be sent to fight in France, were earmarked for the operation.

General Kirke also ordered that two armoured divisions of almost three hundred light tanks and a cavalry division were to be kept in reserve. If any airborne invasion by German forces took place, he instructed, the invaders were to be 'cordoned off by such troops as are available until the armour or horseback troops arrive to deal with them'.

The proposed deployment of novice soldiers unused to modern mobile warfare would probably have done little to calm the anxieties of the locals if they had known anything about Operation Julius Caesar. Nor would the fact that there was a shortage of equipment for them. Yet the men of the 55th Division were speedily moved into Suffolk while the 18th Division headed for Norfolk – each group establishing garrisons along the coast and settling into a not always easy alliance with local inhabitants.

There is no doubt that the ordinary soldiers soon got bored. Most of them had too much time on their hands and very little money in their pockets with which to seek amusement – after deductions, it was estimated that many only had a shilling (5p) per day to spend. Nonetheless, a great deal of voluntary work was carried out to provide these men with comforts and keep them amused.

Plans had also been put into place in case East Anglia should become isolated from the government in London by an enemy invasion. It was to have its own regional 'Government of East Anglia' under the charge of a commissioner, Sir Will Spens, a canny Scotsman and former vice-chancellor of Cambridge University. His authority throughout the area in the event that the worst might happen would be absolute.

The concept of an autonomous regional body such as this was unique in British history. The 'government' was also to have its own 'war room' (in Cambridge) and a series of secure lines of communication to the local authorities, the Air Raid Precautions (ARP) organisations, the police and fire services and the armed forces throughout Suffolk, Norfolk and Cambridgeshire in readiness for any German invasion.

Plans were also put in place for 'War Zone Courts' to deal with civilian offenders or public unrest. Two judges were available to travel immediately by police car to any area where suspects had been arrested. Trials were to take place in a market town 'nearest to, but outside, the fighting area in which the arrest has been made'. There was even a suggestion that, in a real emergency, martial law should be declared, but an official directive from London informed Sir Will Spens, 'In the event of invasion by sea or air, the military authorities have such powers as military needs and the general situation requires, without any declaration of martial law.'

Secret these plans may have been from the people, but the truth was that, ever since the declaration of war, events throughout the region had gone a long way towards preparing them for the crucial and dangerous days of that summer when Britain stood at the crossroads of its fate. The war was to prove the first really to involve civilians. Certainly, East Anglians and Londoners had experienced raids from the Zeppelin bombers in World War One, but now everyone was to be affected by regulations of all sorts, food rationing, shortage of clothing and hardware and the restrictions of national security.

The winter of 1939–40 had also brought the coldest spell to East Anglia for 45 years with day after day of leaden skies and freezing temperatures, testing everyone's resolve. On 17 January, the River Thames froze for the first time since 1888, and ten days later the whole country was swept by the worst storm of the century.

For those who lived on the east coast, each day presented scenes that would not have looked out of place in the Arctic Circle. Snow blocked many of the roads and railway lines, and on the beaches about ten yards of the sea along its edge was 'frozen to a white hard snow in the waves', according to one eyewitness. There was no letup in this weather in February, either, which brought about widespread sickness. Severe colds and influenza were reported everywhere, hitting the working population throughout the region.

As if all this were not hard enough to bear, food rationing came in on 9 January, with each person being allocated four ounces of bacon or ham, a similar amount of butter and twelve ounces of sugar per week. To obtain their meagre supplies, housewives were required to present ration books to their shopkeepers, who would cut out the appropriate coupons.

Meat rationing followed on 11 March, although this had a less dramatic effect on East Anglia than many other parts of the country. In general, the country people found their own solution for the shortage, taking to the fields with their guns and traps to kill rabbits, pigeons and even, occasionally, blackbirds.

Drink and cigarettes became increasingly scarce, too. Many public houses started to ration their customers and as the price of a pint rose – to one shilling and threepence (7p) by 1944 – so did the making of home brews and illegal spirits. For smokers, the utility cigarette known as a Pasha was little better than the roll-your-own varieties made from any number of plants and leaves, including chopped straw, blackberry leaves and shredded chrysanthemums! Even under such circumstances, spirits were not entirely dampened, as another Mass Observation Unit representative discovered:

> In the smaller coastal villages like Snape, Butley and Hollesley, etc it would be possible to spend several hours in a village pub without realising there was a war on. The position can best be summarised by saying that the people are quite ready to say they don't like the war, but quite ready to stick it.

The darkness of the long winter nights on the east coast was, though, made even more impenetrable by the introduction of the 'blackout'. It was now an offence punishable by law to allow any chink of light to filter from a doorway or window during the hours between dusk and dawn. Many people found life at night very difficult, if not actually dangerous, and large numbers of them admitted to staying in for fear of falling over things if they went out, or else getting lost and unable to find their way back home in the Stygian gloom.

The cinemas and most dance halls remained open to offer at least some form of public entertainment, although in the aftermath of air raids the attendances would invariably drop for a day or so. 'Dressing up' and going out was a thing of the past for the majority of women, too, because of the shortage of clothing. The unwritten rule became to buy 'something sensible', and many girls gave up nylon stockings and wore scarves instead of hats. There was a minor fashion craze for a few months in the summer of 1940 for the Anti-Concussion Bandeau – 'designed by a nerve specialist to ward off the harmful effects of concussion from bombs and to protect the ear drums'.

Those less public-spirited individuals who did go out at night sneakily carrying a torch – or used a match or cigarette lighter – were in danger of being hauled up before the local magistrates and fined up to £1 – then quite a considerable sum of money when it is appreciated that the average weekly wage for an agricultural worker was 50 shillings (£2.50).

In order to prevent disaster on the roads after dark, cars were allowed to use one headlight – though this had to be screened with narrow slits – and there was a blanket speed limit of 20 m.p.h. once dusk had fallen. Drivers were also encouraged to camouflage their vehicles – 'sacrificing their gleaming colours in case they should ever find themselves in a tight corner', as a government pamphlet warned – by applying matt-finish cellulose in light brown, medium green or black.

Throughout that long, dark winter the only lights to be seen at night with any regularity were the beams of searchlights crisscrossing the skies like agile white fingers searching for enemy raiders to alert the guns of the AA batteries. Occasionally they would mistake RAF fighters for German raiders hedge-hopping towards their targets and incidents of 'friendly fire' were not unknown. But, friend or foe, many inhabitants of the east coast were condemned to sleepless nights by the sound of huge bombers droning overhead to be followed by the roar of pursuing fighters. As if this were not disruptive enough, the wailing of air-raid sirens only compounded the nightly misery.

When aircraft crashed, it was the responsibility of the army to go to the scene and put an armed guard around the wreck. However, in the more remote districts of East Anglia, the men in khaki uniforms often arrived a poor second to locals and the inevitable curiosity seekers. The carnage of twisted metal and bloody bodies that all of them found provided another rich source of material for local gossip – usually greatly elaborated in the retelling.

Probably the most universal sign of the emergency conditions in 1940 was the gas mask that everyone was supposed to carry. Some 38 million had been distributed to every man, woman and child, with special respirators for babies and infants. In March, the government announced that there was reason to believe the Germans were planning a new form of aerial bombardment, possibly using germ warfare, and new filters for the masks were hastily made available.

To underline the dangers, all citizens were urged to have their gas masks checked frequently by the ARP and to take full advantage of the 'demonstration meetings' held by the wardens to hammer home the message of never being without the ubiquitous mask in its little cardboard box. Those who were compelled to wear the masks – even if only at the demonstrations – never forgot the weird experience or the unpleasant smell of the rubber.

For those nearest to the coast there were constant reminders of the invasion threat. Barrage balloons, known as 'pigs', hung in the sky – 66 feet long by 30 feet high, inflated with hydrogen and able to reach heights of 10,000 feet. All along the coastal roads and lanes could be found ugly antitank and antiaircraft traps, sandbagged weapon pits and hidden explosive charges known as 'Bosche Bumps'. Even the beaches were ringed with pillboxes and 'dragon's teeth', tangled with barbed wire and studded by a variety of steel and concrete bulwarks.

The men who built these constructions – such as A B Kenell from Essex – always remembered the long hours of back-breaking work on remote stretches of coastline.

I was on the defences of the coast; first on tide-work, erecting long iron spikes set in concrete on the beaches. Being below the high-tide mark, what a race we had to beat the incoming tide. Working all hours of the day and night, by moonlight often enough, to finish our section, working in bare feet and legs in the cold sea water and trousers rolled above the knees.

The population of East Anglia also changed dramatically. The passing of the Emergency Powers (Defence) Bill in August 1939 meant that foreigners living in the area were classified as enemies. Germans, Austrians, Italians and those of obscure or suspicious origins were rounded up and sent to camps where they were categorised as Class A (instant internment), Class B (restricted movement) or Class C (allowed free).

A month later, on 1 September, the evacuation of children from London began with hordes of youngsters arriving by train or paddle steamers into Lowestoft and Felixstowe. Although many people in East Anglia considered the whole business heartrending and did their best to help this 'peaceful invasion' of the young, others were less cooperative and steadfastly refused to house children even after radio appeals. One landlady in Southwold was quoted as saying, 'I'd rather have forty soldiers than two of those children.'

By the following spring, however, the situation was being rapidly reversed. In May, all expectant mothers and disabled and handicapped children were moved out of the area, to be followed in June by 5,500 children transferred to South Wales. Before the month was over, a total of 25,000 youngsters had been evacuated from a ten-mile coastal band stretching from Norfolk through Suffolk to Essex, Kent and Sussex.

The adult population of many of the east coast towns also dipped remarkably, too, as the tempo of raids grew in the summer of 1940. In Walton-on-the-Naze, it was estimated that 70 per cent of the inhabitants had shut up their homes and left, and in Clacton the prewar figure of 25,000 residents had fallen to under 5,000 by the early autumn. Not surprisingly, the usual influx of tourists had failed to materialise – Yarmouth was to get just 750 for the entire season – and many businessmen who relied on this trade for their livelihood spent the summer closed and boarded up. Shopkeepers and hoteliers alike complained that the constant BBC broadcasts referring enigmatically to 'enemy planes over the East Coast' did nothing to encourage visitors. The owner of one small boarding house in Lowestoft – which had lost half its normal population – described his situation in a few, heartfelt words to another Mass Observation Unit representative:

It's a life of continual apprehension. The raids are so sudden that they are almost over before the noise of battle has begun. We hear the roar of hostile planes unseen in low cloud, the thud of bombs, the bursts of machine-gun fire and then it's over.

In May 1940, however, two events occurred that were to have great significance to the country – and East Anglia especially. On 10 May, Winston Churchill was appointed prime minister of an all-party coalition government following the resignation of the appeasement-driven Neville Chamberlain. Twenty days later, the German *blitzkrieg* of the Low Countries resulted in the capture of Holland and Belgium to add to their seizure of Norway and Denmark, leaving France within their grasp.

While the first piece of news about Churchill undoubtedly lifted the spirits of many people on the east coast who knew of his concern for their region, the second meant that the all-conquering Germans were now just sixty miles away across the North Sea. Along the coast as far north as Felixstowe there were people who said they had been hearing the unmistakable rumble of gunfire for days.

On 31 May, Miss Bunty Carr, a resident of Woodbridge, wrote in her diary,

A new rumour has started – that invasion is expected tonight and all are to be ready. Played tennis with school-master until 9.30 p.m. He said, 'This reminds me of Drake.' Mother said, 'No one but *you* would think of playing silly games at a time like this!'

Four days later, the encircled British troops in France were dramatically rescued from Dunkirk by a motley fleet of little ships – not a few of which had sailed from the harbours of Norfolk, Suffolk and Essex. The stories told by the exhausted and bloodstained soldiers about the inexorable progress of the Nazis left the men from the east coast who silently piloted them home in no doubt about the intent of the enemy.

Less than a month later, on 1 July, German troops stepped ashore on the Channel Islands and the first piece of British territory fell under the jackboot. The news did not make for comfortable reading on the east coast, as another of the Mass Observation Unit representatives found while compiling his 'Suffolk Village Report Number 170', dated July 1940: 'A woman in Shingle Street told me, "My, they are getting close now. I reckon they'll be over here before long. They're waiting their chance." '

The anonymous woman's remarks are interesting for two reasons: first, because Shingle Street, where she lived, would soon feature in one of the legendary stories of a German invasion of Britain; and, secondly, because she was far from being the first person in the area to feel that the threat of invasion was real and imminent.

The history of England, in fact, reveals that this picturesque and largely unspoiled stretch of East Anglian coastline has been a target for dangerous and greedy invaders for almost *nine hundred years*.

Chapter 2

The Invasion Coast

An early-morning autumn mist was still hanging in little swathes across the estuary of the River Orwell as the first of the fleet of French sailing ships from Boulogne hove into view. Along both sides of the estuary, groups of people could be seen gathering to get a view of the fleet that was approaching from the North Sea. For weeks there had been rumours of the coming of the 'She Wolf of France' and her army – and now it was happening on 24 September 1326.

Invasion had, in fact, been a threat here since the days of the Romans. The evidence was there to see in the chain of forts they had built in the fourth century to repel the Saxons, which stretched from Brancaster in Norfolk to the south coast. Later the Vikings had crossed the North Sea, intent on raiding but staying to settle, as did their successors, the all-conquering Normans. Thereafter, for centuries traders from Europe and even further afield sailed into the Orwell and upriver to Ipswich, ultimately turning it into the largest trading port in England.

These latest arrivals, however, had no thoughts of commerce in mind. Isabella of France was set on invasion and bringing about the downfall of her husband the king, Edward II, the first of the English crown princes to bear the title of Prince of Wales. Her action – just like those before and those to come – has earned the shoreline from Norfolk through Suffolk and Essex to the Thames Estuary the title of 'the Invasion Coast'.

The woman who stood on the deck of the leading ship was a striking figure with long, blonde hair, high cheekbones and wilful eyes. She was the daughter of King Philip IV, and her exploits would earn her the sobriquet of the 'She Wolf of France', not to mention a unique place in history. The famous English poet, Thomas Gray, for one would help to immortalise her in his great work *The Bard* (1757):

> *She-wolf of France, with unrelenting fangs,*
> *That tearest the bowels of thy mangled mate.*

There was, however, more curiosity than fear among the peasant men, women and children gathered on the banks of the Orwell as Isabella's fleet of ships sailed purposefully to the port. In her absence from the country, people had grown tired of the king's incompetence and extravagant ways and wondered what his former child-bride would do in the company of her son, Edward, her lover, Sir Roger Mortimer, and an army of almost three thousand battle-hardened troops. That they took Ipswich with very little loss of life and were soon marching inland collecting supporters along the way as they sought out Edward II indicates this invasion was not altogether unwelcome.

Isabella was the daughter of King Philip and Joanna of Navarre and had been married to Edward in 1308 when she was just twelve years old. The first time she had met her husband was at the church door in Boulogne and her education was largely obtained in the royal court, where she learned quickly. The beautiful girl also soon found that her husband preferred sports, crafts, the theatre and his male friends to her.

Accepting her lot, Isabella became adept at playing politics with those who courted the favour of her ineffectual husband, forever at loggerheads with his noblemen, who finally revolted against him. She accompanied the king when he fought in vain against Sir Robert de Bruce at Bannockburn in 1314 and – having narrowly avoided capture – proved her skills as an

23

astute mediator under the baronial control that ensued. However, stories of Isabella's escape and her devotion to the nation helped to make her very popular with the people and she compounded this respect by giving birth to a son, the future Edward III, at Windsor in 1312.

In 1325, exasperated to the point of 'mortal hatred' with Edward's 'friends', Isabella left for her native France with her son and her lover, Roger Mortimer – whose escape from the Tower of London she undoubtedly helped to engineer. There she gathered an army from the Low Countries and a year later landed in Suffolk to carry out a *coup d'état*. The favourites of the king who had been responsible for much of the unrest in the country were captured and executed, while Edward himself was tracked down and imprisoned in Berkeley Castle, Gloucester. Thereupon he was formally deposed and Isabella and her consort became regents of England. Not long afterwards, Edward II was found murdered in his cell, in all probability by the couple.

Isabella's good fortune did not last for long, however. In 1327, her son, the new King Edward III, was crowned and two years later ordered the execution of Mortimer and his mother's imprisonment at Castle Rising in Norfolk – just a few miles from where she had stepped ashore in such triumph less than five years earlier. Although she was to be accorded all the privileges of a dowager queen with a full company of knights, squires and ladies-in-waiting, Isabella was banned from appearing in public and confined behind locked doors until her death in 1358.

Legend was far from being finished with her, though. Her reputation as a beauty with a wicked temper, coupled with the mysterious death of her husband, soon had rumour hard at work. She was not lying in her coffin, it was whispered, but rising from her coffin on nights of the full moon as a white wolf with fiery eyes and blood dripping from her teeth. Even today, when the moon is full, the she wolf of France is said still to roam the battlements of Castle Rising howling in the darkness

– a reminder of the first, and only, successful invasion of the east coast, which many other eyes would look at greedily in the centuries to come.

It was the French themselves who next sought to invade East Anglia, in August 1386. Not long after Edward III had ascended to the throne of England, Charles IV, King of France, died, leaving no direct heir. The young Edward promptly claimed the throne through his mother, Isabella – Charles IV's sister – and commenced the Hundred Years War between the two nations.

According to E S Creasy, professor of history at London University, in his book, *The Invasions of England* (1852), there were 'repeated projections of invasions by the French' and regular incursions on the south and east coasts by their sailors. He continues, 'But there is one scheme for the conquest of England by France which was organised during the reign of Richard II on such a formidable scale that, though most modern historians pass lightly over it, must be brought fully to the reader's notice.'

Creasy cites as his authority a 'graphic narrative' by Sir Nicholas Harris Nicolas drawn from contemporary sources. Explaining how in 1386 the Duke of Lancaster had taken away the best troops in England to Spain to claim the crown, the new French king, Charles VI, decided to use their absence to attack and conquer England. Nicolas's account is an eerie, almost word-for-word, foretaste of the German plans in 1940:

> France had never witnessed military preparations of such extent and variety as were made in the summer of this year for the invasion of England. The spirit of William the Conqueror seemed to have revived in Charles VI and every other object appeared to be forgotten in the desire to subdue this country. There was not a large vessel from Seville to Prussia which the French could lay their hands on that was not impressed for the expedition. Never were

there seen so many large ships as filled the harbour of Sluys, or were on the coast between Sluys and Blankenberg, amounting to thirteen hundred and eighty seven sail.

The ships were mostly double-sailed vessels with long prows. There were larger ships for carrying horses and a selection of huge boats known as 'dromons' to transport the military equipment and provisions. One of the leaders of the invasion, the merciless and brutal Constable of France, Sir Oliver de Clisson, nicknamed 'the Butcher', was so confident of success he had a prefabricated 'wooden house' built, which was to be conveyed in pieces across the Channel and put together in England, 'for the lords to lodge in and sleep securely at night'.

The French plan was to attack in mid-August. One force would head for southern England, another for the Thames Estuary and London, while a third would make for East Anglia and the great ports of Ipswich and Yarmouth. Once they were landed, England was to be laid to waste. All men were to be put to death and the women and children carried off to slavery in France. As the French went about their preparations, a feeling of overconfidence – even arrogance – was very evident in their attitude, as Nicolas has reported:

Money was no more thought of than if it had rained gold and silver from the clouds, or if it were pumped up from the sea; and the impatience of the knights to embark was even exceeded by their young king. All the great lords vied with each other in the equipments and ornaments of their ships, which were gaily painted and gilt, having their arms depicted upon them and their masts covered with sheets of gold leaf. One knight, Sir Guy de Tremouille, expended no less than ten thousand francs in adorning his ship. Rich banners, pennons and standards floated everywhere and the profusion and splendour of the expedition was everywhere evident.

News of all this activity did not take long to reach England. Accounts suggest that some Londoners became 'like timid hares or mice', pulling down their houses and preparing to abandon the city. Many others, though, spoke up defiantly: 'Let these Frenchmen come – and, by God, not one of them shall return to France!'

Plans to defend the country were put in the hands of the navy – in particular two veteran admirals, Darcy and Trivet, who were appointed on 9 July and began to recruit men-at-arms and archers to augment the crews of their meagre fleet of just forty large ships. In August, the Earl of Arundel was instructed to assemble companies of soldiers for the defence of the south coast. The following month, as the conviction grew that a major French thrust would be inflicted on the east coast, a fleet of ships was also posted to Yarmouth to lie in wait for the invaders.

Across the Channel optimism started to turn to irritation as England's greatest ally, the weather, in the shape of torrential rain and storms, continued throughout the autumn to make sailing from the French ports impossible. An advance party of some 72 ships did venture to cross on 28 September, but, when they were in sight of Margate, heavy seas forced them to turn back. Not all of the vessels reached port safely: seven were wrecked and three carrying parts of the Butcher's collapsible house along with a large number of guns and ammunition were captured by Sir William Beauchamp, 'whereupon the prizes were brought into Sandwich and the Constable's fortification was immediately erected for the defence of the town'!

A second squadron of invaders fared no better on 31 October. The ships had proceeded twenty miles when another violent storm forced them to return to Sluys, where several were wrecked as they tried to enter port. As Christmas neared with the now bedraggled-looking fleet still at anchor, the angry and frustrated Charles had no alternative but to delay his grand plan until the spring. Everything must, though, remain at the ready, the king insisted, as he took himself back to the comforts of Paris. However, the lack of action and finances soon caused a number of the disenchanted noblemen to slip away from the ports under the cover of the winter darkness. Many of the ordinary soldiers, now penniless and starving, went on a rampage of theft and destruction through Flanders and Picardy, making them seem more like invaders than compatriots to the terrified peasants who abused them with, 'Go, go to England – and may never a soul of you come back!'

Come the spring, however, it was the English, now properly armed and buoyed by the small successes of the late autumn, who took the initiative on a 'D-Day' morning in early 1387, as Sir Nicholas Harris Nicolas has described:

> As soon as the weather permitted the English ships to sail, they fell upon the enemy's vessels and put some of them to flight. They burnt or captured the greater part of the fleet, and carried off the stores, among which were two thousand gallons of wine, which supplied the wants of England for a long period. As soon as news that the expedition was broken up was brought to London, the joy was almost universal, and a great feast was given to those who had been employed in guarding the coast.

The Dutch were the next to test the resolve of the people of the east coast. In 1667 a raiding party from a man-of-war arrived at Hole Haven on Canvey Island in the Thames Estuary and did what the French had failed so abysmally to do almost three hundred years earlier: land on the English shore. This incursion, too, has pre-echoes of what would happen on the east coast in 1940.

For years prior to this invasion, Holland had been England's chief commercial rival in overseas trade. Britain's assumed sovereignty of the seas was a source of annoyance to many enterprising Dutchmen and, although hostilities between the two countries had been patched up by a number of pacts, relations remained strained. It was then, after the Dutch had suffered a number of defeats at the hands of the English, that an opportunity occurred to exact revenge.

In 1666, as a result of lack of funds squandered on his 'mistresses and parasites', the king, Charles II, ordered the English fleet to be laid up at Deptford, Leigh-on-Sea and the naval dockyards in the River Medway. As a result only a few small ships were kept afloat and fit for service and the streets of London were soon full of unpaid and starving seamen. E S Creasy explains what happened next:

> The great admiral of Holland, Michiel De Ruyter, and her greatest statesman, Cornelius De Witt, took advantage of this neglect to deal us a home-thrust. They equipped a large and powerful fleet of seventy vessels, with which in June 1667, they sailed from Holland and rode undisputed masters of the British seas making projects for landing.

An Essex clergyman, the Reverend Ralph Josselin, of Earls Colne, was one of the first to spot the incursion of the Dutch, noting in his diary of 6 June that the 'Dutch are off Harwich and seemingly intent on seizing and occupying positions on our coast'. The news was quickly conveyed to London, where the king ordered Lord Oxford 'to rouse the men in the eastern counties and prepare them for repelling any landing attempt made by the enemy', according to historian F G Whitnall, describing the events in *The Invasion of 1667* (1959).

Lord Berkeley was given command of the military at Harwich and, accompanied by a party of young volunteers, set out to thwart the Dutch. The great diarist Samuel Pepys, who was among the group of councillors responsible for administering navy affairs, was sceptical of the plan and believed the young men would be of little use 'except to debauch the country-women thereabouts'.

Although there is little evidence that either of their lordships had much effect, shots were exchanged between marksmen on the Harwich docks and the lurking ships before the Dutch fleet sailed away down the coast. Their next port of call was the daring raid on Canvey Island.

The two dozen men who stepped ashore at Hole Haven moved quickly among the farmhouses and barns close to the waterfront. The horrified local inhabitants could only huddle in fear as the seamen looted valuables and foodstuffs before hurrying back to their ship. The raid was over almost before anyone could sound a warning and the bemused people of Canvey were left to recover as best they could.

A local landowner, Sir Henry Appleton, incensed by the attack, quickly put pen to paper to write to the secretary of state, reporting that 'the Dutch have landed on Canvey Island and plundered it, damaging barns and eight houses and taken several small boats'. The secretary's response in sending a troop of Scots musketeers from the battery at Sheerness to help the islanders was a case of too few, too late.

Far worse was in store when De Ruyter's ships entered the Thames Estuary and became the first – and last – fleet to enter these waters in defiance of English powers. The nineteenth-century historian John Davis describes these significant days in his book, *Holland* (1847):

The Dutch ships having cast anchor near the mouth of the Thames, Cornelius de Witt proceeded with the squadron to Sheerness, which was taken by surprise. It was destroyed as untenable, and the fleet, re-united, directed its course to Chatham. The English had, on the alarm, adopted such measures of defence as the time and circumstances per-mitted, by sinking vessels to impede the passage of the Medway, throwing across it a strong chain, protected from behind by four men-of-war and two frigates, and by a battery of eight guns on the shore on each side.

Despite a fierce exchange of fire, several Dutch boarding parties managed to get into the dockyards and play havoc with the remnants of the British fleet lying there. The *Royal Oak* and the *Royal James* were both badly damaged and the *Loyal London* was left a blazing wreck. An even greater humiliation was piled on the English when the 100-gun battleship *Royal Charles* was seized and converted into De Ruyter's new flagship.

Seemingly content for the moment with having bloodied their enemy's nose and secured some magnificent booty, the Dutch fleet sailed for home, leaving the English to find scapegoats for the debacle that had overwhelmed them. Just before the end of the month, however, they returned once more, as the Reverend Ralph Josselin noted in his diary of 27 June: 'The Dutch have again come up near us. They have put a stop to all trade and forced us to defend the whole shore.'

On 2 July, De Ruyter's maturing plan for invasion was put into effect. On a cold, grey day, an army of some two thousand Dutch soldiers with muskets and cutlasses were disembarked from sixty vessels lying off Harwich. Under the cover of an oily smokescreen provided by the ships, the men stormed onto a windswept shingle spit to attack Languard Fort, built in 1626 to protect Harwich harbour, which it overlooked. Here a garrison of four hundred men under the command of Captain Nathaniel Darell represented the port's last line of defence. The Dutch first had to knock out the fort's cannons before they could go any further – or even start thinking about putting infantry ashore.

The ensuing battle between the two forces is a story of resolute defence and the inability of the attackers to scale the fortress. Shielded by the building's immense walls, Darell's marksmen had time to pick off their blue-coated adversaries as soon as they came into view of the ports or parapets. The encounter lasted for under an hour, before the Dutch withdrew to their ships – which had apparently not fired a shot at

Languard during the entire encounter, probably for fear of hitting their own men – leaving some seventy dead or dying on the beach. There was no doubt in the mind of Darell that, if they had not prevailed, De Ruyter might well have gone on to take the east coast and certainly forced the English into a humiliating peace treaty.

One immediate repercussion of the Dutch 'invasion' was the decision by Charles II to reinstate the English fleet. It was a wise move because five years later De Ruyter returned once again to confront the English off the east coast. This time he was met by a new, refurbished navy, and the two fleets clashed off the Suffolk coast between Southwold and Lowestoft in what became known as 'the Battle of Sole Bay'. On the morning of 28 May 1672, the lord high admiral, James, Duke of York, scored a stunning victory and effectively destroyed Dutch sea power in the North Sea. The only sad moment for those on the English side was the sinking of the *Royal James* – the self-same ship that had been set on fire by the Dutch at Chatham and yet survived to fight another day.

In the intervening years, the people of Harwich had honoured the bravery of the defenders in Languard Fort, while the Canvey Islanders had completed the restoration of their properties. The nightmare of invasion soon faded on the island, although the fort on Languard Point was destined to remain as a monument to a special moment in history. Both places, though, would continue to share the distinction for the next 130 years of being the only locations in England on which enemy troops had left their footprints – until a new incident occurred that would also prove yet another curious precursor to events in World War Two.

Sunday, 2 July 1797, started as a normal enough summer morning at Clacton. At the time a collection of scattered farmsteads, rustic cottages and enclosed fields above a sandy shore, the area was undisturbed as a lot of the men, women and children had gone to church. On the deserted beach – which a century later would become one of the most popular holiday resorts on the east coast – a few fishing boats lay in the shadow of red clay cliffs varying from twenty to forty feet high. Although these cliffs were almost perpendicular in some parts, there were other places where the marks of footprints indicated it was possible to climb up to the community divided into two villages, Great and Little Clacton.

Despite the fact that England was again at war with France and Napoleon Bonaparte, the tranquillity of Clacton beach was usually disturbed during the day only by the occasional sloop beaching to deliver a cargo of chalk or to collect grain from the local farmers. Under the cover of darkness, though, smugglers sometimes picked the locality to land their illicit cargoes, safe in the knowledge that the customs officers had little chance of catching them on a coast that was plagued by such men.

However, on this Sunday morning a revenue cutter under the command of Captain James Adams happened to be in the vicinity and he and his crew were to be eyewitnesses to another 'invasion' of the east coast. As the boat sailed on patrol from Harwich past Walton-on-the-Naze, a member of the crew pointed urgently at a sail on the horizon just off Clacton. Captain Adams raised a spyglass to his eye. It took him only a moment to identify the ship: she was French. Closer examination as the cutter closed in revealed that she was a lugger, probably a privateer. So what was she doing here?

As the customs boat drew nearer, there were signs of feverish activity on board the lugger as she tried to turn and head out to sea. Instead, the French captain managed only to ground his ship in the unfamiliar waters. Almost at once, a dozen figures were seen to leave the ship, wade ashore and disappear in a mad scramble up the cliff.

As soon as Captain Adams reached the French vessel, he lowered a boat and sent a small party of men in pursuit. They, too, climbed up the nearest incline and were soon racing from farmhouse to cottage rousing people to sound the alarm that invaders were probably on the loose. Kenneth Walker, who has told the story in 'When the Enemy Landed on the Essex Coast' in *Essex Countryside*, June 1977, takes up the drama:

> There was no knowing what this desperate body of men might do, and children would have been called home, and doors hastily barred, while the able bodied men, seizing whatever weapons lay at hand, were mustered to aid the revenue officers in their search for the enemy. It was decided to seek military assistance, but the nearest troops were then at Colchester. Sir William Hope, in charge of the Eastern District, was nearer at Wivenhoe, and a messenger was therefore sent to him hot foot. As soon as the General heard the news, he dispatched an express to the barracks at Colchester to advise the garrison that Frenchmen had landed at Clacton and were committing depredations in the area.

According to a contemporary account, it was not until 4 p.m. that the message reached the garrison, but a detachment of the Warwickshire Fencible Cavalry were soon galloping along the road to the coast. The French seamen, in the meantime, had made themselves scarce and were believed to be in hiding, hoping for darkness to fall and give them the chance of stealing a boat somewhere along the coast to get back to France.

Captain Adams and his men proved formidable trackers, however. Assisted by an ever-growing band of farmers and labourers, they finally hunted the 'invaders' to Holland-on-Sea, some three miles to the north. The sailors were quickly surrounded, Kenneth Walker writes, and, after a fierce fight, were overpowered and conducted back to the beach where they had landed:

> They were secured aboard their own vessel and so conveyed to Harwich and thence presumably to some

prison hulk. The cavalry had been within five miles of the coast when they were told their services were no longer required and they therefore returned to Colchester. So ended the enemy 'invasion' of Essex.

Well, not quite. One Frenchman had evidently hidden himself when the rest of his colleagues were surrounded and remained under cover for the whole of Sunday night. The next day he reached Great Holland and was trying to steal a boat when he was seized by its owner. The customs officers from Harwich were once again called on the scene to arrest the man and cart him off to join his compatriots.

Just as the people of London celebrated the ending of the French 'invasion' in 1387, a party was held for Captain Adams and all those who had taken part in the successful arrest at the Ship Inn at Great Clacton. At the same time, plans were also made for a military camp to be established at Clacton and the sea defences strengthened. Later, barracks would be built at Weeley and other fortifications erected along this stretch of coast.

At the time, local people probably felt they had removed any threat of a French invasion. They could not have been more wrong.

Evidence suggests that it was not until the following year that fears of a real invasion began to spread in East Anglia. But, as E S Creasy has explained, Napoleon Bonaparte was initially not keen on such a plan:

It may be doubted [Creasy says] whether the project which the French vaunted of invading England in 1798 was real, and whether the preparation of ships along the coast had any other purpose than to divert the attention of England from the real object on which the ambition of Bonaparte was then concentrated – the conquest of Egypt. His opinions as to attempting an invasion of England at that time are probably correctly stated by [Louis] Thiers [in his *Histoire de la Revolution Française* (1823–7)]. This historian, describing how the French, immediately after the Treaty of Campo Formio with Austria was signed, created an army called 'The Army of England' and how they caused the coasts to be inspected and flotillas prepared, proceeds to say that, 'Bonaparte seemed to approve this great movement, but at heart he disliked the plan. To land 60,000 men in England, to march to London, and to enter the capital, did not appear to him the most difficult part of the business. He was aware that it would be impossible to conquer the country and to establish himself there; that he could at most ravage it, despoil it of part of its wealth, throw it back, annul it, for half a century; but that he must sacrifice the army which he had brought over and return almost alone after a sort of barbarian invasion.'

The attitude in England towards the French threat was not, though, one of complacency, and the defences along the east coast were strengthened, as well as consideration being given to a military presence on the shore. An enquiry by General Roy of the Light Dragoons identified the area between the Orwell and Hollesley Bay as the most vulnerable. But as G M Willis has pointed out in his essay, 'The Threat of Invasion' in the *East Anglian Magazine*, September 1950, the marshy terrain would defeat the object of cavalry patrols:

The situation was serious on Hollesley Bay. There the smooth water afforded an ideal landing-place, and stores and artillery could have been unloaded with ease in Orford Haven. Again, due to the abundance of marshes and of rivers which could be crossed by ferries, a system of cavalry patrols was impracticable, though, General Roy reported, enough was left of Orford castle to make a good infantry position.

If the French had landed at Hollesley Bay, the first defensive position would have been at Martlesham, where it was hoped to concentrate 20,000 men, with the next position at Ipswich. In the event that the invaders continued to advance towards Colchester, another formation would endeavour to stop them at the appropriately named Gun Hill on the River Stour.

As it transpired, of course, Bonaparte directed all his energies towards Egypt and the spectre of invasion did not arise again until the dawn of the new century. By then the French leader had developed a quite different attitude towards the English – very similar to that of Hitler one hundred and fifty years later – as Creasy explains:

In 1801, Napoleon, now first consul and virtual despot of France, conceived in earnest the idea of transporting his victorious armies to England and endeavouring to crush on their own soil the islanders, whom he had found in every part of the globe his most obstinate and dangerous foes. He ordered an immense flotilla of gun-boats and flat boats to be built in all the ports of the channel; and in the month of July 1801, nine divisions of gun-vessels and all the troops they could embark were assembled in Boulogne harbour, whence they were to attempt the passage to England.

Admiral Horatio Nelson, who had been born on the Norfolk coast at Burnham Thorpe, was a leading figure in England's defensive measures, and for a time commanded the naval squadron detailed to protect the coast from Orford Ness to Beachy Head. Nelson estimated that, if the French attempted to invade, about 200 to 250 flat-bottomed vessels would be sent from Boulogne in separate waves carrying up to 100,000 men. As many as 20,000 of these soldiers would be landed between sixty and seventy miles eastward of London, he thought, with the same number westward of the capital.

It was precisely this difficulty of establishing *where* the enemy might land that exercised the mind of Lieutenant-General Sir James Craig, the commander of the eastern district. He insisted to the Duke of York that it could 'only be guesswork' – and because of the French lack of knowledge of the coast they might well land 'where they did not intend to'! In order to make the most of his troops, Craig decided to concentrate them in a few central points – Ipswich and Bromeswell Heath – from which they could march at short notice to any threatened spot such as Hollesley Bay, the Orwell–Deben beaches or Harwich Harbour.

Certainly the most important reaction to the possibility of invasion was the creation of the Loyal Volunteer Regiments, the prototype of the Home Guard who would stand ready for the Germans the following century. The idea had been sparked by a pamphlet, *Plan of Defence Against Invasion*, written in 1797 by Captain James Burney, a retired naval officer who had sailed with Captain Cook on the *Discovery* on his third voyage, and after the latter's death become commander.

Burney argued that security was 'the first blessing of life' and with the future of the nation at stake it was vital to have a plan to repulse any foreign invasion. He stated his plans in these words:

> That in London, and in all the counties near, and likewise in the counties near the Eastern and Southern coast of the Kingdom, there should be taken in each parish separately, an account of all the male inhabitants in every house, of whatever description, between the ages of 18 and 55 capable of bearing arms. That the names of such shall be enrolled, and they required to attend, at a time and place appointed by each parish for themselves, on one forenoon in each week, for the first three months, to be embodied, regulated and exercised.

The appeal had an immediate effect. The first Loyal Volunteers were assembled in the autumn of that year and by May 1803, when war had been declared with France, their ranks had been increased to about 460,000 men – no small achievement considering the much smaller population of England at the time.

The training of this militia – all of whom worked during the week and in the main attended sessions in the evening and at weekends – consisted in making them proficient in the use of muskets and pikes and instruction in how to make beacons of straw, faggots and tar to set alight in the event of an invasion at night. Most of the volunteers were dressed only in greatcoats, but the top units were eventually provided with complete uniforms (usually in green in contrast to the scarlet tunics of the regulars) paid for by wealthy patrons. Some were even invited to go on full-time duties for periods of up to four weeks of paid service. According to contemporary accounts, two of the really crack units of volunteers were the Wells Volunteer Infantry in Norfolk and 'the Sharp Shooters' of Hollesley Bay.

The men from Wells were apparently regularly exercised on the beaches at Cromer and Mundersley, which were considered to be particular danger spots for invasion. The force's nearness to Kings Lynn meant that they benefited, uniform-wise, from a movement set up there by a group of well-meaning ladies to make flannel underclothes for volunteers on night patrols.

The Sharp Shooters were led by a veteran seaman, Captain Thomas Broke, of whom it was later said, in histories of the volunteers,

He transformed all the spirit of the sea into the land service and made his troops ready for action in every respect. They rush to the beach, skirmish behind hedges, trees and banks, fire and load lying on the ground with admirable dexterity and perform an exercise which is generally neglected by volunteer corps, that of using the bayonet.

Groups of volunteers were, in fact, set up all over East Anglia and their units were usually commanded by ex-army officers, occasionally the local vicar. They were frequently inspected by officers of the regular army, who commented on their appearance and proficiency when they were going through 'different evolutions'. After such manoeuvres the men were sometimes treated to a slap-up dinner of roast beef and plum pudding with barrels of strong beer.

The main coastal towns had similar volunteer bands of 'Sea Fencibles' – fishermen who patrolled the beaches and gave service afloat if required. The largest number of these men were based between Harwich and Aldeburgh, and in November 1803 one local resident wrote to a friend, 'We are in daily expectation of a visit from the other side of the water, but our coast is now tolerably-well guarded and the town volunteers come on wonderfully in their exercise and firing.'

A test one Saturday morning later that month to try out the daytime warning system in the event of invasion – the raising of red flags from church towers – went badly wrong when rumour insisted the French fleet had actually been sighted. In fact, the flags were merely being flown to determine the speed of communication between Lowestoft and Diss and many villagers had not been informed it was only a rehearsal.

Aldeburgh, which had its own cannon constantly primed for invasion, was also the setting for an amusing 'invasion' story. It was told by the Reverend George Crabbe, who reported that the gun was fired one night just after midnight after heavy gunfire had been heard at sea, at which a volunteer on the quay had called the local soldiers to arms. Clifford Morsley recounts the finale in his article, 'Ready For Napoleon' in the *East Anglian Magazine* of March 1966:

It seems that everyone was awakened except the clergyman. When his son eventually roused him and said, 'The French are landing,' Crabbe coolly replied, 'Well, old

fellow, you and I can do no good. We must await the event.'
An hour or so later his son returned to report that
everything was quiet again; but his father had long since
gone back to sleep. Several folk were quite sure the French
had been testing the state of preparedness of that part of
the coast, but others were equally certain it was just
another false alarm.

The east coast was to experience many more false alarms
during the following months. However, the completion of a
number of impregnable Martello towers – first suggested in
April 1798 by the military engineer Thomas Vincent Reynolds
as a replacement for the existing open batteries – helped to
settle the worries of the east coast commanders. No fewer than
twenty of these stolid, brick-built structures were placed at
several of the most vulnerable spots in Suffolk, including
Languard Point, Bawdsey and Orford Ness, with four in
Hollesley Bay – two at each end of the long sweep of beach.

It was claimed that fifteen to twenty men with sufficient
stores and ammunition could hold out behind the thick walls of
these towers. Their guns could sweep the beaches, making
landings extremely difficult, while, even if the enemy got past
the fortification, they could continue to harass the invaders
from the rear.

Napoleon, like other leaders before and since, prevaricated
and delayed over invading England. Although he was still
consumed with a desire, as Clifford Morsley wrote, to 'completely subdue the English' and believed 150,000 troops could
secure such a victory, 'the sea and its elements rolled between
him and his anticipated prey'. There was also the problem of
the powerful British navy augmented by captured enemy ships,
while his own fleet of men-of-war had been decimated in
actions abroad. Nelson's estimation of the size of fleet required
for an invasion proved rather smaller than that of the French
themselves.

The emperor's strategists reckoned that at least 1,200 flat-bottomed vessels of varying sizes would be required to land on the shelving English coast. These would be divided into three groups. The first, two-masters armed fore and aft with heavy cannons carrying a hundred soldiers and their arms and ammunition, would lead the invasion. A second similar group would transport field pieces, artillery wagons, horses and provisions enough for twenty days. Finally, there would be a third group of large, lightweight boats with sixty oars – each rowed by soldiers who were then expected to fight! A second flotilla of eight hundred vessels would follow containing the rest of the men and ammunition.

In England, while all this planning was going on, the French were expected at virtually any moment. But in reality the building of the fleet and the training of the soldiers in landing tactics took up all of 1804 and much of 1805. Manoeuvres were regularly carried out at sea, occasionally within sight of the enemy coast, prompting interventions by the English navy that proved costly to the French in terms of men and equipment.

On 3 August 1805, Napoleon finally believed the time was right to strike. He had little idea of the defences that had been organised against him and in any event was convinced the English would put up little resistance to his troops, as he confided to Admiral Decres: 'The English know not what awaits them. If we have the power of crossing for but twelve hours, England is no more!' Once again a vaunted French invasion fleet was ready to set sail cross the Channel – and once more it was destined to failure.

East Anglia's hero son, Horatio Nelson, now commander-in-chief of the navy, was ready to face his moment of destiny. Aware of what was going on across the Straits of Dover, he had already harried the pride of the French fleet all over the Atlantic and organised attacks on the invasion craft at Boulogne and the other Channel ports, severely reducing their numbers. Then, at daybreak on 21 October, with a fleet of 27 ships he faced 33 of the enemy under the command of Admiral Pierre Villeneuve off Cape Trafalgar. If he lost the engagement, it would certainly give the French the signal to begin their long-delayed embarkation against England.

The rest, of course, is history. During the fierce exchanges, Nelson was shot and died three hours later as the battle was ending in a famous English victory. The French fleet was annihilated and with its destruction went Napoleon Bonaparte's dream of invading England. The dream itself, however, was far from dead and one hundred years later would become the obsession of another European nation – not once, but twice, in just forty years.

It was Germany who replaced France as the bogey of English invasion fears in the twentieth century. In fact, as early as 1900 the first of what would become a flood of novels and works of nonfiction predicting a German takeover of the British Isles was published. The first of these was *How the Germans Took London* by T W Offin, a sensationalist 64-page paperback, which demonstrated just how simple such an attack might be. It was evidently inspired by the recent Boer War, which had shown up the inadequacies of Britain's military organisation and stressed how the shadow of German militarism was lengthening and broadening over the nation.

Less than three years later apparent proof of Germany's intentions was laid out for everyone to read in *Der Weltkrieg: Deutsche Traume* by a Leipzig historian, August Niemann. Although full of bombast against Britain's arrogant stance as one of the world's leading powers, the book was still translated into English by J H Freese, retitled *The Coming Conquest of England* and published in both Britain and America, where it became something of a *succès de scandale*. A quotation from the author's Preface clearly indicates its anti-British tone:

Are things to come to this pass, that Germany is to crave of England's bounty – her air and light, and her very daily bread? In my mind's eye I see the armies and the fleets of Germany, France and Russia moving together against the common enemy, who with his polypus arms enfolds the globe. The iron onslaught of the three allied Powers will free the whole of Europe from England's tight embrace. The great war lies in the lap of the future.

Despite the book's finale, in which England is 'utterly defeated' by the invasion of the three powers after an unopposed landing on the Firth of Forth in Scotland, English-language readers could take comfort from a note by J H Freese: 'The translator offers no comment on the day-dream which he reproduces here – the meaning and the moral should be obvious and valuable.'

However seriously Niemann's book was taken, it was certainly popular enough to encourage other writers and publishers to jump on the bandwagon for German-invasion books. The pseudonymous *The Writing on the Wall* by 'General Staff' appeared in 1906 with another emotion-charged Preface: 'The object of this work is to call the attention of the public to the absolute unpreparedness of our land forces for the tasks which they may be called upon to perform.' Again, German forces triumphed, landing this time at various points on the east coast between Clacton and Lowestoft. A striking feature of the book was the inclusion of sketch maps of the 'Lines of Advance of the Invading Divisions'.

Two other authors less reticent about their identities shared General Staff's concern that the east coast was the Germans' most likely target for invasion. Captain Henry Curties, a retired army officer turned novelist, declared in *When England Slept* (1909) that the enemy would attack on a wide front from Newcastle to the coast of Surrey. John Blyth in his tale of a devious and cowardly enemy, *The Swoop of the Vulture* (1909), had the German fleet flying a white ensign as it approached Lowestoft and Yarmouth and then opening up on the defenceless ports with all guns blazing.

Undoubtedly, though, the most influential of this group of authors was William Le Queux, a forty-year-old French-born journalist who had worked for years in England and claimed to have been a spy. His book, *The Invasion of 1910: With a Full Account of the Siege of London* (1906), was written in a documentary style and had been created after 'an extensive motor tour of all the imaginary battlefields and a careful survey of the German occupation methods during the Franco-Prussian war'. It became a huge bestseller, helped by its initial newspaper serialisation and an enthusiastic Introduction by the country's leading soldier-statesman, Field Marshal Earl Roberts, who shared the author's fear of a German invasion: 'The catastrophe that may happen if we still remain in our present state of unpreparedness is vividly and forcibly illustrated in Mr. Le Queux's new book which I recommend to the perusal of everyone who has the welfare of the British Empire at heart.'

This book, too, was illustrated with authentic-looking maps and sketches – notably those of the IV German Army Corps landing near Cromer and an 'Appeal for Calm' by the mayor of Norwich after the invaders have occupied Yarmouth and Lowestoft and set up their headquarters in Beccles. Some of the most vivid writing in the book describes the battles between English and German forces in Colchester and Chelmsford and the ultimate 'Massacre of the Germans in London'. Unlike its predecessors, Le Queux's book envisaged an English triumph.

The success of this book prompted Le Queux to abandon fiction for fact, and he produced two books with Field Marshal Roberts that continued to warn of the German threat, *The Great War* (1908) and *Spies of the Kaiser* (1909), followed by *German Spies in England: An Exposure* (1914), in which he wrote,

East Anglia has been the happy hunting ground of Spies and the counties of Norfolk, Suffolk and Essex have been very thoroughly surveyed and every preparation made for a raid. It was found – as far back as four years ago – that next door, or in the vicinity of most village post-offices near the coastline of these counties, a foreigner had taken up his residence, that German hairdressers and jewellers were everywhere setting up shops where custom did not warrant it; that Germans took seaside furnished houses or went as paying guests in the country, even in winter; while, of course, the number of German waiters – usually passing as Austrians – had increased greatly.

Le Queux insisted that German spies and sympathisers had located the position of the Royal Navy's minefields off the east coast and were signalling or transmitting this information to enemy submarines lurking in the North Sea. 'We must not be blind to the danger of a German invasion,' he signed off his book, 'any more than we should relax, for an instant, our preparations to meet it should it come.'

Ridiculous as some of William Le Queux's claims may seem today, his books and those of the other writers helped to fuel the public's concern about invasion, as Henry Wills has written in his *Study of UK Defences* (1985):

When the German Army advanced through Belgium to Ostend in the First World War, it was thought possible that an invasion of the UK could be undertaken by a force of 70,000 men, carried in barges, each holding 500–1,200 men. These barges, normally working the Rhine and other inland waterways, would have been escorted by secondary units of the German navy, while the main units of the British and German navies fought a major battle elsewhere. At the end of 1915 the Royal Navy, weakened by losses and by the Gallipoli operation, could only have intervened in a landing 24–28 hours after the initial attack. It was then thought that up to 135,000 men could have been landed in that period of time. However, by 1917 the number was reduced to the original estimate of 70,000 men. With the 24–28 hour delay for naval intervention, the British defence scheme was to prevent the capture of a port in that time, necessary to sustain an invading force.

Recognising the public's anxiety, the British general staff initially allocated six divisions of the regular army to the east coast. Even when they were later augmented by members of the Territorial Army, the number of regulars was never allowed to fall below four divisions of infantry and one of cavalry. Despite the fact that the threat of invasion – which was then viewed as more a large-scale raid than an all-out attempt to conquer the country – receded as the war went on, it was never totally discounted in official circles.

There is other evidence to support this view. M P Trotter, who was the commander of the Thetford Company of the Sixth Battalion of the Norfolk Regiment, has recalled how another famous invasion novel, *The Riddle of the Sands* by Erskine Childers (1903), about an invasion attempt in flat-bottomed boats from the Frisian Islands, was the inspiration for an army exercise in which he took part in 1912. He told *Norfolk Fair* that he and his men were asked one weekend to help the navy and army to patrol the coast of Norfolk, as they would be doing in wartime:

> The Fleet and Transports were going to carry out the idea in *The Riddle of the Sands* to see if it was possible for them to get to the East Coast without being spotted. I billeted myself in a coastguard cottage at Weybourne and patrolled the coast on my cycle that weekend. But I saw nothing, nor did anyone else, and the Fleet got to Whitby without being seen.

The conviction that the Germans would invade this area if they came was apparently also held in the offices of *The Times* in London, according to a diary entry by one of their journalists, Michael MacDonagh, in May 1915:

> Early in the war the danger of invasion was seriously born in mind. I have been kept on duty in the office all night in readiness to be sent to the East Coast if necessary, to describe the landing of the Germans. This precaution was taken on the advice of our Military Correspondent.

In fact the east coast did suffer German attacks during World War One. The very first action occurred within hours of the outbreak of hostilities when a German minelayer, the converted liner, *Königin Louise*, was surprised operating off Harwich on 5 August and sunk by British naval forces. A day later, the British light cruiser HMS *Amphion* struck one of the German mines and also sank – taking to the bottom of the North Sea some of the German seamen she had rescued only a short while before from the *Königin Louise*.

Far more frightening for the people of East Anglia was the appearance of enemy aircraft overhead later in the year. Ruby Marson, a teacher at Tattersett School near Fakenham, kept a diary of these incursions, which she called *What I See of the War*. Extracts were later published in *Norfolk Fair* and make illuminating reading:

> October 13th. This horrible war has been raging since August. I have always known from my earliest days that I should live to see war in England. I have seen very bright lights in the sky at different times. I wonder what they can be? Can an aeroplane fly so high that in half light it is invisible?
>
> November 1st. Mr. Hurn told me he saw an aeroplane flying from Tattersett towards the coast – making for the

Burnham direction. He asked me if it was a Britisher? I said, 'No, only a German scout learning the country to guide the Zeppelins across presently.' How they all laughed at me, but time will prove.

Indeed, only two days later Miss Marson was proved tragically right when Zeppelins attacked Lowestoft, Southwold and Yarmouth. According to the *Norfolk News* of 3 November, they dropped eighteen bombs which 'shattered windows in all directions and set fire to several buildings, though no one was injured'. It was believed that the raiders were trying to demolish the railway stations and harbour works.

Early in the new year, the schoolteacher saw several more grey shapes high in the sky over Norfolk and one night even heard a noise close overhead 'that sounded like a threshing machine'.

January 14th. I have been told two aeroplanes followed each other over Syderstone. I'm not a bit satisfied that these are British machines. I think they are German hydroplanes learning the country by night for a bomb-dropping raid presently. I wonder if any of the soldiers on guard troubled to report them? They would simply say, '*Our* scouts are busy' and not dream of Germans.

After a report that bombs had been dropped on Sandringham on 20 January, there was a lull in activity, Miss Marson notes in her diary. On Easter Monday, however, she refers to another topic of concern: 'April 15th. When I ask young men why they don't enlist they answer, "Look at those about here – they have too many soldiers now." I answer, "These are guarding our shores. Wait till they move and the Germans will soon be here."'

The young woman's powers of prophecy were again proved not far short of the mark when, two days later, Lowestoft and Yarmouth were again bombed by Zeppelins. C R Temple, a schoolboy in Yarmouth at the time, later recalled the event in *Norfolk Fair*:

I had been kept up late because my dad was coming home on leave. When he arrived we heard a peculiar noise from somewhere outside, like a traction engine. Gradually the noise got louder and louder, so dad opened the door and looked out and there immediately above us was a large, cigar-shaped object which was making the noise. It was one of the German Zeppelins which had followed dad's train into the Beach Station – or so it was said at the time! We looked at it with something of amazement and just a little fear. We saw men walking about in one of the gondolas and quickly shut the door. Shortly afterwards we heard explosions. It had dropped its bombs on to Crown Road and St. Peter's Plain, killing a Mr Sam Smith, a cobbler, and an elderly spinster, outright.

The next morning I went along to view the damage and found houses terribly wrecked at St. Peter's Plain, craters in the road, walls knocked down and the windows and masonry in the nearby St. Peter's Church badly damaged and broken. The York Road Drill Hall, which it is said was aimed for, escaped damage, but nearby houses did not escape. After the raid all town lights were extinguished, thus locking the door after the horse had escaped.

In the following months, however, the improvement of England's air defences – with searchlights, antiaircraft guns and fighter squadrons in an organisation called the Air Defence of Great Britain – saw the Zeppelin threat steadily diminishing until they became no more than memories to people such as the prescient Miss Ruby Marson. In another diary entry in November 1915 she ponders:

I was very troubled by all these raids because I felt so help-less. I have asked myself whether the Zeppelins are fitted up with wireless installations to enable them to reach their targets. Is there someone who can read the messages transmitted from an airship? I wish I could find out.

Fate was to supply the Tattersett schoolteacher with the answer to her question – though not in the manner she might have predicted. For, almost a quarter of a century later, another Zeppelin flew over the east coast just prior to the outbreak of a second war with Germany that the people of England – and East Anglia especially – had hoped would never happen. By then, the messages from the German airship could be read and were helping to justify faith in an invention that it was hoped would ensure, once and for all, the country's safety from invasion.

In fact, this prized possession was to make the possibility even *more* likely than ever before.

Chapter 3

A Shadow Over Britain

The RAF Fighter Command operations room in Bentley Priory, Stanmore, on the outskirts of London, was functioning with its usual unflustered efficiency on the morning of 3 August 1939. The stylish mansion that had once been the home of a prior and earlier in the century a girls' boarding school, now housed dozens of offices and, ten metres underground, the RAF's vital command post. Here men and women methodically plotted the movement of all aircraft across the skies of Britain – and it was from here, in the event of a war, that the aerial defence of the country would be directed.

Built on two levels with a gallery overlooking a huge map of the British Isles and Western Europe, this centre of operations was technically known as the 'filter room'. The route or 'plot' of any aircraft approaching Britain was received from radar stations and checked against the known movements of friendly aircraft. Information about unidentified – or perhaps hostile – aircraft would then be passed to the group and sector operations rooms for action.

Although the WAAFs in their radio headsets and the uniformed RAF officers poring over the map were working away methodically as they had been trained, there was for all of them – and in particular the duty officer, Flight Lieutenant Walter Pretty – an almost tangible sense of foreboding in the air; a need for special vigilance now that the nation's relations with Germany were deteriorating so rapidly.

Then, just after 11 a.m., a signal was handed to Pretty. It told him that a 'very large blip' had been located above the clouds over the North Sea heading in the direction of the east coast. The officer's finely trained mind slipped into action. He and his team had been told to keep a special watch on those parts of the coast where it was thought possible an enemy action might occur. Could this be the beginning of the threat?

Almost instinctively, Pretty suspected the object must be an airship. The data he was handed *could* have indicated a large group of aircraft, but that seemed doubtful. More likely the blip was a Zeppelin. But, if his conclusion was right, *what* was the purpose of the giant airship?

Flight Lieutenant Pretty came up with an answer almost as quickly – and correctly. It had to be a spying mission to discover whether the British were in possession of radar, as Louis Brown has explained in his definitive study of this aspect of the war, *A Radar History of World War II* (1999):

> The notion that the flight was espionage occurred quickly, but the Air Force personnel already knew a fundamental law of electronic warfare. When you see a suspected electronic snoop on your radar, he has already seen you – so if you turn off your set you have given him proof of your function.

Pretty knew this – and he also knew he should do *nothing*. No air-raid alarm was to be sounded and no fighter squadron scrambled. He just had to keep a close check on where the airship went and what it did. Of course, the situation would have been very different a quarter of a century earlier – but this airship was using the clouds and overcast sky to keep well out of visual range. It had to be on a military mission and not a bombing raid.

The flight lieutenant alerted the other group and sector operations rooms to keep track of the intruder. At a point about 45 kilometres east of Lowestoft, the blip turned north and – for just a moment – Pretty had what he called a 'whimsical notion' to send a message to the airship informing the crew of their actual position. Moments later, though, the Zeppelin seemed to adjust its course and continue flying northwards just offshore.

The lowering clouds over the east coast did not, in fact, break until the airship had reached Aberdeen with the RAF tracking every mile of her progress. There, the sudden appearance of the intruder with its unmistakable German insignia produced an immediate surge of worried phone calls from local residents to the Auxiliary Air Force base at Dyce. Within minutes, Squadron Leader Findlay Crerar had taken off to reassure the public there was nothing to worry about. In his passenger seat was a cameraman to photograph the airship in order to identify those who were flying her.

The craft was, in fact, the new LZ-130, *Graf Zeppelin*, the sister ship of the LZ-129, *Hindenburg*, which had been destroyed in the horrendous fire at Lakehurst, New Jersey, in May 1937. It was known that the Zeppelin had not long completed its trials and was currently on charter to Colonel Wolfgang Martini, *General der Luftnachrichtentruppe* (director general of the Luftwaffe's signals and radar division). It was known, too, that he had already made several similar trips over neighbouring countries to the east and west of Germany.

There was, therefore, no doubt in Flight Lieutenant Pretty's mind – nor those of his superiors to whom this information was relayed – that Martini was intent on electronic espionage to discover whether or not Britain had a radar defence system. The German colonel was a career serviceman and scientist with an outstanding knowledge of communication systems. He had played an important role in developing the country's own type of radar system and was keen to test it under actual conditions.

Martini had decided on the LZ-130 for his spying missions because of its capacity to carry heavy equipment along with an extensive team of technicians, headed by Germany's top specialist in the field, Dr Ernst Breuning. The thorough colonel also preferred the airship's leisurely pace because it allowed his men more time to investigate any interesting signals they might pick up.

As the airship continued further north, Pretty and his colleagues had no trouble picking up its large-amplitude signals and even noted its course when it unintentionally veered overland at Hull. Louis Brown provides the finale to this first shadow of invasion over Britain:

> The trip continued far enough north for examining any signals that might have come from the Scapa Flow naval base, but none of the Thames Estuary. The original route would have covered these stations and the entire coast, but the weather – England's old ally – intervened, causing the airship to pause near Bawdsey as it changed course. There have since been a dozen versions of the Zeppelin espionage flight, frequently conflicting and eliminated by subsequent research, but all agree that Martini found no trace of British radar. The suspected reason is that no one in Germany conceived of radar on such long wave-lengths, of such a low pulse repetition rate, or of radiating over such a wide front as the British operated.

The one element of the trip that did cause genuine alarm at the time was the German airship's 'pause' near Bawdsey. Unknown to all but those working there – plus a few senior government officials and service chiefs – the remote peninsula on the east coast in Suffolk was the place where radar had been developed and was now being perfected. Indeed, several of the Bawdsey scientists were convinced the airship's change of course was no accident and they were now 'marked for destruction when the war began', according to radar historian A P Rowe.

As inhabitants of one of the country's most secret sites, they had good reason to be worried.

In August 1939, Bawdsey, at the southern end of Hollesley Bay and just over eight miles from Harwich, was undeniably a very sensitive locality. It was home to the 'all-seeing eye' of radar, the brilliant electrical invention that would prove so vital to Britain in pursuing its lonely war against Germany.

Radar had initially been developed on Orford Ness, an isolated splinter of island at the other end of the bay, and then moved into Bawdsey Manor at the mouth of the River Deben. Professor Robert Watson-Watt, the superintendent of radio research at the National Physical Laboratory, had first proposed the concept that radio echoes might detect aircraft as early as 1935. He had been consulted after the admission by the RAF chiefs at a defence meeting that their fighters were practically incapable of intercepting enemy bombers if they attacked the country. A solution was urgently required.

Watson-Watt's first experiments on Orford Ness produced encouraging results. In February 1936, it was decided to purchase Bawdsey Manor to provide proper laboratories and comfortable living space for the team of radio-physicists and technicians turning the great man's vision into a reality. The elevation of Bawdsey, poised seventy feet above sea level and standing in its own estate of 150 acres, greatly increased the scope of Watson-Watt's experiments – categorised as 'radio direction finding' (RDF). Later, this would be imaginatively changed to 'radar' – a word reading the same forwards or backwards – and more suitable when the later lightweight versions classified as 'air interception' (AI) were fitted into fighter aircraft to help detect enemy bombers during the night battles of 1940–1.

Soon enough, however, the erection of steel and wooden masts – rising between 240 feet (for receivers) and 360 feet (for transmitting signals), towering above the tree line at Bawdsey – was being noticed by local residents, as Gordon King has written in *Flight Over the Eastern Counties Since 1937* (1977):

> These towers caused a great deal of local gossip and speculation. The supposed purpose of them ranged from death-rays to rays for stopping aircraft engines, and tales circulated of cars which for no apparent reason stopped in the vicinity of Bawdsey, the drivers being informed by Service personnel that their trouble would cease at such and such a time. Whether with official backing or not, the stories went the rounds and maybe helped in some small way to camouflage the true purpose of the establishment.

Left largely undisturbed, Watson-Watt's scientists got on with their work and by late 1937 had drawn up plans for a string of twenty radar stations – named 'chain homes' and abbreviated to 'CH' – stretching around the coast from the Isle of Wight to Scapa Flow. They were able to detect aircraft flying above 10,000 feet and possessed ranges varying from 50 to 125 miles.

The cost of building these stations exceeded £2 million – but by September 1938 the majority were on continuous watch. In order for the operators to gain expertise, all types of flights over the country were monitored – varying from daily commercial flights in and out of London's main airport at Croydon to the flight of Prime Minister Neville Chamberlain's Lockheed airliner to Germany. As Derek E Johnson says in his book, *East Anglia at War 1939–1945* (1978), about another fact that could have done little for the peace of mind of the resident scientists, 'The observers at Bawdsey could follow the arrival of aircraft from Europe more accurately than the controller at Croydon Airport. One thing they did notice was that the *Deutsche Lufthansa* aircraft nearly always flew low over Bawdsey when they approached England.'

When Watson-Watt conducted Winston Churchill on a tour of Orford Ness and Bawdsey in June 1940, it proved a memorable experience, but the scientist later confessed in his book, *Three Steps to Victory* (1957), 'We did our tricks for him, and foolishly tried to explain to him what was inside some of our black boxes'.

Churchill may not have fully understood the technicalities of radar – but he was certainly in no doubt of its importance. Nor did he doubt that Bawdsey might feature on any list of locations the Germans would want to take in the event of an invasion. On his return to London, he promptly wrote a memo to the air minister, Sir Kingsley Wood: 'These vital R.D.F. stations require immediate protection. We thought at first of erecting dummy duplicates and triplicates of them at little expense, but on reflection it seems to me that here is a case for using the smoke-cloud'.

A Suffolk historian, Christopher R Elliott, who investigated the history of Bawdsey, has explained what is meant by this 'smoke-cloud' in an article for the *East Anglian Magazine*, June 1967: 'Elaborate steps of all kinds of ingenuity were taken to confuse enemy agents. "Artists" even came and went with their paint boxes and "bird watchers" kept a keen eye everywhere.'

In fact, the nation was desperate for means of deceiving the enemy in the early months of the war. Many answered the call, but perhaps no one more unlikely – or successful – than the novelist, Dennis Wheatley, the top-selling British author in the thirties, who dreamed up a whole series of anti-invasion proposals, many geared to his favoured east coast.

I first met Dennis Wheatley in 1974, when he was living in an opulent flat in London's fashionable Cadogan Square, Knightsbridge. A florid, egocentric personality who wore his dark hair parted rigorously down the centre of his head, he was a man of strong opinions, but a good conversationalist and generous host.

I had been told before meeting him in his first-floor flat with its lofty rooms and rich furnishings, that he was someone who aroused conflicting opinions in those who spent time with him. I was cautioned, too, that few escaped his liberal dispensing of wines without a hangover the next day, and when, inevitably, I had to use his lavatory, to look out for the framed letter from King George VI thanking him for his war work that hung behind the door. I was not disappointed in either of these respects.

For many years, Wheatley claimed that the Official Secrets Act had prevented him from talking about his work during the war. He was, though, less reticent thirty years on in the final decade of his life.

From our conversation it was clear that he believed Hitler had intended to invade Britain. But what was really surprising was a story he had heard that some Germans *did* actually land in the country. Indeed my talk with him on that winter night in London was to prove one of the cornerstones when it came to writing this book.

Born at the turn of the twentieth century into a family of Mayfair wine merchants, he was a cadet on HMS *Worcester* before serving as a gunner officer with the 36th (Ulster) Division in World War One. He fought at Passchendaele, Cambrai and St Quentin before being gassed and invalided from the army. Wheatley returned to the family business, but sold it in 1932 to follow his dream of becoming a writer. His first novel, *The Forbidden Territory*, published in 1933 proved an immediate success – being reprinted seven times in seven weeks – and in his career as a popular novelist of tales of espionage and high adventure he never looked back.

In the early months of 1939, Wheatley was combining his activities as a bestselling novelist, society figure and partygoer with writing occasional articles for the national press. His combat experiences in World War One – plus following the events in the Spanish Civil War – had given him an especial interest in the threat posed by Hitler. The result was an article for the *Sunday Graphic* in which he urged people to lay in stores of tinned food in case of an emergency. The paper offered a prize for the best list of 'sustaining items' and received more than 14,000 entries.

'That April, war was very much in the air,' he told me, 'and I invented a game called Invasion. It was played with small counters of three shapes, representing the army, navy and air force, on a large map. The moves depended on throws of the dice by each player in turn. Geographia, a subsidiary of Hutchinson, published it and it was a great success.'

When war was declared in September, Wheatley, then 43, offered his services to the newly formed Ministry of Information. Annoyed when he was summarily rejected despite his experience as a novelist and journalist, he decided instead to aim higher and made use of a family friend to get an introduction to MI5. Once again, the man whose spy thrillers were being read all over the world found himself being denied entry to the real world of espionage.

Frustrated but not downhearted, Wheatley threw himself into writing a new novel, *The Scarlet Impostor*, a topical novel featuring his dashing hero, Gregory Sallust, set during the early months of the war and forecasting – prophetically – a conspiracy to assassinate Hitler. He considered it his best work and was delighted when the critic of the *Evening Standard* hailed it as 'the first great spy story of the war'.

However, while Wheatley was hard at work on another book that winter, he was startled to receive a visit from MI5 – the very people who had rejected his services. His name had apparently been found in some files left by William Joyce, the notorious 'Lord Haw-Haw', after the traitor had fled to Germany to offer his services to the Nazi Party. Wheatley was amused at the contents of the file – but very relieved they were not being taken seriously.

'There was a copy of a report by Joyce to his Nazi masters,' Wheatley explained. 'In it he said that, because I had a number of Jewish friends, I was not quite clean on that aspect of their policy. But, in all other respects, after the invasion, when able collaborators would be needed, I would make a first class *Gauleiter* for northwest London!'

While Wheatley had been busy at home, however, Joan, his wife, had succeeded where he had failed and got a job with MI5 at their 'office' in St James's Street. There she was in charge of petrol allocation and served occasionally as a driver. One particular journey she undertook was to change Dennis Wheatley's war completely. He repeated the story during our conversation and liked to think of it as a real-life adventure as dramatic as anything he had created in his fiction.

'The date was 27 May 1940,' he said, 'the day on which unknown to the public the evacuation from Dunkirk had begun. My wife was driving and her passenger was Captain Hubert Stringer, an army officer engaged in counterespionage, who was sure that Hitler's next move would be an invasion of Britain. He told her, "I've been given the job of thinking up ideas for resistance to invasion, but mine is normally police work and, apart from the routine stuff we already have laid on, I don't seem to be able to think of much we can do."

'My wife thought of me at home upset because I couldn't help the war effort. "Why don't you ask my husband?" Joan said to him. "His speciality is original ideas and I know he would jump at the chance of trying to make himself useful." As soon as I heard this I pushed my new Gregory Sallust novel, *The Black Baroness*, to one side and worked nonstop for fourteen hours writing seventeen thousand words for the first of my "war papers", *Resistance to Invasion*.'

Wheatley's paper was devoted to ideas that he believed could be implemented speedily to delay and hopefully stop a German landing that he envisaged 'would be confined to the coast from Cromer in the north to Beachy Head in the south'. He postulated the Germans would come in 'fleets of innumerable fast, shallow-draught motor boats holding from 20 to 40 men each'.

To counter the invasion – particularly if it was concentrated on the estuaries and rivers of East Anglia – he suggested erecting booms with mines attached and a barrier of hundreds of miles of fishing nets to foul the propellers of German landing craft. The widespread use of fire should also be considered in the form of 'Fire Ships' that could be anchored just behind the net barrier. These would be filled with crude oil and ignited as the invasion fleet approached. 'Flaming Oil', too, might be spread over the water to ignite enemy craft. Even rowing boats packed with high explosive could be detonated by shore parties 'causing confusion among the invaders', Wheatley wrote.

Further suggestions in *Resistance to Invasion* looked at measures that might be implemented on the shore: vast piles of old junk, obstacles of glass and nails to pierce the boots of the enemy, and the commandeering of every available yard of barbed wire. Even the old Martello towers might be pressed into use again, Wheatley said, along with pillboxes, 'tiger traps' and a variety of booby traps, especially antitank measures. On the Norfolk Broads, he felt it was important to set up antiaircraft floats 'covered by shore artillery to prevent landings by German troops in seaplanes'. The novelist also wanted secret forces of regular troops to be stationed on barges on the Broads as well as in the Essex creeks.

Finally, Wheatley argued that concealing the names of localities from the invaders was vital – 'particularly to the threatened area on the East Coast where all evidence of identity should be eliminated'. He even suggested with typical élan, 'we should not try to conceal what we cannot keep secret' and drop leaflets over German troop areas that might read:

Come to England this summer for your holiday and sample the fun we have prepared for you. Try bathing in our barbed-wire bathing enclosures. Try rowing in our boats which will blow up as you touch the tiller. Try running up our beaches covered in broken glass. Try picnicking in our lovely woods by the coast and get a two-inch nail through your foot. Try jumping into our ditches and get burnt alive. Come by air and meet our new death ray (this sort of lie is good tactics at a time like this). Every Nazi visitor guaranteed death or an ugly wound. England or Hell – it's going to be just the same for you in either!

When Colonel Stringer received the paper he was immediately impressed and copies were soon circulating through the higher echelons of the War Office. A week later, Dennis Wheatley was given another assignment – to put himself in the position of the German High Command and imagine *how* they would plan an invasion. Again he let his imagination loose for another 48 hours – fuelled, he told me, by three magnums of champagne and more than two hundred cigarettes – producing a document twice the length of the first which he called *The Invasion and Conquest of Britain*.

In this paper, Wheatley envisaged Hitler and his generals planning a five-day operation. As the Nazis already had every shipyard in Europe under their control, they would be able to institute a vast naval building programme. Then, utilising the combined German and Italian navies and air forces along with every liner, cargo ship, seagoing barge and motorboat that could be found, this awesome force would carry a 'picked force of 600,000 men' to secure a foothold on the country from the Kent coast to East Anglia, with airborne troops striking in at the Wash and Bristol to form a pincer movement.

He believed that the Nazis would initiate a ferocious programme of bombing of both military and civilian targets and might also try infiltrating troops disguised as parachutists, concealed in cargo ships, by submarine, and even by swimming, 'equipped with water-wings and water-tight bundles containing clothes, arms and rations'. Secret agents and fifth-columnists would certainly be on hand to aid the invasion, Wheatley believed, probably armed with doped cigarettes and chocolates to distribute to soldiers and civilians alike.

The author of *The Invasion and Conquest of Britain* was in no doubt that the Germans would stop at nothing to achieve their objective and would use the same brutality against the English as they had employed in Europe. They believed that 'the conquest of Britain means the conquest of the world' and would advocate the use of poison gas and bacteriological warfare to protect Nazi troops, 'though this is a matter for the chemical section and the final decision in both cases lies with the Führer'.

Long after Dennis Wheatley had submitted this document, he was to learn that the 'top brass' at the War Office had conceived a quite different approach by the Germans. He later claimed without a hint of false modesty, in an article for the *Evening News* in 1969,

> They had not envisaged the possibility of airborne landings designed to cut England into three sections and had placed the main landings on the coast of Suffolk. As a result, a special Committee under General Denning and Air Marshal Slessor was set up to re-examine the probabilities. My paper was studied by the Committee and afterwards Slessor told me that large parts of it had been adopted in their new and final approach.
>
> After the war, when the documents of the German General Staff were seized and examined, it transpired that in 'Operation Sea Lion' – their plan for the invasion of Britain – I had been right in all my major assumptions! Having thoroughly frightened myself, I at once sat down to write a third paper of 12,000 words, *Further Measures for Resistance to Invasion* which I dispatched to all those who had received my first two papers on 28 June.

In this Wheatley proposed the holding of 'Invasion Weekends' in which 'every able-bodied person in the kingdom should report to police stations and be allocated jobs such as digging trenches, making road barriers, strengthening defences and collecting every sort of material that might prove useful'. He also thought that special armbands should be issued to troops to enable them to be distinguished from any Germans disguised in British uniforms, and urged the setting up of a shadow government in Scotland, 'in the event of Mr. Churchill and other resolute members of the Cabinet being assassinated'.

No sooner had the novelist delivered his third manuscript, than he began work on a fourth, *Village Defence*, proposing that each community should be responsible for organising its own defence and self-sufficiency in the event of an invasion. With arms now pouring out from the factories and in from overseas, it would be possible to arm thousands of civilians – with the coastal villages having preference. 'We all know the fire power of modern weapons and that a single man with a Tommy-gun may quell a mob; but *you* are not going to stand about to be shot at, like nitwits, in a crowd.'

Wheatley wanted all men between the ages of 16 and 45 to form the first line of defence, with the older men and women of the village organising the supplies. The local Scout troop and any women with horses could provide means of communication, while even children could be encouraged to help the war effort by setting up a 'Bush Telegraph' using their toy drums and trumpets to signal an invasion. Most importantly, he wanted no one in the villages of East Anglia and the south coast to show any mercy to the invaders. In a paragraph headed 'Kill Your Man', he wrote straight-faced:

When you see the enemy do not have compassion on him if he happens to be a young, fair-faced boy. Remember that if that young German had a little more brains and guts he would be in the Nazi Air Force, then switch your mind

65

back to the women and children of France and Belgium who were mercilessly massacred by machine-guns from the air. If he had the chance, that German would do the same thing to your wife and children, and should they become refugees he *will* do it at the first opportunity if you let him live. Therefore, whenever you get the chance, don't hesitate, but shoot to kill. *That is your duty*. And you owe it to your friends and your country!

The novelist's profusion of ideas did not dry up there, either. He wrote further papers on 'Aerial Warfare' and 'A New A.R.P. Policy' and by August he had produced almost half a million words and set a number of military and political minds busy thinking. Churchill, for one, said that Wheatley was capable of 'magnificent conceptions', while King George VI – who had once bought wine from his business and now enjoyed his novels – also became an avid reader of his 'war reports'. Air Marshal Sir Lawrence Darvell probably best summed up the consensus of opinions when he wrote later, 'Wheatley's ideas were fresh, iconoclastic and challenging and had an influence out of all proportion to the expectations of their author.'

Looked at today, these documents – which were passed from the files of the War Office and the Air Ministry to the National Archives after the war and remained classified for over a decade – are a mixture of common sense and practicality, with the occasional odd, unusual and even outlandish idea. Yet they are all written with the verve of a popular novelist. Even he admitted to me during our conversation that some were 'a bit like comic opera' – but nonetheless he believed there was a germ of possibility in every one.

In the autumn of 1940, Wheatley was again asked for his ideas about what should be done in the future when the war was ultimately won. He has recalled the instructions he was given on this occasion in his memoirs, *The Time Has Come*, published shortly after his death on 10 November 1977:

It is a testimony to the Prime Minister's absolute confidence in victory, and his determination to secure Britain's future, that in September 1940, when our fortunes were at their lowest ebb, he ordered his Joint Planning Staff to produce for him a paper on the following problem, 'When we have won the war, what steps ought we to take to prevent Germany launching a Third World War against us in twenty years time?'

The directive came with a note, 'give to Wheatley', with a PS that he should be allowed a longer time for contemplation. When finished, *After the Battle* ran to 120,000 words – but like its predecessors again offered some surprising ideas, not the least of them a simple, if quite appalling, 'final solution' to the menace of Germany. Its population had to be reduced to numbers 'insufficient to go to war with any first-class Power', the novelist stated bluntly. Amid the welter of detail as to how this might be achieved, he wrote that the country would have to be reduced from a population of 80 million to 40 million and 'deprived of her great industrial zone in the Ruhr, so in no state ever again to launch a major war'.

When I met Wheatley some thirty years after he had written this document he seemed surprised that I should be shocked at such a radical proposal to 'cull' the German people – not all of whom had been die-hard Nazis – and divide their nation into smaller states such as Bavaria, Bohemia and Silesia.

'That was the advantage of being a free agent,' he smiled, lighting up yet another cigarette. 'I said what I liked. I wasn't frightened I should be sacked or sent to Iceland.'

Not wishing to pursue this issue, I returned to the subject that had begun our conversation – the likelihood of Britain's being invaded by Germany.

'There were a lot of stories around at the time about what the Germans might or might not do if they landed,' he explained, 'which is the reason why I enjoyed writing those "war papers". There was a chap at the War Office who told me that a little group of Germans had actually come ashore on the coast of Suffolk. They were most probably reconnoitring for a landing place. Somewhere near where that nuclear power station was built at Sizewell.'

The story caught my interest at once. Did he know any more details?

Wheatley took another sip of wine and shrugged his shoulders. No, it was just something he remembered hearing during those hectic days of the summer of 1940 when he was constantly in and out of the ministry buildings in London, meeting with the 'top brass' of the armed forces and assisting the work of the Joint Planning Staff.

Was it just another of his inventions, I wondered, a tale he planned for one of his ingenious novels and somehow never got around to using? I had come to appreciate during our talk that he was a man who had always loved being privy to secrets and classified information and took pleasure in dropping titbits to his society friends for added kudos. But this was something that had happened long ago.

I did know, however, that he had a particular soft spot for the east coast of England. He had gone on holiday there as a child, spent some of his time as a cadet at Harwich, and had close friends he visited regularly at Aldeburgh and Cromer. I also remembered that one of his early novels, with the appropriately prophetic title *Dark August*, written in 1934, is set on this coast around the little community of Shingle Street.

The plot describes an England a few years hence about to be taken over by communists. After a group of revolutionaries, the 'Greyshirts', seize Scotland and Wales and march on London to secure their final triumph, a party of dedicated royalists, including the indomitable Gregory Sallust, Kenton Wensleadale, a prospective MP for Mid-Suffolk, and a pretty young secretary, Anne Croome, flee from the panic and chaos in the capital to set up a last defence in Shingle Street. Here they fortify the village for a siege and try to defy the marauding Greyshirts with fake signs: WAR DEPARTMENT – ENTRANCE FORBIDDEN. The story continues:

> The first ten days at Shingle Street had seen the transformation of that quiet hamlet into a pulsing centre of strange and seemingly unconnected activities: the second saw them take form and cohesion. The fortifications were now almost completed and a long line of breastworks linked the Martello Tower on the south with a redoubt on the north, screening the whole village and the stockaded enclosure on the landward side. The occupants had also acquired three Lewis guns and eight shotguns and hoped to be able to put up a performance which would lead the enemy to think the garrison was far stronger than it was.

When the Greyshirts finally mount an attack on the little community, the results are stark and horrifying, as Wheatley recounts: 'One by one the houses seemed to leap into a blinding sheet of flame as the projectiles struck them, and then disappear, so that the remnants of the burning hamlet began to take on the appearance of a row of black and jagged teeth which were being steadily extracted.'

For the young secretary, Anne, a still greater horror awaits when she runs down to the beach after the first bombardment. There in the darkness she finds piles of bodies and a group of people trying to help the dying, while stretcher-bearers are busy removing the corpses. In desperation, she sets off to get help – and hours later stumbles into the suburbs of Ipswich, where she is confronted by a man who bars her way and demands to know what she is doing:

> 'Communists,' muttered Anne, 'they're going to burn them.'
> 'Eh! What's that?' he questioned with a quick glance. 'Where have you come from?'

'Shingle Street,' she flung at him with a terrible effort. 'They'll be burnt alive unless I can get help!'

As in all the best adventure stories – and especially those by Dennis Wheatley – help arrives in the nick of time, in this case with a counterrevolution led by the Prince Regent, who defeats the Greyshirts and restores law and order in Britain. Shingle Street, though, is left with terrible scars of explosives on its buildings and the awful memories of the bodies on the beach.

In an extraordinary example of prescience – and with the mere substitution of the word 'Nazis' for 'communists' – Wheatley had described a series of events that would occur *in reality* in the little hamlet just seven years later. But, remarkable as this coincidence is, it was Dennis Wheatley's hint of a real German landing a few miles up the coast from the location of his novel that stuck most clearly in my memory. Later it, too, would re-emerge during my search for the truth about where the eagle landed.

It is, though, important to remember that at this point in time Wheatley's anti-invasion ideas – practical, possible or wholly improbable – were all part of a great national resolve in the summer of 1940 to prevent such a threat from becoming reality – a threat that had been growing ever since the idea had first been sown in the mind of Adolf Hitler, and was even now filling a top-secret British file with the curious title of Operation Smith.

Chapter 4

Hitler and Operation Smith

To the army motorcycle dispatch rider travelling through the beautiful Cotswold countryside on a June morning in 1940, the war and the London blackout he had left behind earlier now seemed a million miles away. As he had ridden through Hounslow and on to Reading and Newbury, his spirits had gradually lifted until by the time he sped past the Marlborough Downs and was nearing his final destination in Tetbury, Gloucestershire, he was even whistling to himself.

The rider was a regular serviceman attached to the War Office and, with a young wife and baby who had been evacuated from the capital to Wales, he was glad of any opportunity to get out of the smoke for a few hours. He wished he could ride on to see them after he made his delivery in Tetbury, but he knew this was impossible. It was the first time he had made this run, but another rider who had done it several times gave him instructions on how to find Chavenage Manor on the outskirts of Tetbury. His motorcycle clattered through the town's rows of ancient buildings before taking a side road out into the rolling Cotswold Hills.

The man's destination was an Elizabethan manor house that was now being used as an administrative branch of the War Office. Ever since the previous year when war with Germany seemed likely, Parliament, the Cabinet and the three armed forces had made plans to relocate in the event of London's being attacked and perhaps destroyed. Parliament would sit in Shakespeare's birthplace, Stratford-on-Avon, with the War Cabinet moving to Hindlip Hall, near Worcester. The Admiralty's new HQ would be in Malvern, the Air Ministry in Worcester and the War Office in Droitwich. All five groups had, in the meantime, set up secondary administrative offices at different locations across the countryside to cope with the anticipated flood of papers and documents relating to the war.

Tetbury was typical of these places, run by a small group of army personnel and female clerks. Like all such departments, it had been given a codeword, 'Smith' in this case, and among the documents the motorcyclist was carrying in his panniers were several files bearing this prefix and all embossed with a red stamp, TOP SECRET. Each contained information that had been received at the War Office's main building in Whitehall about the possibility of a German invasion.

The man from London was happy to reach his destination and hand over the material to a duty officer. If he saw the slightly puzzled look on the face of the officer as the man opened the files, he took no notice of it. He was just anxious to get something to eat before making the return trip to London.

The frown that crossed the officer's face – a new man just assigned to Tetbury – was due to the fact that the information he glanced at was undoubtedly very sensitive. It seemed to be details of how Hitler was planning to invade England. But where had it originated, he asked himself, and why had it been sent to Chavenage? With a shrug of his shoulders, the officer decided the only thing to do was to keep the files under lock and key until he was given orders what to do with them. As soon as he had done that, he, too, went off for a meal break.

What neither of these men knew was that they were the victims of an administration error. Just a few weeks earlier, Winston Churchill had decided that any information relevant to an invasion threat should be referred to as 'Operation

Smith' – unaware that the War Office had already appropriated the name for its minor branch in the Cotswolds.

The threat – now growing in momentum every day – had been revealed thanks to the cracking of the Germans' Enigma code machine by which all top-secret information was passed between their army, navy and air force. However, the German codename *'Unternehmen Seelöwe'* (Operation Sea Lion) was still unknown – it would not, in fact, be discovered until 21 September – and hence Churchill's chance selection of 'Smith' and the confusion it caused, as R V Jones has explained in *Most Secret War* (1978):

> It turned out that the War Office had its own 'Operation Smith' that was concerned with the invasion. It was the code name for the movement of one of its minor administrative branches from its current headquarters in Tetbury to some place further north if the Germans should have invaded and posed a threat to south Gloucestershire. The result was that when the Bletchley teleprints were received in the War Office, duly headed according to the Prime Minister's instructions, they were immediately sent to a Colonel in Gloucestershire, who no doubt impressed by the service that the War Office was providing but realizing that the material was too secret for general circulation, locked them in his safe and told nobody.

In hindsight, Winston Churchill could not have chosen a more commonplace name for a more momentous and deadly plan.

The sheer magnitude of what was being planned across the Channel was indeed awesome, as Egbert Kieser has written in his 1987 study of events from the German standpoint, *Hitler on the Doorstep: Operation 'Sea Lion'* (published in English in 1999):

> This – in terms of the dimensions of its preparations – greatest operation in German military history, made the

world hold its breath during one summer: an invasion of the British Isles by German forces after the rapid overthrow of France was but a logical next step, because Great Britain was the only opponent still left.

According to Kieser, Hitler first considered a plan for invading England on 21 May 1940, the day on which the German panzer troops reached the coast of France and were able to gaze across at the glistening White Cliffs of Dover. Although the Führer would not issue his directive for 'Operation Sea Lion' for another two months, it was Admiral Erich Raeder, the commander-in-chief of the German navy, who brought up the subject that he himself had been contemplating since not long after the declaration of war. He, if anyone, was the 'godfather' of the plan to invade England.

Raeder was a clever and much respected naval veteran who had risen to the top of his service after working as chief of staff to Admiral Hipper in World War One, and then been made head of the *Oberkommando der Marine* (OKM) in October 1928. His immediate ambitions were to build a fleet on parity with France and eventually one to challenge all the other major maritime powers. Construction began immediately on three *Panzerschiffe* (pocket battleships), followed by plans for a fleet of eight more of these battleships, three aircraft carriers and 72 U-boats. In 1939, Raeder was promoted to *Grossadmiral* and such was the progress in building the ships that it seemed his objective of creating a world-class navy was attainable.

However, Raeder undoubtedly had an ambivalent attitude towards his Nazi overlords – in particular Hermann Goering, *Oberkommando der Luftwaffe* (OKL) – although there was no question he admired Hitler for having restored Germany to what he considered her rightful place among the great powers. But the evidence suggests that Hitler had not thought of crossing the Channel before Raeder conceived the idea in the winter of 1939, as Kieser has stated in his book:

During a visit by Raeder to the Chief of Naval Command on 6 November 1939, talk turned to the continuation of the war after a possible victory over France. Would the Führer decide to starve Great Britain out by means of a blockade or intend to land on the islands with masses of troops? Hitler had just designated 12 November 1939 as the date for the attack on the west.

Raeder was well aware of Hitler's sudden whims that would be followed by a demand for action, and decided not to leave such a possibility to chance. On 15 November, under conditions of great secrecy, he created a small team headed by Vice Admiral Otto Schniewind to examine the military, naval and transportation aspects of 'a possible invasion of England'. The men set to work with a will and a week later Raeder was presented with a document entitled 'Study Red', which concluded,

> If a victory in the West or a stabilisation of the front permits forces to become available, a landing operation across the North Sea to the south coast on a large scale would appear to us to be a possible means of forcing the enemy to sue for peace.

There were, however, several crucial conditions to be met if such an invasion was to succeed. The Royal Navy had to be eliminated or kept away from the landing area and attacks by submarines prevented during the crossing. The enemy coastal defences must be destroyed. And – most important of all – the RAF had to be driven from the skies.

Raeder decided to send copies of 'Study Red' to the OKL and the *Oberkommando des Heeres* (OKH), headed by General Walter von Brauchitsch, who instructed a Major I G Stieff to prepare a counter-report, 'Study Northwest'. In this, the army experts expressed concern at the numbers of troops available because of the campaigns going on in Europe. What they *were* agreed upon was that any invasion should be centred on the *east* coast, and it has been suggested that one of the influences on their thinking was a book that had been published in 1934 just a year after the Nazis had come to power and caused a sensation. It was *Raum und Volk im Weltkrieg!* (Germany – Prepare for War!) by Dr Ewald Banse, in which he proposed occupying Holland, Belgium and the northwest coast of France. Although officially denounced in government circles, the book became a bestseller. What may have been particularly significant as far as Major Stieff was concerned was this paragraph by the fulminating doctor:

> When invading England an important region to be occupied is East Anglia for the Great Ouse which flows into the Wash and a number of streams flowing into the Blackwater Estuary which are separated from the source of the Ouse by a few miles only, make the peninsula into a regular island which provides an invading army with safe and roomy quarters, from which it can threaten London (which is quite close and without natural defences on that side) and also the industrial Midlands not far away.

Just how influential Banse's book was on the military thinking will never be known, but Kieser draws together the strands of the differing viewpoints:

> Taking the difficulties into consideration that the *Kriegsmarine* had been confronted with in 'Study Red' in assuming a landing on the English southern coast, Major Stieff and his team moved the landing north between the Thames estuary and the Wash. Air Division 7, reinforced by the 16th Infantry Regiment, were to take the ports of Yarmouth and Lowestoft in an airborne operation, while one infantry division and a brigade of cyclists landed in the ports from the sea. South of the ports, a further

76

infantry division was to land on the open coast near Dunwich and on Hollesley Bay in front of Ipswich, in order to prevent enemy counter-operations from there. A second landing wave consisting of two panzer divisions, a motorised infantry division and a reinforced infantry division, was to follow.

Stieff's team also had in mind a diversionary landing north of the Humber. This was intended to divert attention further away from the primary objective, London. Once the German forces had been landed on the coast of East Anglia, they believed, it would be possible to cut off the capital's lines of communication and seize the greatest prize.

The Luftwaffe was, however, far from enthusiastic, claiming that it could not meet the requirements of the other two services. 'The planned deployment is therefore only possible under a condition of total air superiority and even then, only if complete surprise is guaranteed,' the OKL reply stated bluntly.

All of this debate was behind Raeder when he put the idea to Hitler for the first time on 21 May. At this meeting – to quote the *Grossadmiral*'s own account – the two men 'discussed in private details concerning the invasion of England on which the Naval Staff had been working since November'. Hitler's reaction was, apparently, negative, since he was convinced the embattled British would 'come to their senses' and seek a negotiated peace.

The admiral, of course, knew his leader's attitude could change at any moment, and gave orders for a list to be drawn up of the numbers of ships available for short sea crossings including the shipping resources of the recently conquered nations. He wanted inland vessels on the list, too: barges, tugs and motorboats, complete with details of their suitability for landing operations plus the space available for cargo and troops. A daunting estimate soon came through that up to 750,000 tons of shipping – in the main cargo ships of around 7,500 tons – would be required.

A topographical study of the English coast from the Isle of Wight to the Wash was also instigated, with special attention being given to beaches where a landing might be attempted. Much of the information that came to hand indicated that the southern shore would be treacherous because of the numerous sandbanks and rocky ledges and it would be essential for pilots with up-to-date information to travel on the landing craft. Fair weather at all times would be critical.

When this information was passed to Raeder in early June, it also contained a memorandum, 'Studie England', by Rear Admiral Karl Fricke, the head of the OKM's Operations Division. In this he proposed a possible landing area between Portland Bill and Great Yarmouth as the crossing would be shorter, the landing beaches were easier and more numerous and the country behind was less heavily populated and less easy to defend. Fricke also believed that an invasion on the east coast could be launched from harbours between Denmark and the Scheldt that were more secure from the RAF's reconnaissance and bombing. In an estimation – and a comparison that must have made Raeder shudder when he read it – the rear admiral concluded his report, 'The crossing of the Channel is similar to the crossing of a river, in which, because of the width and peculiarities of the waters to be crossed, the *Kriegsmarine* as the branch of the services specifically trained for this sort of thing, is to be employed.'

Hitler, though, remained cool to the idea when his navy chief raised the idea again on 20 June – despite the fact that circumstances in Europe had changed dramatically. The French had just sought an armistice, Italy had joined in the war, and the forces of the Third Reich now controlled much of Europe.

If ever there was a moment to press home the advantage and invade Britain this was surely it. Instead, according to Raeder, with typical unpredictability Hitler talked about a plan for settling Jews on Madagascar and pondered on a scheme for invading Iceland bizarrely codenamed 'Icarus'.

The passing of another month and the continued lack of any sign of Britain's capitulation gave Hitler cause for second thoughts. On 16 July, exercising his authority as chancellor of the German Reich and supreme commander of its armed forces, he issued what would become famously known as 'Directive No. 16': 'Preparations for the Invasion of England'. The purpose of this statement was made abundantly clear in its opening paragraph:

As England, in spite of the hopelessness of her military position, has so far shown herself unwilling to come to any compromise, I have decided to begin to prepare for, and if necessary to carry out, an invasion of England. This operation is dictated by the necessity of eliminating Great Britain as a base for which the war against Germany can be fought, and if necessary the island will be occupied.

Hitler continued more specifically:

A landing should not be undertaken for the purpose of overthrowing England *militarily*, which can be achieved by the *Luftwaffe* and the *Kriegsmarine*, but only to give the *coup de grâce*, if necessary, to an England which is economically paralysed and impotent in the air. It cannot be expected that such a state of affairs can be achieved before late August or early September.

A third paragraph indicated that the Führer had decided on a landing point for the invasion. It was *not* to be the isolated and more vulnerable east coast, but on a front over two hundred miles along the south coast:

The landing operation must be a surprise crossing on a broad front extending approximately from Ramsgate to a point west of the Isle of Wight. Units of the *Luftwaffe* will

79

do the work of artillery while the *Kriegsmarine* will do the work of engineers. I ask each of the fighting services to consider the advantages, from their own point of view, *of preliminary operations* [my italics] such as the occupation of the Isle of Wight in advance of the full-scale invasion, and to inform me of their proposals. I shall be responsible for the final decision. Preparations for the full-scale operation must be complete by the middle of August.

Hitler then issued a series of orders to the German forces to implement what was originally codenamed '*Unternehmen Löwe*' (Operation Lion), which he personally later changed to the more apt 'Operation Sea Lion'. It was a document that would represent a turning point in both World War Two and the future of the author himself.

Even Raeder, who had been anticipating that such a change of mind might occur, was stunned at the speed of Hitler's decision. It was, after all, only eight weeks earlier that he had first discussed the idea of invasion and previously it had been the Führer's custom to give the orders for attacks on countries – for example Czechoslovakia and Poland – at least four to five *months* in advance.

But there was no arguing with Hitler's instructions. The Führer said he would be in sole charge and all the invasion forces would take orders from him.

It seemed evident to Raeder as he read the orders for Operation Sea Lion, that the OKM was to be responsible for transport across the Channel and fighting the Royal Navy, while the Luftwaffe would prevent air attacks and strike at the English coastal defences and any front-line troops. The OKH would simply get into the armada of ships, cross the Straits of Dover and capture a largely impotent England. Raeder could be forgiven for feeling he had a daunting, even impossible, task.

Goering, of course, had already begun the Luftwaffe's offensive against Britain with a series of probing attacks intended to discover the strength of the RAF. Following the publication of Directive No. 16, he stepped up his plans – not to mention his boasts that it would take only a few days for his pilots to destroy Fighter Command and four weeks to finish off the RAF. What followed during the summer days after the beginning of the Battle of Britain on 10 July is now one of the proudest pages in the English history of the war.

In Britain, of course, the public knew nothing of Hitler's invasion order. But at the Reichstag on 19 July, while ostensibly promoting a number of his senior officers – notably Goering, who was given the unprecedented rank of *Reichs- marschall* – the Führer offered the British a final chance to avoid disaster. In a broadcast to the German people, he declared, 'In this hour, I feel it my duty before my conscience, to appeal once more to reason and common sense in Great Britain as elsewhere. I consider myself in a position to make this appeal since I am not the vanquished begging favours, but the victor speaking in the name of reason. I can see no reason why this war must go on.'

As if to drive home the extent of the Führer's generosity, his speech was translated into English and printed as a leaflet under the banner headline A LAST APPEAL TO REASON. Many thousands of these were scattered by German aircraft across the eastern counties of England to become the object of amusement and even derision, not to mention instant collectors' items!

Along the coast of France and parts of the Low Countries, feverish preparations were going on by the Germans to prepare for invasion. Ever-increasing numbers of ships of all shapes and sizes began to assemble, while on the beaches large numbers of soldiers went through arduous landing exercises. The ports to be used for embarkation were also checked for feasibility and damage as a result of the recent battles. Boulogne and Calais were operational and Dunkirk two-fifths so. Another port just along the coast, Gravelines, which was destined to feature in a strange invasion mystery about burned corpses, was passed 'usable for smaller vessels'.

Estimates of the available military strength of the German forces at this time make revealing reading and provide a vivid picture of the grand scale of Operation Sea Lion. The *Kriegsmarine* had assembled 155 cargo ships totalling over 700,000 tons, plus 1,277 barges and lighters and 470 tugs or steam trawlers to tow them. These barges had been fitted with concrete floors, ramps and drawbridges to enable them to carry heavy vehicles such as armoured cars and medium tanks. The basic units for transporting the men – referred to as *Schleppzugs* (tug-trains) – would consist of a tug or steam trawler towing two barges with a complement of 300 soldiers. The whole armada would be accompanied by 1,200 small naval craft, including minesweepers, patrol boats and launches for additional artillery.

The Luftwaffe, for its part, had 25,000 airborne troops on standby – of whom almost 7,000 were paratroopers – along with 750 Junkers, 52 transport planes and 150 gliders. The OKH, in turn, was moving the 6th and 9th Armies to the coast. The invasion troops would cross in two waves: the first consisting of six divisions of 90,000 men with panzers, machine guns and antitank guns plus 4,600 vehicles; the second of seven divisions of 170,000 men armed with heavy weaponry and more than 34,000 vehicles. A total of 260,000 men and more than 40,000 vehicles, not forgetting 62,000 horses and 26,000 bicycles!

None of this preparation had gone unnoticed by the RAF, who were flying increasing numbers of reconnaissance flights to add to the mounting information being collected about Operation Smith. Colin Smith has recalled these heady days for the Germans as they prepared for their 'gigantic river crossing' in *Why Hitler Sank Sealion* (1974):

Morale among the German soldiers preparing for the operation was high. They had great victories behind them and they sang cheerfully: 'We sail away to conquer Eng-el-land.' But many of them, from central Germany, had never even seen the sea before and it was discernible that units from the Baltic coast, who did know something of the sea, adopted a more cautious attitude. However, all lined up in French ports and on beaches to practise disembarking with their barges and for swimming lessons. One general went bathing with his staff: when they came out they were amazed to find that their car was being engulfed by the incoming tide.

While all this was going on, Admiral Raeder sent another memorandum to Hitler stressing again the importance of air supremacy in the invasion as well as the threat posed by the Royal Navy 'to throw in all its forces to achieve a decision'. Once again, he was summoned to a meeting with the Führer on 21 July. Reiterating that he believed the war had 'been decided but Britain will not admit the fact', Hitler told his *Gross-admiral*, '*Seelöwe* seems to be the best way of ending the war in our favour. We should at the same time pursue diplomatic initiatives with Spain, Russia and Japan, though these will inevitably be long and difficult since the world seems to expect that England will be saved by a miracle. Invading Britain would be a very daring operation because, even though the sea crossing is short, there is more to it than a large-scale river crossing since the sea is dominated by the enemy. We cannot compare it with the invasion of Norway, which required only a single sea-borne crossing.

'Tactical surprise is unattainable. The enemy is utterly determined, defensively prepared and dominates the intervening sea. The Army will require forty divisions and their supply will be extremely difficult since we must assume that no supplies will be available for them in England. The prerequisites are absolute control of the air, the use of heavy artillery in the Straits of Dover and effective protection from

mine barriers on the flanks. The main landing must be carried
out by 15 September and, if all the preparations are not
complete by the beginning of that month, other plans will have
to be discussed.'

Hitler's more reasoned argument – not to mention his
rejection of the idea that the operation was just a 'large-scale
river crossing', which had never pleased Raeder – may well
have made the commander-in-chief feel his mission was not
quite so impossible. However, before the next interservice
meeting scheduled for the last weekend of July, the Führer was
to have yet another profound change of heart.

'On 23 July he [Hitler] had attended a special performance
of *Götterdämmerung* at Bayreuth,' Michael Glover has
explained in *Invasion Scare 1940* (1990), 'and left the opera
house with the conviction that he must attack Russia. For the
moment this decision was not communicated to the three
services, but within the Supreme Command of the German
Forces a study group was established to work on a plan.'

Hitler allowed Raeder and the other service chiefs to
continue with their plans for Operation Sea Lion until the end
of the month. And then at a meeting on 31 July he dropped his
bombshell: the way to defeat Britain would be to attack Russia,
he declared unequivocally. The thought of switching the target
of attack from the small island of Britain to the vast wilderness
of Russia must have been mind-blowing to the assembly of
Germany's military chiefs.

'We must eliminate Britain's hopes, which are based on
Russia and America,' Hitler told his officers sitting in stunned
silence around the conference table. 'If her expectations of
Russia fail, America, too, will fall out as the elimination of Russia
increases Japan's threat to the United States in the East. If
Russia is smashed, Britain's last hope is gone. The sooner we
smash Russia the better. Five months will see the end of it.'

But five months would not, of course, see the end of Russia –
nor would it signal the end of the plans for Operation Sea Lion.

Something, though, very significant occurred that same week-end in England. It was an incident that would represent the nearest the Germans ever came to an invasion. But, before this previously unrecorded moment in history, it is essential to discover how the English were preparing for an invasion that many were convinced had been coming for months – and, in the case of one particular person, for years.

Chapter 5

The Man Who Prophesied Invasion

The streets of London were buzzing with a new rumour in the early days of July 1940. Hitler, it was whispered, had apparently secretly flown over London to observe the state of the people who were frustrating his ambitions and see for himself the possibilities for invasion. The story was obviously untrue, but it did the rounds of the city public houses and clubs until briskly dispelled in the press.

Yet the story was not without foundation. It had originated from a little book, *The Flying Visit*, written by the journalist and intelligence officer Peter Fleming, which had been vigorously promoted by its publishers, Jonathan Cape, and achieved a far greater notoriety than they – or the author – could have imagined.

It is perhaps understandable in a country desperate for any news about the Germans and their plans that the plot of *The Flying Visit* should have inspired this kind of gossip. Though why Fleming's tale of Hitler's being forced to parachute into Henley, Oxfordshire, after his aircraft had been exploded by a bomb in a thermos flask, should have been credited as true for even a few days is still a puzzle. The book's illustrations by David Low, one of the war's greatest cartoonists, certainly underlined the farcical nature of the story in which the Führer is ultimately dropped *back* into Germany because no one in authority knows what to do with him. But, even so, there could be no denying its impact on the general public.

The Times was among the national newspapers to report the stir and offer a clue as to why the novel had generated such tittle-tattle:

> The most topical of the new books is *The Flying Visit* in which Peter Fleming plays with the fancy that Hitler once came to England – not by invasion but accident. It is an idea full of possibilities since Hitler must be human enough to feel some curiosity about a land that means so much to him. He is shown to be quite mystified by the common man, picking his way over unfamiliar country in the blackout. The humour of the book is chiefly in the Government's embarrassment at finding the arch enemy in their midst!

The Führer was, of course, still safely ensconced in Berlin hoping that the English would surrender without the necessity of an invasion. Peter Fleming, for his part, was surprised and amused by the furore and added a postscript to later editions of *The Flying Visit*:

> Several people have questioned the good taste of publishing, in so grave a situation as today's, a story in which the Arch-Enemy is treated as a comic figure. They may be right. If they are, I have made a miscalculation and I am sorry. That he has now done to Holland, Belgium and France what he did in 1939 to Poland can hardly be said to alter the quiddity of the man. A sense of humour and a sense of proportion (or perspective) are essential and happily almost indestructible elements of any civilisation. I shall be disappointed if this anecdote at the expense of a criminal is rejected merely because his crimes are being committed too near home.

Both Fleming and his younger brother, Ian – destined to create the famous James Bond – were involved in espionage:

Ian at the Naval Intelligence Division and Peter at MI5 and the Special Operations Executive (SOE). Earlier in the year, in fact, the two men had been involved in an actual invasion scare that may well have inspired Peter Fleming's book.

According to John Pearson, Ian's biographer, in June 1940 the brothers were tipped off about a possible invasion at Southend. An allegedly genuine letter from a German agent had warned that in the early hours of Whit Sunday a battalion of parachute troops would descend on the resort. The Chiefs of Staff made plans to deal with the raid and, as nothing could be released to the press, the two Flemings got themselves accredited as official eyewitnesses to report the 'Battle of Southend' in order to confound the inevitable lying reports of German propaganda. Pearson explains in *The Life of Ian Fleming* (1966):

> On the Saturday Ian and Peter rushed off to Southend in a staff car and joined a party of naval officers stationed on the roof of a large hotel on the seafront, keeping their vigil throughout the evening to the sound of 'The Lambeth Walk' from the blacked-out ballroom below. But nothing happened; and as dawn broke on Whit Sunday the two official eye-witnesses drove back to London, speculating in general on the strangeness of human affairs and in particular on the perversity of whoever had written the warning letter.

Peter Fleming did not let the experience go to waste, however. Apart from *The Flying Visit*, he returned to the subject again in 1957 to write *Invasion 1940*, one of the earliest and still most highly regarded studies of the period. The book was based on his personal experiences as well as access to the archives of the three military services and is one to which I have had frequent recourse while writing my own version of the extraordinary events of that summer.

*

The man who comes out most strongly in both of Peter Fleming's books – as he did in the events of World War Two – is undoubtedly Winston Churchill. His prescience about Hitler long before 1940 marked him out as an exceptional politician, and his leadership skills during the five years of the conflict would establish him as one of Britain's greatest-ever statesmen. This was the man who had spent years in the political wilderness on the Parliamentary back benches railing against the general apathy towards the arming of dictators and the threat they represented to the nation's security and independence. Indeed, there were some parliamentarians in the early thirties – when Churchill was a Constitutional MP for Epping, supporting the Conservatives – who regarded his beliefs as verging on the obsessional.

The Parliamentary record, Hansard, reveals that Churchill was warning against the possibility of invasion as early as 1934, when he proposed that some of the 30,000 unemployed men in Britain might be put to work building earthwork defences around airfields. Two years later he aired his concern again when addressing a question to Sir Thomas Inskip, the former attorney general and now Prime Minister Stanley Baldwin's minister for the coordination of defence: 'Can the honourable member inform the House what would happen if 200 German aircraft, each carrying 50 men, were discovered making towards, say, Newcastle, with a further one hundred following behind with stores and ammunition.'

Sir Thomas consulted the Air Ministry and informed the House that the Germans were 'more likely to attempt a high level of bombing attacks than an airborne invasion'. If any such attempt *was* made, the minister said, the Territorial Army would be ready to move quickly to any threatened point.

Clearly unhappy with this answer, Churchill responded by pointing out that there were at present only four Territorial Army divisions. 'Surely in their present state of training and equipment, they could not make headway against a quarter of their number of trained and regular storm troops? If they were raised to full strength and given three months' training in each year, and mechanised to a high degree, they would be an effective deterrent.'

But his words fell on deaf ears, and, when the war that he had feared *did* break out three years later, there were MPs who had scoffed who could only sit uncomfortably in their seats whenever he appeared in the house. Then, on 7 October 1939, newly installed as first lord of the Admiralty, Churchill returned to the subject without a hint of triumphalism, offering a brilliant new suggestion: 'Why do we not form a Home Guard of half a million men over 40 – if they like to volunteer – and put all our elderly stars at the head and in the structure of these new formations? If uniforms are lacking, a brassard would suffice and I am assured there are plenty of rifles.'

It would, however, take eight months for this idea to be put into effect. On 14 May 1940, after the rapid German advance in the Low Countries, the new secretary of state for war, Anthony Eden, broadcast an appeal on BBC radio. He asked for all men between the ages of 17 and 65 who were 'capable of free movement' to join a force of Local Defence Volunteers (LDV). It would be their duty to help guard strategic points, man roadblocks and carry out a variety of other tasks to relieve the hard-pressed regular army, including keeping a watch out for aerial invaders.

Eden had become particularly concerned at the constant flow of reports from embattled Europe about the skill of German parachutists. There was, he said, an anxiety among the British people that, *if* Hitler attempted to invade, the first wave of troops would come by air, although he was 'anxious to quash ridiculous rumours that the parachutists might be disguised as policemen, bus conductors, labourers, even as women with sub-machine-guns in their blouses or skirts'.

He wanted the LDV to be the eyes and ears of the nation in case of such an eventuality: 'The purpose of the parachute attack is to disorganise and confuse as a preparation for the landing of troops by aircraft. The success of such an attack depends on speed. Consequently, the measures to defeat such an attack must be prompt and rapid. This appeal is directed chiefly to those who live in country parishes, in small towns and in less densely populated suburban areas.'

The function of these 'Parashots' – as the press dubbed them – would be to watch for any hostile parachute descents and try to shoot the paratroops before they landed. Failing that, they were to mop up the enemy before they could become organised.

The response to Anthony Eden's appeal was immediate. Within a week, a quarter of a million men had enrolled, all competing to be the first operational unit. Contemporary evidence suggests that this honour belongs to a patrol at Babraham in Cambridgeshire who were on duty 'armed and in uniform' on the evening of Saturday, 18 May, to guard the telephone exchange at St Andrew's Street. Some mystery surrounds what these uniforms might have been, but the weapons were almost certainly shotguns.

An LDV officer based in southwest Cambridgeshire later recalled for a Mass Observation Unit representative a typical early day in the life of one of these units, whose initials had already caused more than one joker to claim they stood for 'Look. Duck. Vanish.'

> They rushed out rifles to us with ten rounds each along with denim overalls. I remember a handful of rifles dumped on the billiards table of the village inn, with ducklings waddling in through the door, and the air of subdued excitement and anticipation everywhere one went. 'Any news of the invasion, sir?' you would hear someone say. On being told there was no news, another voice would add, 'Well, I suppose it will be coming in due course.' And everyone thought it was, and appeared to be utterly unafraid, although we were raising an army as ill-

equipped as that of Monmouth at Sedgemoor to face the most highly trained and mechanised troops in the world.

News of the Parashots soon reached German ears, and many recruits to the LDV spent the following weeks chuckling over the fulminations of Lord Haw-Haw in his broadcasts from Germany. In one of these he thundered, 'The British government is committing the worst crime of all. Evidently, it permits open preparations for the formation of murder bands. The preparations, which are being made all over England to arm the civilian population for guerrilla warfare, are contrary to the rules of international law. German official quarters warn the misled British public and remind them of the fate of Polish *franc-tireurs* and gangs of murderers. Civilians who take up arms against German soldiers are, under international law, no better than murderers, whether they are priests or bank clerks.'

In another radio tirade, he quoted from letters to the British press in which the strangest suggestions had been offered about how to deal with German parachutists. A reader of the *Daily Mirror* advised putting miniature sewing machines under the seats of bicycles left standing around so that, when German soldiers tried to ride them, they would be automatically sewn to the saddle! Other correspondents proposed arming the LDV with lassoes to catch the paratroopers or alternatively providing them with such 'lethal' weapons as boomerangs.

But, even as more would-be 'killers' were queuing up outside police stations across the country to sign on for the units, Churchill was dictating a memo to Eden on 26 June: 'I don't think much of the name "Local Defence Volunteers" – I think "Home Guard" would be better.' Two weeks later the name was changed.

Females were also taking on voluntary war work, signing up in large numbers for the Women's Voluntary Service – the WVS – and carrying out all manner of duties, including running reception centres and mobile canteens, as well as helping families who suffered from the German air raids. Formed originally in 1938 to assist the ARP, the WVS eventually ran to a membership of over a million.

One of Churchill's earlier memos had expressed his concerns about the vulnerability to invasion of certain areas of the country. He highlighted particularly the part of the East Anglian coast not far from his own Essex constituency where there were two kinds of terrain ideal for a German attack. They might well, he said, 'try to land on some of the gently shelving beaches' in order to give their tanks access to London and the industrial Midlands. Alternately, they could land at Harwich, or Weybourne near Sheringham, where there was deep water close in shore. He continued: 'Have any arrangements been made by the War Office to provide against this contingency? I do not think it likely, but it is physically possible.'

The result of this idea was, of course, the implementation of 'Operation Julius Caesar' under the jurisdiction of General Sir Walter Kirke, the commander-in-chief of the Home Forces, one of whose team was General Sir Robert Haining, a distant relative of the author and another reason for my particular interest in this chapter of the war.

When Winston Churchill became prime minister on 18 May his first broadcast to the nation was, once again, devoted to the theme of invasion. 'We must expect that, as soon as stability is reached on the Western Front, the bulk of the hideous apparatus of aggression will be unleashed on us,' he said in his familiar stentorian tones. 'After the battle in France abates, there will come the battle for our island. *That* will be the struggle.'

Following the dramatic evacuation of Dunkirk, the prime minister was in an even greater passion to rouse the people when he addressed Parliament on 4 June. He began by assessing the situation with an acknowledgement to Britain's proud history.

'I would observe that there never has been a period in all those long centuries when an absolute guarantee against invasions, still less against serious raids, could have been given to our people,' he said. 'There was always the chance, and it is that chance which has excited and befooled the imagination of many continental tyrants. We are assured that novel methods will be adopted, and when we see the originality of malice, the ingenuity of aggression, which our enemy displays, we may certainly prepare ourselves for every kind of novel stratagem and every kind of brutal and treacherous manoeuvre.'

At this, Churchill paused, looked around the packed house, and delivered the lines that would stir the nation, ensure his place in history and continue to resound down the years as one of the great calls to arms: 'We shall defend our island, whatever the cost may be. We shall fight on the beaches. We shall fight on the landing grounds. We shall fight in the fields and in the streets. We shall fight in the hills. We shall *never* surrender.'

In East Anglia – as in the rest of the country – people rallied to the prime minister's call and quickly began taking what action they could to make an invasion as difficult as possible for the enemy. Aside from all the building of fortifications and other practical tasks, there were, for example, concerted, if largely futile, efforts to catch fifth-columnists – the men and women believed to be in sympathy with the Germans and prepared to carry out subversive activities, be they spying or sabotage, even setting up landing strips for the Luftwaffe.

Although one redoubtable brass hat in the Home Forces insisted that such traitors and secret agents were likely to be 'the best behaved and the most sleek people' and police stations and military headquarters received thousands of reports of suspicious activities, few fifth-columnists were ever caught. Nevertheless, many a stranger in a community had to endure the pointed finger of suspicion, as did the occasional churchwarden, local philan-thropist, or even men with beards or dark glasses, as whole districts of the country were gripped by spy fever.

Peter Fleming, who knew all about such things, wrote of this period:

> Throughout the land disturbing reports based on equally nebulous evidence were passed from mouth to mouth and from Ministry to Ministry, from the police to the military and from the military to the police. Flashing lights, bridges blown too soon or not at all, punctured tyres, cut telephone-lines, misdirected convoys – in whatever went amiss the hand of the Fifth Column was detected, never the normal workings of muddle or mischance, confusion or plain cowardice.

Churchill's new all-party government was, of course, reacting to the situation in all sorts of new and intriguing ways. An Invasion Defence Executive was set up in Whitehall under the appropriately named General Sir Edmund Ironside to monitor whatever evidence there might be of German intentions. After studying the tide tables, for instance, they came to the conclusion that there was only one week in each lunar month when the conditions would be suitable for an invasion attempt. During that week the most vulnerable beaches were at points further northward each day with conditions for a landing in Suffolk being suitable five days before those in Norfolk.

At the same time, orders were also given to create an underground resistance movement that would begin to function only *after* a German occupation. This highly secret organisation, commanded by Major Colin Gubbins, recruited men from all over the countryside to form cells of fighters ready to harass the enemy. Units were quickly under wraps in Norfolk, Suffolk and Essex, with special attention being given to the area of Suffolk around Woodbridge, which – prophetically as far as our story is concerned – was felt to be a location the invaders might try to occupy first.

At the end of May, the names of all streets, towns, villages and railway stations began to be obliterated. Roadside signposts were also removed and all milestones uprooted. A correspondent to *Picture Post* suggested that one way of misleading an airborne invasion might be to adopt the name of a town in another locality: 'For example, all civilians in, say, Norwich, if met by a parachutist and asked the name of the town should at once reply, "This is Bristol". All residents in the same town would give the same reply.'

Apart from roadblocks, the curiously shaped 'pillboxes' also began to appear like a rash across the countryside, especially in Suffolk and Norfolk. The mile upon mile of these immensely solid, reinforced concrete structures, mostly hexagonal but occasionally circular, were intended to prevent invading enemy columns from rushing about the countryside, even if the main defence lines had been penetrated. The authorisation for the building of pillboxes had been given by Churchill himself – and in fact many of them are still to be seen today in the middle of fields, at road junctions, by railway embankments and rivers and even on beaches, having defied all efforts to remove them and remaining as among the last surviving relics of the war.

Special defences were also erected along the east coast shoreline – in particular around Harwich, by now one of the country's most important naval bases. Booms were put in place across the estuary and also the five-mile-wide mouth of the Wash. Floating booms were also positioned around a hundred miles of vulnerable coast, augmented later in the summer by tall fences of steel scaffolding laced with barbed wire and booby-trapped with mines.

People living along this coast were perhaps more surprised by the sudden arrival of a fleet of vans with aerials poking through their roofs. They took up positions on headlands from Sheringham on the north Norfolk coast to as far south as Felixstowe. They were, it transpired, part of the 'Y Service', which had been set up to listen in to German radio broadcasts emanating from Luftwaffe planes, German E-boats and any other Nazi war machines within range, in the hope of picking up a warning of invasion. Packed with high-frequency receiving and monitoring equipment, the vans were staffed by German-speaking operators – a number of them Wrens – with orders to pass any intercepts to filter rooms at Harwich and Immingham.

Peter Fleming also tells another, rather more curious, story of the attempts to pick up invasion information. A water diviner serving with the Royal Engineers claimed he would be able to assess the imminence of invasion and was given a posting to Felixstowe in early July. The officer maintained that his gift would enable him not only to locate but also estimate the size and rate of growth of the supply dumps the Germans were accumulating at the invasion ports. Fleming adds,

Accurate data of this kind would obviously be a valuable guide to the enemy's state of readiness and the diviner was supplied with aerial photographs and other materials calculated to stimulate his extra-sensory powers. Although he achieved nothing to the purpose, this was probably his finest hour.

All the time these precautionary measures were busy being put in place, the government was anxious that people should 'stay put' if an invasion *did* occur. To reinforce this message, on 13 June the Ministry of Information released a drum-beating leaflet, 'If the Invader Comes'. Here are three typical paragraphs:

Do not believe rumours and do not spread them. When you receive an order, make quite sure it is a true order and not a faked one. Most of you know your policeman and your

ARP warden by sight, you can trust them. If you keep your heads, you can tell whether a military officer is really British or only pretending to be. If in doubt, ask the policeman or ARP warden . . .

Be ready to help the army in any way. Do not block roads until ordered to do so by the military or the local authorities. In factories and shops, all managers and workmen should organise some system by which a sudden attack can be resisted . . .

Do not give the Germans anything. Do not tell them anything. Hide your food and your bicycles. Hide your maps. See that the enemy gets no petrol. Remember that transport and petrol will be the invader's main difficulties. Make sure that no invader will get your car, petrol, maps or bicycles.

With an almost Pythonesque touch of humour, the Ministry shortly afterwards issued a second pamphlet, 'How Shall I Prepare to Stay Put?', which was full of good advice and useful tips for spotting – among other things – a real British military officer as distinct 'from someone only pretending to be one'. It was particularly hot on ensuring personal safety: 'Make ready your air raid shelter. If you have no shelter, prepare one. If you can have a trench ready in your field or garden, so much the better, especially if you live where there is likely to be danger from shells.'

One enterprising East Anglian publisher cashed in on the public mood by printing a line of small cards for display in the home. They read cheerily, WE ARE NOT INTERESTED IN THE POSSIBILITIES OF DEFEAT – THEY DO NOT EXIST. An appeal was also launched by the dynamic newspaper magnate Lord Beaverbrook of the *Daily Express* directed at housewives and encouraging them to hand over their household utensils to help aircraft production. The man who would later be appointed by Churchill as minister of supply urged his readers:

We will turn your pots and pans into Spitfires and Hurricanes, Blenheims and Wellingtons. Everyone who has pots and pans, kettles and vacuum cleaners, hat pegs, coat hangers, shoe trees, bathroom fittings and kitchen ornaments, cigarette boxes, or any other articles made wholly or in part of aluminium should hand them over to the local headquarters of the Women's Voluntary Services.

Although there was undoubtedly already a great deal of scrap aluminium in the country, the response to Beaverbrook's appeal was still huge. Later, metal fixtures and iron railings were added to the list and were soon piling up in great heaps everywhere.

Children, too, were urged to collect waste paper, scrap metal, textiles, bottles and even old bones – anything that could be recycled, in fact. These youngsters – who were nicknamed 'cogs' – even had their own theme song: 'There'll Always be a Dustbin'.

A week after the publication of the Ministry's second document about staying put, the government announced the establishment of a 'Defence Zone' – a twenty-mile-deep strip of the coast stretching from the Wash to the Thames to prevent interference with military movements. No one was to visit the area without a permit. Peter Fleming has written of this decision:

The authorities' obsession with a landing in East Anglia was underlined when all aliens, not only those of enemy origin, were instructed to seek special permission if they wished to remain in Buckinghamshire, Hertfordshire, Middlesex or Northampton. They were also forbidden to possess cameras, telescopes or nautical charts.

By July, the Home Guard was already better trained and organised and on Churchill's orders the volunteers were to be increasingly entrusted with coastal defences. Much-needed modern weaponry had also found its way to the Parashots. In the second week of the month, 55,000 Thompson sub-machine-guns and 800,000 Ross .300 rifles had safely reached the country across the Atlantic from America. The prime minister directed that these arms should be rushed to the areas where they were most needed, in particular East Anglia. Eight thousand items arrived in ten lorries in Cambridge and were delivered to the Corn Exchange prior to distribution.

Unfortunately, as soon as the packing cases were opened, the weapons were found to be coated in thick grease. Within hours, however, more than a hundred women volunteers had been found to clean them. Although the ranks of housewives and young girls were quickly swelled to almost 250, it still took two weeks for the arms to be ready for distribution.

As if – perversely – to confirm the German view of the Home Guard as 'murderers', the men were also issued with lethal devices known as 'Molotov cocktails'. These were made from bottles filled with a mixture of petrol, paraffin and tar oil to which a fuse was attached at the neck. To use one, the fuse had to be ignited and the bottle hurled at its target. The resulting explosion was said to be big enough to set fire to a tank and incinerate its occupants. *That* was the claim, anyhow.

Once again Lord Haw-Haw could not resist a cry of outrage. 'Suicide academies have apparently been set up all over Britain,' he wailed. 'The headmasters are cunning blackguards who teach their inmates how to make bombs at the modest cost of two shillings each, how to poison water supplies by throwing dead dogs into streams and how to kill sentries noiselessly from behind.'

Beaverbrook's *Daily Express* followed up this 'initiative' with another campaign, 'A Hand Grenade Dump By Every Village Pump', urging citizens to defend themselves when the enemy materialised. Any schoolboy who could throw a cricket ball could certainly learn to handle a grenade, the paper maintained in a call to take up arms that must have horrified some of its older readers.

No matter how prepared the nation was becoming, however, there was still a lack of agreement among the military and politicians as to where a German invasion might land. On 12 July, for example, Naval Intelligence reported that it might be possible, with favourable conditions, for the enemy to land 12,000 troops in small landing craft between the Wash and Dover, plus another 5,000 men between Dover and Land's End. Alternately, 50 transport ships sailing from German-occupied ports might put ashore 50,000 men between Rosyth and Southwold. The Joint Intelligence Committee, though, calculated on 18 July that as many as five divisions could be transported by sea and 12,000 men by air. They would all be dispersed between the Wash and Newhaven, intent on encircling London.

Churchill, of course, was quick to interject his own view in a memo:

I find it very difficult to visualise the kind of invasion all along the coast carried in small craft. Except in very narrow waters it would be a most hazardous and even suicidal operation to commit a large army to the accidents of the sea in the teeth of our very numerous armed patrolling forces . . . I believe the main danger is from the Dutch and German harbours, which bear principally upon the coast from Dover to the Wash.

After a few more days' deliberation, the prime minister penned another memo – this time to his old stamping ground, the Admiralty – headlined 'Action This Day'. It outlined an idea for laying a curtain of mines behind a German invasion fleet and by so doing containing it in a trap. He wrote:

If an invader lands during the night or morning, the flotillas will attack him in the rear during the day, and these flotillas will be heavily bombarded from the air, as part of the air battles which will be going on. If, however, when night falls a curtain or fender of mines can be laid inshore, so as to cut off the landing-place from reinforcements of any kind, these mines, once laid, will not have to be guarded from air attack, and consequently will relieve the flotilla from the need of coming back on the second day, thus avoiding losses from the air and air protection.

By the high summer of 1940 no one in Britain could be in any doubt that Winston Churchill – the man who had for so long prophesied invasion – was leaving no option unexplored in his determination to prevent the nightmare occurring. As he remarked to one of his colleagues, 'I think that no idea is so outlandish that it should not be considered and viewed with a searching, but at the same time, I hope, with a steady, eye.'

It was this admiration for the iconoclastic thinking to which he was so devoted that had also inspired Churchill to authorise the setting up of a remarkable group of experts with a very special mission. These men would be part of one of the most extraordinary and clandestine organisations dedicated to defeating plans for the invasion of Britain of this – or any other – war.

Chapter 6

The Wizard War

The tall, insistent man who arrived at reception in Block North of Admiralty Archway in Whitehall on a July morning in 1940 was clutching a small briefcase in one hand and an envelope of papers in the other. His eyes glinted with an inner conviction and he repeated several times to the immaculately uniformed Wren behind a desk that he had a plan that would prevent the Germans from ever landing in Britain.

The girl listened to the visitor with a patience born of experience with naval types of all ranks and dispositions. Although she was responsible for the coming and going of visitors to the various departments in this adjunct of the Admiralty straddling the wide thoroughfare of the Mall leading to Buckingham Palace, it was only in recent weeks that a slow but steady stream of obvious eccentrics had begun to clamour for admission to the Department of Miscellaneous Weapon Development (DMWD) office, a single, large room situated directly over the arch.

From what the girl knew, this new department consisted of a group of naval scientists ready to put to the test any idea – no matter how outlandish or bizarre – that might help the war effort. Their job was to evaluate ideas for new weapons and devices and, if feasible, see them through the development stage. It was a task that often meant considering well-intended but wildly impractical proposals from civilians as well as members of the armed forces.

Among those other personnel at the Admiralty who had heard of the existence of the DMWD, it already had a nickname, 'the Department of Miscellaneous Wheezers and Dodgers'. But to anyone else they were a unique and clandestine organisation whose activities would not be removed from the secret list until a decade after the end of the war.

The men had been brought together as part of Winston Churchill's belief in promoting creative thinking. If the Nazis were to be defeated – if they were even to be prevented from conquering Britain – he knew a vital part of the battle would be waged between the best minds in Britain and Germany. It was a conflict he was to term 'the Wizard War'.

Because the young Wren knew that the DMWD had the blessing of the prime minister – and its organisation's chief, Lieutenant Commander Charles Goodeve, had given instructions that no one was to be turned away unless he or she was obviously a lunatic – she took the man's name and address and directed him to the organisation's office. Mr J W Wilton from Framlingham, Suffolk climbed the stairs full of expectation, following a path that would be well trodden in the days and months of the war that lay ahead.

Already the 'Wheezers and Dodgers' had started investigating a string of ideas, from practical countermeasures for German sea mines and antiaircraft devices to decidedly strange proposals for firing Thermite (a mixture of aluminium powder and metal oxide, which gives off great heat when ignited) into the air to 'seize up' the engines of Luftwaffe aircraft and a machine gun operated by centrifugal force. The gun idea had apparently been quickly dismissed by one of the scientists, as it was immediately evident that even the very lightest model would have to weigh several tons. But nothing, it seemed, could stem the tide of ingenious proposals.

The member of the team who met Wilton in the DMWD office, with its spectacular views to the Palace in one direction and Trafalgar Square in the other, soon found himself in a similar situation when his visitor opened his briefcase and placed a sheath of notes and diagrams on his desk. The illustrations showed what was obviously meant to be a 'death ray'.

The machine was curiously mounted in the basket of a naval balloon and was intended to be 'fired' at the German hordes as they attempted an invasion. Wilton's specifications also contained details of what the man in the basket would require in the way of protective clothing, signalling devices and even provisions to allow him to stay aloft for long periods of time.

The scientist looked patiently at the drawings and then read the neatly handwritten explanation of the idea. He saw almost at once that there was a single, vital element missing. There was nothing specific about the 'death ray' *itself*. He politely asked his visitor why.

The look of confidence did not waver for a moment on Wilton's face. Nor did it leave after he had been courteously thanked for coming all the way up to London at such a dangerous time.

'Oh, there is no need to worry about that,' the man from Suffolk had replied with a knowing wink. 'The Admiralty has access to secret archives and there are bound to be several death rays there. Just take your choice.'

The man given the orders in May 1940 to set up the Department of Miscellaneous Weapon Development was Canadian-born Lieutenant Commander Charles Goodeve. A direct and restless man in his mid-thirties, with prematurely white hair and piercing blue eyes, he had earned a degree of Master of Science and the Gold Medal at the Engineering Institute of Canada before being awarded a scholarship to University College in London. Here he combined his interest in chemical and electrical engineering – ultimately becoming the university's reader in physical chemistry – as well as pursuing a life-long passion for the Navy.

Signing on for the Royal Naval Volunteer Reserve (RNVR), Goodeve had spent the decade before the war serving primarily on battleships and destroyers with a period at sea on mine-sweepers and submarines. On shore, he had won a reputation as an excellent private consultant in chemical and electrical engineering, revealing an amazingly clear and analytical mind never afraid to employ unorthodox methods to solve complex problems.

The early days of the war saw him working on various devices to protect British ships from German mines. It was not long, either, before he had his first taste of the sort of wild schemes that would later cross his desk in the 'Wheezers and Dodgers'. It took the form of a memorandum that had been sent to Rear Admiral William Wake-Walker at the Admiralty – a Churchill appointee assigned to supervise all ideas for countering enemy mines – and dealt with the idea that had been proposed by a 'well-meaning individual' to use *fish* as mine detectors. The memo to the rear admiral read,

> It has been suggested that a means of causing magnetic mines to explode harmlessly may be found by attaching small but strong permanent magnets to flat fish and distributing these fish over the sea bottom. The fish, moving in search of food, would, at short range, bring mines under the influence of a magnetic field and consequently cause an explosion. The questions are (1) Whether the influence of a magnet which could be carried by a fish would be effective; and (2) Whether the scheme is possible from the 'fish' point of view.

Wake-Walker's response to the writer's quite ludicrous suggestion provided Goodeve with a perfect object lesson in the kind of humour he would be called upon to employ when dealing with similar crackpot ideas in the future:

1. The suggestion contained in your 191/D 478 is considered of great value.

2. As a first step in the development of this idea it is proposed to establish a 'School for Flat Fish' at the Royal Naval College, Dartmouth. Candidates for this course should be entered in the first place as Probationary Flat Fish, and these poor fish would be confirmed in their rank on showing their proficiency by exploding a mine.

3. A very suitable source of candidates to tap would be the Angel Fish of Bermuda, which, though flat, swim in a vertical plane.

4. With the success of this scheme it may be necessary to control fried-fish shops.

5. It is requested that you will forward, through the usual channels, proposals as to the necessary accommodation, and a suggested syllabus of the Course.

There was, however, no sign of levity in the rear admiral's voice when he informed Goodeve that Churchill, then still first lord of the Admiralty, wanted to set up a 'think tank'. Churchill was alarmed at the navy's lack of close-range weapons to deal with the German attacks on North Sea shipping and Wake-Walker believed the versatile Canadian was the man to find the solutions.

Goodeve was given authority to assemble a small team of scientists and technicians. They were assigned office space in Admiralty Arch and ordered to report to Vice Admiral James Somerville, the 'Inspector of Anti-Aircraft Weapons and Devices', a veteran of the East Indies, now chair-bound with lung problems. Somerville was one of the great characters of the navy and his designation was quickly shortened by his subordinates to 'Instigator of Anti-Aircraft Wheezes and Dodges' – from which, in turn, Goodeve's men earned their epithet. Both Wake-Walker and Somerville assured the lieutenant commander he would have a completely free hand – but they wanted results, 'and soon'.

Fired by the challenge, Goodeve lost no time in recruiting his team. To each of the sixteen men who ultimately made up the group he said the same thing: 'You will have no set hours and no official leave. You will be required to work all night as well as all day – and seven days a week if necessary. You will see many secret documents. Don't talk to *anyone* about what you see.'

Two members of this group are particularly relevant to our invasion story – Nevil Shute, best remembered today as a bestselling novelist, and Alec Menhinick, for a time the holder of a world motorcycle speed record.

Like Goodeve, Nevil Shute was a man of great passions – though in his case it was for aeronautics. Such, indeed, was Shute's success in this field that he took to writing almost by chance and for years afterwards remained surprised at his international success.

He was born Nevil Shute Norway in 1899, and his Cornish ancestry included a Captain Norway, who was killed on the deck of the packet boat, *Lady Mary Pelham*, during a skirmish with an American frigate, *Privateer*, in the early days of the War of Independence in 1812. Nevil, too, had an adventure-filled childhood. While still in his teens he witnessed some of the early manifestations of the Sinn Fein rebellion in Dublin and for a time worked as a rescuer with the Red Cross. After serving with the army in France during World War One, Shute developed an interest in aeronautical engineering. In 1924, he joined the staff of the company that was building the R100 airship and later became the ship's chief engineer. After the disaster of the R101 in 1930 put an end to airship building in Britain, he devoted his time to the manufacture of light aircraft and such was his success that he soon became managing director of his own factory in Southsea.

In 1938, however, with war looming on the horizon, he resigned from the company. His mind was actually buzzing with an idea for a novel, *What Happened to the Corbetts* (1939), about a small English family bombed out of their Southampton home and forced to take refuge on a houseboat. In introducing one of the many later reprints of the book during wartime, Shute said, 'I wrote this story to tell people what the bombing attacks would really be like . . . I was right in my guess that gas would not be used and in the disruption of civil life that would be caused by high explosives. I overlooked the importance of fire.'

The writing of this realistic and detailed story, just eighteen months ahead of fantasy becoming reality, highlighted Nevil Shute's enquiring, perceptive, not to say prophetic, mind. When he was commissioned into the Royal Naval Volunteer Reserve it was only a short step to a summons to the Admiralty and an invitation to join the 'Wheezers and Dodgers'.

What had brought the burly, pugnacious Shute to the attention of Goodeve was apparently a gliding torpedo that he had been involved in designing for the Fleet Air Arm. But the first meeting of the two men was anything but auspicious, as Shute was to write later in 1956:

In my time I have met many cranks, and this man bore all the external hallmarks. Here, I thought, was a crazy inventor who had sucked in the simple admirals to the point when they were allowing him to set up a staff to mess about with graph paper and slide rules instead of fighting the Germans. If I got involved in this, I thought, I should be very safe, but other men would win or lose the war within the next three months. If I didn't, if within three days of joining the Navy, I refused point-blank to do what the Navy wanted me to do, I might well find myself cashiered before I got my uniform. The subsequent work of the D.M.W.D. shows how very, very wrong I was in every single particular.

His wartime experiences were also to prove invaluable to Nevil Shute when he took up authorship again. Following a move to

Australia for health reasons, he wrote a string of novels that all became bestsellers. Notable among these are *No Highway* (1948), which featured metal fatigue as the cause of aircraft disasters and was published just before the first of the Comet jet crashes that occurred for exactly that reason; and *On the Beach* (1957), a tale of nuclear disaster that was filmed two years later by Stanley Kramer with Gregory Peck and Ava Gardner.

Among Shute's closest friends at the DMWD was Alec Menhinick, a man of similar ingenuity and delight at a challenge. Although Menhinick had been a member of the RNVR since he was sixteen, he was actually rejected for war service because of weak eyesight. Irritated rather than infuriated, he instead found the perfect haven for his talents in the ranks of the new secret research organisation in Admiralty Arch.

Like his friend, Menhinick was born in Cornwall and had been something of a free spirit ever since his youth. He particularly loved motorcycles and speed and in 1932 set a new motorcycle world record by travelling at 105 m.p.h. along the Royston-to-Newmarket road near Cambridge. With this achievement on his CV, the young man was even more staggered when, after the navy refusal of his services, he applied to join the army early in 1940, but was curtly informed he was 'not safe' to be a dispatch rider!

Instead, though, Menhinick managed to secure a commission as a second lieutenant to the Royal Army Service Corps (RASC) and soon found himself posted to Suffolk. He recalled this period of his life later in an undated personal interview.

'It was the time when the invasion scare was at its height,' he said. 'So the army sent me off with four four-inch guns, twenty-six soldiers and a daily rum ration to a naval Coastal Forces base at Felixstowe, HMS *Beehive*. We were expected to hang around and repel the enemy with those four ancient pieces of ordnance. I reckoned that if I remained attached to the base for long enough there was a sporting chance the army would forget me. But instead, after three weeks of sitting around, I was ordered to hand over the guns and my men to an army unit at Wickham Market. So I asked for a transfer and they sent me to the "Wheezers and Dodgers" still wearing my Army uniform!'

Although Menhinick was no scientist, Goodeve wanted to utilise the record breaker's mechanical knowledge and ice-cool nerve under dangerous conditions. He was to be responsible for organising and conducting the trials for all the weird and wonderful inventions being developed by the DMWD. It was to provide four exciting and dramatic years that he never forgot.

Like other 'Wheezers and Dodgers', Alec Menhinick soon learned that the kind of experimental work he was involved in could be very life-threatening. Within a week of his arrival on the staff, he found himself wounded and swimming for his life in the North Sea after the ship on which he had been testing a rocket weapon was unexpectedly bombed and sunk by a passing Dornier DM17.

He and Nevil Shute were also privy to some of the wackier ideas of that summer of 1940. In the wake of Mr Wilton came several other suggestions from correspondents living on the vulnerable coast of East Anglia. One writer thought that the enemy bombers flying over the region at night could be destroyed by the use of searchlight beams that solidified on contact with the Nazi planes. 'The aircraft must be struck repeatedly by the searchlight beam until it plunges to the earth,' the man explained, adding, in terms that would surely have delighted his predecessor from Framlingham if he knew, 'The method of solidifying the rays is merely a matter of research and development.'

Another writer, from Oulton Broad, who claimed to be an expert on the Norfolk waterways and beaches, put forward plans for electrocuting German troops as they attempted to wade ashore. High-tension cables of electricity placed on the seabed covered by the tide would kill anyone who touched them. It was once again left to the DMWD's secretary to reject the suggestion politely, explaining that the department felt the huge amount of power required to achieve such a stunning blow would cause the sea to boil long before even a single invader had been electrocuted!

They were also asked to test an invention with the wonderful nomenclature of 'the Wroxham Roaster'. The ideas had been submitted complete with a detailed drawing and specifications for the amount of gelignite and lengths of cord needed to detonate it by a Royal Navy man, Sub-Lieutenant Gerry Friggens, who had grown up on the Broads. The 'Roaster' was intended to be detonated from the shore when any German flying boats attempted to land and could also be triggered if the aircraft's floats caught the cords strung just below the surface of the water.

Menhinick and the inventor carried out a number of tests on Wroxham Broad, which indicated that the device might be successful in practice. The man from the DMWD, however, never forgot the noise of the explosions or the fountains of water that spurted into the air, disturbing the neighbourhood for several weeks. He was often fond of recalling that the racket had earned Sub-Lieutenant Friggens – who was, of course, known in the area – some unrepeatable variations on his name.

Both Shute and Menhinick shared the concern that the east coast was vulnerable to invasion – and each had his own project with this as an objective. The pair had been particularly motivated by a story told to them of a coaster on the North Sea run that had only a single Lewis machine gun for its defence. It appeared that, when the crew had exhausted their ammunition against one attacking enemy aircraft, they had resorted to flinging lumps of coal in impotent defiance.

As a result of the work of the DMWD, British shipping was to benefit with improved methods of lighting the night sky as well as direction-finding gadgets that enabled their guns to be aimed more accurately. The scientists also carried out experiments with camouflage, acoustic warning equipment and antiaircraft systems utilising huge rockets and wire-netting devices.

With his specialist knowledge of aeronautics, Nevil Shute took particular pains in devising countermeasures against the low-level and dive-bomber attacks occurring with increasing frequency along the east coast in the summer of 1940. One of his solutions was a terrifying device perversely called the 'Pig Trough' that could be fixed onto the deck of a ship and fired at any attacker. The job of testing the prototype fell to Alec Menhinick, who decided to carry out the trials off the Arran Islands of Scotland, far from the seas where it would be required.

To keep the weapon pointing vertically in even the roughest weather, it had been fitted with a trough-shaped swing mounting into which were packed fourteen rockets carrying two-pounder shells. As Menhinick discovered when he loosed off the first trial shots in the direction of an imagined attacking aircraft, the 'spread' of the rockets was such that they were far more likely to hit a raider than the 'directional' fire of a Lewis gun.

Thanks to Shute's ingenuity and Menhinick's thoroughness, the 'Pig Trough' became the first rocket weapon to be installed on merchant ships. It at last gave crews something to hit back with at their tormentors.

Shute's other project that summer was the 'Radiator', a rocket projector that could be installed near the mouth of any coastal river and fired on any approaching landing craft. The device was simplicity itself, firing salvos of ten two-inch rockets horizontally. Like the 'Pig Trough', it did not have to be accurate, as the enemy boats would certainly attempt to land in clusters.

Menhinick was again put in charge of testing the invention and returned once more to Suffolk – though with rather more to do on this occasion. A secluded stretch of water just to the west of Aldeburgh was chosen as the proving ground for the latest example of Shute's inventive genius.

One of the trial firings, however, went badly wrong because of a short-circuit in its tumbler switch, which resulted in a shattering explosion. Of this Menhinick reported later, 'It must have awakened the dead all along the Suffolk coast!' What *was* certain was that the blast had been heard by mystified residents as far apart as Felixstowe and Lowestoft. Nevertheless, the 'Radiator' passed its trials and was confidently installed at a number of locations along the east coast to await the arrival of the invader.

Although a number of the concepts researched by the men in Admiralty Arch did not actually come to fruition until after the threat of a German invasion had long passed, their impact on the British war effort was undeniable – though, sadly, recognition of the fact would be years in being acknowledged.

One other idea that the DMWD scientists took up briefly as a possible anti-invasion strategy was the use of flame-throwers, as Gerald Pawle has written in his book, *The Secret War 1939–1945* (1956), which features the work of the Department of Miscellaneous Weapon Development:

> Of all the less orthodox methods put forward to discouraging German visitors, the use of flame in various forms seemed to hold a special fascination for naval minds. Perhaps it was an obsession springing subconsciously from the far-away days of Drake and his fire ships. At any rate the view was widely held in naval circles that 'England will again be saved by fire', and technical objections were brushed aside.

Goodeve, it seems, had little time for the idea of using flame for coastal or harbour defence, but his team did look at two suggestions. The first was a plan for arming motor torpedo boats (MTBs) based at Felixstowe with 'guns' to project jets of creosote at German E-boats. The other was a flame-thrower mounted on the poops of ships plying the east coast shipping lanes that could be directed at diving Luftwaffe aircraft. Faced with such a pillar of fire, it was believed, the pilot would have to pull out of his attack or fly through it and risk destruction.

Strangely, although Churchill was aware that the Germans had used flame warfare during World War One, he did not press the 'Wheezers and Dodgers' on this issue. *Flammenwerfer* had, after all, been only a primitive weapon then and the enemy had never made any significant advances in this particular aspect of warfare. For once, the great man was in for a surprise later that summer when the most bizarre stories of flame warfare began to spread.

For the moment, the prime minister was more preoccupied with ideas for making the Germans aware that the nation was not just lying dormant waiting to be invaded. In fact, he was planning to revive an idea he had seen at first hand over half a century earlier for taking the battle to the enemy – the commando raid.

What, of course, he did not know was that the Germans were making similar plans – and actually had *two* secret units already jostling to be the first to set foot in England.

Chapter 7

Scallywags and the GB Kommandos

It was just before midnight on Monday, 24 June 1940. The sky was starless and the sea on which the little flotilla of boats was silently heading towards the coast of France was like a millpond. On shore, there were no lights or signs of human activity. In the boats, the men with blackened faces, their balaclavas pulled down to just above their eyebrows, breathed nervously and prepared to begin a new chapter in the history of warfare.

The location was the shoreline between Boulogne and Berck-sur-Mer and the date probably the very nadir of the war for Britain. The evacuation of Dunkirk had taken place less than three weeks earlier and the French had just signed an armistice with the Germans that would come into force the next morning. At that moment, Britain would be absolutely alone against the might of Hitler's army, which had recently been joined by Mussolini's Fascist troops.

But, on that midsummer night, the very first British commando raid was – almost impudently – launched against the enemy.

It was codenamed 'Operation Collar', and 115 officers and men were taking part under the command of Major R J F Todd of the Argyll and Sutherland Highlanders. His orders from the War Office were to split his force into four groups and land at midnight at different points on the twenty-mile stretch of French coast beyond the port of Boulogne. Their objectives on

French soil were to be fairly free-ranging, according to Christopher Buckley, the *Daily Telegraph* war correspondent, who wrote the first account of the embryo force in *The Commandos* (1951):

> It was not a very elaborately prepared raid. It could not have been, for it was only 12 days since a Directorate of Raiding Operations had been formed, and in the intense month of June those who controlled the Armed Forces of the country had many and more pressing matters to consider. The scale of the raid was modest, though not so modest as many which subsequently followed. A force of 200 men was to be landed at various points on the French coast south of Boulogne to obtain information about the nature of the German defences, destroy any installations they might happen across and bring back what prisoners they could. It was most unlikely that the German High Command, which confidently expected a British surrender in a matter of some three weeks, would have taken any elaborate steps to fortify the French coast against a British counter-invasion, and the enterprise, therefore, could have little but a psychological effect.

In fact, there were problems for the operation from the very start and a good deal of improvisation became necessary. The training of the men, the collecting of information about the target area and the planning of the raid had to be done in a hurry. The schedule was not helped when the twenty C-boats that Major Todd had expected developed defects and had to be replaced at the last moment with lightweight motorboats that were fast but crewed mostly by civilians. The restricted space in these boats meant that some 85 fewer men than anticipated sailed out from Southampton on the Monday evening. The tyro commandos rendezvoused off Cap Gris-Nez, where they were told they were only to spend eighty minutes ashore.

The group who landed in the middle of the chosen area at Le Touquet were led by Lieutenant Ronald Swayne. Their mission was to attack the Merlimont Plage hotel, which was believed to have been requisitioned by the German army. Armed with rifles and grenades, Swayne and his men went ashore only to find the building boarded up and empty. Disappointed, they scouted around but were unable to find anybody or anything to attack before they returned to their boat. However, the vessel was nowhere to be seen, as Lieutenant Swayne recalled later in an account for Christopher Buckley:

It was hanging around some distance offshore and we couldn't make contact with it. Some Germans turned up then whom we killed and that created a bit of noise. I'm afraid we bayoneted them. I was armed with a .38 revolver. I'm sorry to say that I forgot to load it on this occasion. So I hit one of the Germans on the head with the butt of my revolver. My batman bayoneted one, and I grappled with another and we killed them. It wasn't really very serious soldiering, I'm sorry to say. And, of course, because we were being rushed, we never got their identity papers, which was very inefficient of us. We also lost a lot of our weapons. Then some more Germans appeared in the sand-dunes and I needed to get the men away fast, so there was nothing else for it but to swim out to the boat.

The other parties of raiders also met with mixed fortunes. One group went ashore at Hardelot and penetrated several hundred yards inland, but returned empty-handed. A second group came across a German seaplane anchorage at Berck, but it was too heavily guarded to risk attempting to destroy any of the aircraft. The third party, led by Major Todd, landed near Boulogne, where they encountered a small group of German soldiers, and a short gun battle ensued in which one of the party was wounded behind the ear. He was to prove the only casualty of the entire landing that night.

The return journey was equally anticlimactic. The eight boats made their way home independently, one of them running into problems when it tried to dock in Folkestone the following morning. A trio of understandably nervous coast guards refused to allow the boat into harbour, since no one on board was carrying any identification documents. The vessel had to remain at sea for several hours before the thoroughly frustrated raiders were finally allowed back on shore.

Such embarrassing moments were not, of course, made public. But a press release was issued to acclaim the first commando raid and give the British public the impression that the country was starting to hit back at the enemy:

In co-operation with the Royal Air Force, naval and military units yesterday carried out successful recon-naissance of the enemy coastline. Landings were effected at a number of points and contact made with German troops. Casualties were inflicted and some enemy dead fell into our hands. Much useful information was obtained. Our forces suffered no casualties.

This classic example of wartime spin on the events of 24 June had the desired effect – although some versions of the story were elaborated in the popular press. One tabloid claimed that one group of the commandos had thrown hand grenades into a café filled with German troops and French 'good-time' girls. Even such falsehoods, though, could not dent the feeling of optimism exemplified in a *Times* leader: 'The point is that this incident is exactly what the public wants.'

The raid had not gone unnoticed by the Germans, either, who countered the same day with an 'official communiqué', which, not surprisingly, was completely ignored by the British media: 'Reconnaissance attacks of weak enemy forces on the north French coast during the night of June 24–25 were repulsed without difficulty.'

As far as those who had set up and taken part in Operation Collar were concerned, the whole landing had been 'amateurish', and it was obvious that a great deal more training and planning needed to be done before the new commandos could venture again onto occupied soil. In the interim, it was to be the turn of a German foray in the opposite direction with very different consequences.

Winston Churchill's idea for the British commandos had been conceived as long ago as the turn of the century. While taking part in the Boer War, he had visualised the formation of well-armed, mobile troops to carry out guerrilla warfare against an unsuspecting enemy. He nicknamed them 'Leopards'.

Forty years later, some of the British officers in the higher levels of the General Staff who were privy to the rather haphazard formation of these units were far less complimentary – referring to the whole idea as an opportunity for 'scallywagging' and the men themselves as 'scallywags'. Later, though, these desk-bound soldiers would have any number of opportunities to regret their words.

Churchill had actually gained first-hand experience of commando-type operations during his time as a war correspondent in South Africa in 1899. After seeing service as a Hussar in Malakand and with the Nile Expeditionary Force, he had resigned his commission to become a journalist, plunging straight into the heart of the action in the Boer War. He was captured in an ambush set up by a group of 'Boer commandos', but managed to escape, returning home a hero with a price of £25 still on his head, which was buzzing with a new idea.

It was perhaps no surprise, then, that upon becoming prime minister in 1940, he began to consider the creation of the kind of special forces that did not exist in the British Army, as John

Parker has explained in *Commandos: The Inside Story of Britain's Most Elite Fighting Force* (2000):

He demanded prompt action to raise commando-style seaborne raiding parties, saboteurs, espionage agents and airborne and parachute troops, the latter having so successfully spearheaded the Nazi incursions into Norway, Belgium and Holland. Thereafter, and in spite of all the other great worries surrounding him, Churchill took great personal interest in nurturing them into being, forgiving early errors and pointing the way forward to the point of insistence.

Indeed, Churchill was very much to the point when he issued his first set of instructions to the Joint Chiefs of Staff in a memo dated 6 June:

The completely defensive habit of mind which has ruined the French must not be allowed to ruin all our initiatives. It is of the highest consequence to keep the largest numbers of German forces all along the coasts of countries that have been conquered, and we should immediately set to work to organise raiding shores on these coasts where the population are friendly. Enterprises must be prepared with specially trained troops of the hunter class, who can develop a reign of terror first of all on the 'butcher and bolt' policy. But later on, or perhaps as soon as we are organised, we should surprise Calais or Boulogne, kill and capture the Hun garrison and hold the place until all preparations to reduce it by siege or heavy storm have been made, and then away.

Urging his chiefs to initiate a 'vigorous, enterprising and ceaseless offensive', the prime minister suggested that even tanks and armoured fighting vehicles might be taken across the Channel in flat-bottom boats to raid inland, cut vital communications and, by using men armed with Tommy guns, grenades and trench mortars, 'leave a trail of German corpses behind them'.

In a nutshell, Churchill wanted to harass and weaken the enemy at every opportunity, as Christopher Buckley later wrote, with the benefits of hindsight, in his book *The Commandos*:

> Perhaps in the truest sense of the term, the Commandos represented a form of 'psychological warfare'. Not only did they provide confidence and battle experience – both sorely needed – to our own men; they contributed to maintain the enemy garrisons across the water in a state of tension and uncertainty, wondering whether anything would strike them suddenly from the sea or from the air; wondering when, where, and in what manner it would strike. For that purpose a special force was needed: shock troops, volunteers trained to a high pitch of toughness, endurance and battle craft.

Following Churchill's directive on 6 June, the War Office began urgently searching for volunteers for this force of 'shock troops' to be known as commandos. The requisite was forty officers and a thousand men, the best of whom would be divided into ten units of about fifty each. They were to be based in the main at coastal areas, where they could live and train. On 12 June, Sir Alan Bourne, the adjutant-general of the Royal Marines, was appointed commander of Offensive Operations – a title that would later be changed to the more familiar Combined Operations. For the honour of serving in this new do-or-die brigade, the officers were to get a daily payment of thirteen shillings and fourpence (67p) with the ordinary soldiers receiving six shillings and eight pence (33p).

East Anglia was to be home to some of the first of these units – the No. 4 Independent Company, by chance, being formed at Sizewell, which, as we shall see, plays a significant part in our story. However, due to an administrative error – one of many that blighted the early days of the commandos – this group were soon afterwards moved to Glasgow, a fact that might have significantly changed the course of events on this part of the east coast.

Such remote locations, far from curious eyes, were ideal for turning men into fighting machines, capable of acting independently and killing without compunction. Here, too, they could build up the physical fitness of athletes; learn endurance by lengthy route marches; and be taught to scale cliffs and swim in full kit. The men also learned to endure extremes of fatigue, cold and heat and the ability to perfect sudden physical assault and close-quarters killing. They were trained to fulfil the designation of 'shock troops' in every respect: expert in daring offensive action and virtuosi in killing.

Small wonder, then, that within a year of the start of their operations against the Germans, the commandos had long since put the memory of Operation Collar behind them. By then they were being angrily referred to by Hitler as 'terror and sabotage troops' who he said acted outside the international Geneva Conventions, while the Nazi propaganda machine labelled them 'murderous thugs and cutthroats' who killed soldiers and civilians indiscriminately and preferred to murder their enemies rather than take prisoners.

As history has since shown, there was an element of truth in this estimation. But as Churchill, the instigator, was to remark with wry satisfaction about the impact of his concept, 'In embattled Britain, desperate times required desperate measures.'

Across the Channel in July 1940, the Germans made preparations to answer the commandos' raids while their troops awaited Hitler's orders to launch Operation Sea Lion. Already, in fact, some special forces units had been established along similar lines to those in England and the men in these groups were flexing their muscles and looking with interest at the rich prize lying

123

just 21 miles away. These units, also volunteers, were known collectively as the Brandenburg Division and they had been trained in the same skills of mobility, initiative, self-reliance, intelligence and endurance as their compatriots in England.

The history of the 'Brandenburgers' is, however, rather sketchy, since their official records were lost during the final days of the Third Reich – though some documents survived and are now deposited in the Imperial War Museum in London. They help to piece together a picture of a group of men who were rugged individualists and merciless fighters, with an equal number of mavericks and misfits. They were intended to serve in small groups using the tactics of *blitzkrieg* on a smaller, more personal basis.

Named after the barracks near Berlin's famous Brandenburg Gate where they had first been assembled, they were charged with the destruction of enemy property such as railway junctions, bridges, crossroads and tunnels – vital to the success of an advancing army – the capture of prisoners and a range of other dubious activities on the fringes of legitimate warfare. They had been set up by the Abwehr (German intelligence service) with a virtual *carte blanche* to carry out any covert activities regardless of convention.

The Brandenburgers reported directly to the Abwehr's head, Admiral Wilhelm Canaris, a former U-boat commander in World War One. A highly intelligent man with a gift for languages, he had experience of espionage from the earlier conflict and, like his compatriot Admiral Raeder in the *Kriegsmarine*, had serious reservations about Hitler. Indeed, it has been suggested that he deliberately formed the special commando force – not unlike Goering's ground units and Himmler's infamous SS – with a view to overthrowing the Führer. Canaris remained as head of the intelligence service until July 1944, when he was implicated in the 'bomb plot' on Hitler's life.

Whether there is any truth in the allegation, there is no doubt that, from the moment of his appointment as leader of the Abwehr in 1935, Canaris busied himself with expanding the service rapidly into three sections. Abwehr I dealt with spying and intelligence gathering; Abwehr II with sabotage and special units; and Abwehr III with counterintelligence. The 'Brandenburg Training Company' – as the unit was initially called on its formation in 1939 – came under Abwehr II and was commanded by Lieutenant-Colonel Heinz, a man who shared his leader's admiration for Lettow Vorbeck, who had operated a commando-style regiment in Germany's African colonies during World War One. Heinz also disliked Hitler, too.

Both men were eager to recruit from the countries on the borders of Germany: the *Volksdeutsche* from Poland, Czechoslovakia, Hungary and the Sudetenland. As the war expanded, the Brandenburgers grew from company to battalion strength, and then became a regiment and finally a division. The ability of the men to pass themselves off as locals proved invaluable in special operations in those countries and all of them received special instruction in languages. The French military historian Eric Lefevre, who has made a special study of the Brandenburg Division, wrote in 1998,

> Their superb linguistic skills led them into many areas of espionage and subversion. The best-known Brandenburg operations were during invasions such as those of Belgium and the Netherlands where they seized bridges and other key points while wearing enemy helmets and jackets. This use of foreign uniforms and other Brandenburg tactics were clear violations of the rules of war, but their influence on later special operations around the world is obvious.

Right from their inception, the training of the Brandenburg commandos was as realistic as possible with live ammunition often being used in exercises. The intensive courses incorporated tactics used by partisans in rural areas and those of urban guerrillas in towns and cities. Later, they were taught the skills of seamanship, mountaineering and parachuting as well as the manufacture and use of explosives. Instruction in mental stamina, the ability to improvise and the capability to survive in any situation were also on the curriculum. Just as Hitler had angrily accused the British commandos of being 'murderous thugs and cutthroats', there were those in his own country who believed the Brandenburgers were 'criminals and renegades'. Like those of the English, too, their first operations were labelled 'amateurish' – but, once into their stride as the German army rampaged across Europe, the Nazi commandos were invariably ahead of the action, making their presence felt with deadly efficiency.

The evidence suggests that two special units were directly involved in invasion plans against England in July 1940. One, the curiously named Great Britain Kommando, had a 'seize-and-arrest' mission to fulfil among the invading troops. The other was the more elusive Pioneer Group 909, which actually considered a preliminary landing and whose fate is shrouded in mystery.

With their daunting reputation, it comes as no surprise to discover that detachments from the Brandenburg Division were earmarked to be among the first units to land when Operation Sea Lion was given the go-ahead. Even as the plans were being drawn up, specially selected officers and men were being put through a special training programme in preparation.

The Great Britain Kommandos were certainly the more unlikely of the two groups. They had been set up to operate in conjunction with the Brandenburg troops by Heinrich Himmler, the infamous head of the SS. Their purpose after the invasion was to arrest or 'take into protective custody' a list of political and public figures and, more particularly, to confiscate the valuable artefacts and paintings belonging to the Church of England and the Roman Catholic Church. These were to be sent back to Berlin, where the best would be selected by Hitler to embellish the *Führermuseum* he was planning to build in the town of Linz to glorify his 'Thousand Year Reich'.*

SS records indicate that Himmler made the decision to set up the undercover group of three hundred Kommandos in the week that the armistice with France was signed. The unit, who were to be led by a senior SS colonel, *Standartenführer* Franz Six, were initially given the codename 'England Operation', but this was soon changed by its ambitious leader to 'GB Kommandos'. Six, a fanatical Nazi devoted to his boss, was given authority to recruit the men he felt most suitable for his operation and, it seems likely, instructed to put aside a few rich pickings from those destined for Berlin to be sent instead to Himmler. Above all else, the unit was to keep its mission a secret from any other Nazi leaders, who might also be looking for the spoils of war.

In order to attract as little attention as possible, the Kommandos went through the same training schedules on the French coast as the other Brandenburg units preparing for the invasion – embarking on and disembarking from landing craft, running up the beaches, firing their weapons and learning to find the best cover in exposed landscapes. True to the Brandenburg tradition, they would be expected once in England to commandeer their own transport to get to London – their primary objective – followed by Bristol, Birmingham, Manchester and Liverpool. After this they were to split up into smaller groups of twenty men and head for the east coast, followed by the Midlands and Scotland. With typical Teutonic thoroughness, all of the men were to be issued before embarkation with pocket torches, map cases, field dressings and gas masks.

* The story of Hitler's obsessive looting of the treasures of the conquered nations of Europe and the legend that has grown up around one of the most extraordinary and valuable of these hoards is told in my earlier book, *The Mystery of Rommel's Gold* (Robson, 2003).

The Kommandos were also given crash courses in colloquial English along with detailed information about the suspects they were to seize. Invaluable for this purpose was the *Sonderfahndungsliste GB* (Special Search List GB), which had been compiled in May 1940 by a lawyer turned secret service agent, SS-General Walter Schellenberg. Known euphemistically as 'The Black Book', it contained the names of 2,820 British subjects and European exiles who had been deemed a threat to the Nazi cause and were to be seized as soon as Operation Sea Lion was successful.

Sonderfahndungsliste GB also contained details of institutions and establishments of particular interest to the Nazis – ranging from newspaper offices to Freemasons' Lodges – as well as many well-known names from the worlds of British politics, literature and the media, including Churchill, H G Wells and even Noël Coward! It was, by any standards, a mishmash of inaccuracies and even glaring factual errors.

The group of Kommandos dispatched to East Anglia would have had much to keep them busy, as the list credited the region with being home to the largest number of suspects outside London. There were many at Cambridge University, for example, and between five and ten members of the military and the then establishment to be rounded up in each of Norfolk, Suffolk and Essex. Among those who could have expected a knock on the door from the GB Kommandos if they had ever reached the east coast were Lord Graham at Woodbridge, Suffolk, a Miss Savery at Thorpland Hall in Norfolk and a chemist, J A Graffy, of 95 Devon Road, Barking.

All of these people were, of course, able to rest easy in their beds that summer and autumn when the invasion failed to materialise. They might, though, have slept a little less easily if they had known how close the other Brandenburg unit came to actually stepping ashore.

The story of Pioneer Group 909 was first mentioned in Peter Fleming's *Invasion 1940*, in which he states that subunits of the Brandenburg Division may have attempted several reconnaissance landings on British soil before the date of the projected invasion:

> No evidence survives to show what role would have been allotted to these protean soldiers in 'Operation Sea Lion'. One of them, captured much later in the war, recalled that they were moved up the coast in August 1940, after undergoing training in 'sabotage and English etiquette'. Some of them may even have been ordered to carry out impostures.

A German military historian, Konrad Burg, spent several years investigating the mystery of Pioneer Group 909 before publishing his findings in a series of three articles in 1965 in *Der Landser*, the long-running magazine devoted to the country's military history. His account began in issue 703 with the German preparations for invading England:

> While the plans for 'Operation Sea Lion' were going ahead in the summer of 1940, several special army units – in particular the Brandenburgers – were being considered for some daring action against the enemy. Such tasks might prove risky, it was felt, but whatever happened they would certainly help to educate the men for the greater task that lay ahead.

During the early months of the year, the Brandenburg Division had been busy developing a very effective radio network using tiny receivers utilising the previously little-used short-wave frequency. These radios could reach distances of up to 4,000 kilometres and provided units with the capability to keep in touch with one another, even when long distances apart. The value of such equipment in an invasion was obvious – as long as it worked under actual conditions.

At this same time, says Konrad Burg, Admiral Canaris and his staff in Abwehr II had been giving considerable thought to how they might attack the British ports that it would be essential to capture in any successful invasion. Much attention had been focused on London and the River Thames, which, it was realised, played a special role in the minds of the English – both economically and psychologically – and was known to be heavily defended. Dover, the Channel port, was also of major importance – but closer to hand and perhaps more vulnerable. There were others, too, on the coast of East Anglia that might be even more successfully attacked *if* the planning was right.

On the orders of Admiral Canaris, a handpicked group of multinational soldiers and experts at the new radio technology was set up. Initially, it was called the Hollmann Unit after the barracks in Berlin where it was based, but this was changed to Pioneer Group 909. The group's very name gave its mission away, says Konrad Burg. These Brandenburgers were intended to land *ahead* of the main invasion thrust:

> The unit was to go to Dover Harbour where the British had placed a steamer which would be scuttled at the first sign of an invasion to block the harbour. They had to occupy this steamer and prevent it being used as a blockade. Then they were to switch their attention to the British coastal batteries on the cliffs.

The planners envisaged that Pioneer Group 909 would use a captured British cargo ship as their means of transport across the Channel. Their short-wave radio would then be used to fool the coastal defences with messages in English until they were safely in the harbour. Despite initial enthusiasm, however, the plan was shelved when it was decided that coming in on a flood tide would very probably drive the vessel onto the steep coast around Dover.

Even before the idea had been put aside, the unit of mainly English-speaking Germans, who had lived overseas before the war, were in intensive training for whatever mission they were handed. In early July, the hundred-strong group were living in accommodation at La Chapelle near Dieppe under the watchful eye of their inspirational and hard-working leader, Major General Forster.

Two weeks later, Pioneer Group 909 were on the move again to Bussum on the coast of Holland. From here, in a captured Swedish steamer and protected by several Luftwaffe fighter aircraft, they carried out a successful trial landing on the steep coast of Heligoland intended to duplicate one in England. On the return journey to France, they were told they would invade dressed as Englishmen, according to Konrad Burg:

At La Chapelle they were familiarised with their individual tasks. Every day there were maps to be studied and for hours they would move around dressed as Home Guards or 'Bobbies' speaking only English and practising British manners. They were to be in the first group of attackers landing to the west of Hastings to create a bridgehead. Once the defenders began retreating inland, they were to push on to the coastal batteries at Beachy Head and cut off the English there.

The fact that the soldiers of Pioneer Group 909 were to be dressed as policemen and members of the Home Guard was to have extraordinary ramifications long after they had taken part in an actual sortie 'somewhere off the east coast' that same month, according to Konrad Burg. He has provided the only details of this event in his account for *Der Landser*:

On a particularly dark night in autumn 1940, a combined operation by this unit with naval personnel and the *Luftwaffe* was carried out. The aim was to land a small group of men on the English coast and, after taking a few prisoners, return in their landing craft to harbour. The result was worse than the pessimists had imagined. The landing craft, protected on either side by the navy and in the air by planes, approached to about 100 metres of the English coast when the order to land was given.

Suddenly flames sprayed out through jets coming from underwater oil pipes, turning with unbelievable speed into a barrier of flames. The landing craft on which the commandos were travelling caught fire. The men who wanted to save themselves by swimming to the English shore were caught in the wall of flames. The seamen in the escort vessels could not help as they were in great danger, too. They had no option but to turn back. To complete the misfortune, English army units opened fire with their artillery and infantry weapons. And, finally, the *Luftwaffe* planes not only fired on the English positions, but also managed to hit some of the hapless German soldiers in the water.

After the debacle, Admiral Canaris apparently tried feverishly to discover what had caused the 'barrier of flames'. He is said to have watched a film of the ill-fated exercise taken from a U-boat, although no trace of this has ever been found. Photographs of an extensive blaze on a watery surface that were allegedly taken at the time by a German secret agent on the English coast and later smuggled to Berlin also proved so indistinct as to be useless. Even on such insubstantial evidence, Canaris concluded that the enemy had apparently devised a way of making the coast unassailable with a wall of flame.

'The heat from this is so great that boats will catch fire at once,' he is quoted by Konrad Burg as saying, 'and even iron components start to melt. Hardly a single soldier from an invasion fleet would reach English soil.'

According to Burg, news of the disaster eventually reached Hitler and it was to signal the end of the Führer's plans for invading England:

> After the disaster of this experimental venture with such heavy losses, 'Operation Sea Lion' was abandoned. No explanation was ever given. There were rumours, but these were put down with draconian methods in both the Army and in Germany generally. The Army leadership – particularly Hitler and his staff – had decided such a venture would end in catastrophe and agreed that an invasion of England was impossible.

In a footnote to his articles, Burg also briefly quotes another version of events. According to this, Himmler had heard rumours that the English possessed a 'flame wall' defence system, but was convinced there was no truth in the stories. Indeed, so confident was he that he offered to carry out a 'sham landing' using SS troops to show such defences were non-existent. His men then set out just like those of Pioneer Group 909 – with precisely the same result.

Whether there is any truth in these incidents as related by Konrad Burg – and though there is no doubt about the existence of Pioneer Group 909, there is much else about their activities that is implausible – 'Operation Sea Lion' was actually far from being abandoned. Indeed, a story was breaking that would lead to the spread of even more remarkable invasion rumours on both sides of the English Channel.

Chapter 8

A Sea of Burned Corpses

The stretch of French coastline running from the Belgian border to Normandy is sometimes referred to as 'the Opal Coast'. The milky-white seas that give the area this name wash onto a craggy coast of wide beaches, estuaries and creeks providing havens for fishing villages and ports from which men have sailed out for centuries to battle the elements of the North Sea – or repel invaders.

At the northernmost point of this area, situated where the River Colne flows into the English Channel, lies Dunkirk, one of the most famous locations associated with World War Two. Today, it is the fourth most important fishing and commercial port in France, a centre for chemical plants and oil refineries, linked to the other northern industrial centres of France and Belgium. But, despite the passage of time, it still bears the scars of those terrible months of conflict when it was so nearly erased from the face of the earth.

Originally a tiny hamlet named Saint-Gilles, it was not until the ninth century that it was given its Flemish name, Dune-Kerke, meaning 'church of the dunes'. For centuries thereafter it was a battleground for the Spanish, the Dutch and the British as they fought for control. In 1662, the English king, Charles II, sold the town to Louis XIV, who extensively fortified it in an attempt to prevent further incursions.

Dunkirk suffered considerable damage during World War One. Indeed, it was not until 1920 that the town was fully restored – only to fall victim twenty years later to the crushing bombardment of German shells and bombs that rained onto the 325,000 British and 40,000 French soldiers struggling to get off the beach of Fort des Dunes into the 'little ships' sent to fetch them across the Straits of Dover to England.

Thankfully, some of the town's most characteristic monuments survived – notably the 59-metre-high belfry, which now serves as a war memorial and tourist office; the flamboyant church of Saint-Eloi; and the nineteenth-century Renaissance-style Hotel de Ville. These few buildings – along with personal testimonies, photographs and records – bear witness to the terrible events that occurred there during the British evacuation, the German occupation that followed, and its recapture by the Allied Forces in 1944.

There are, though, few more extraordinary stories than that of the burned corpses that were washed up on 'the Opal Coast' in the summer of 1940. Rumours suggested they were all that remained of a German force sent to conquer Britain – and the truth behind the accounts of these scorched and disfigured bodies provides an important element in our search for the truth about where the German eagle landed in England.

The story actually begins a little over three kilometres to the west of Dunkirk in the picturesque historic port of Gravelines, situated on the right bank of the River Aa, where it pierces the sand dunes. Like its bigger neighbour, it was originally a small village and also has a history of attacks and bloodshed – not to mention the dubious distinction of being the place where the first of the burned bodies were apparently found.

Gravelines was originally founded in the eighth century by an English missionary, St Willibrord, from Northumberland, and the parish church in the town still bears his name, spelled in French as 'Willibrod'. The early inhabitants were evidently fearful of being attacked and in 1160 they built a *glacis* – a high, sloping bank complete with ramparts and a moat on which invaders were vulnerable to fire from above.

Before the century was out, the River Aa had also been diverted through the town.

However, even this protection could not save Gravelines from seizure by the Duke of Burgundy in the fourteenth century, followed by Emperor Charles V in 1528, who increased the fortifications. These still proved no match for the bludgeoning army of Gaston d'Orleans, who captured the town in 1644 and immediately destroyed the battlements. Perhaps not surprisingly, this decision rebounded on Gaston just eight years later when Archduke Leopold marched into Gravelines with his superior forces.

After years of protecting the western borders of the Spanish Netherlands, as they then were, from France, Gravelines finally came under the rule of the French monarchy following the Treaty of the Pyrenees in 1659. Thereupon the fortifications were rebuilt by the great French engineer Vauban with the extremely effective star-shaped defences that are still visible today.

Gravelines earned its real place in the history books in 1588 when the English fleet routed the Spanish Armada within sight of the port. The Armada was on its way to invade England and had stopped to pick up an invasion army – a host of battle-hardened troops who had already subdued a revolt in the Spanish Netherlands. However, this army was not ready to embark and the alerted English decided to take advantage of the delay and set fire-ships ablaze and drift them into the middle of the Spanish fleet. Captain Henry Whyte, one of the English captains who played a part in this action, later recalled the events in a dispatch, 'The Battle of Gravelines', dated 8 August 1588:

When the enemy's fleet came to anchor, it was devised to put them from their anchor, and seven ships were allotted to the fire to perform the enterprise. Among the rest, the ship I had in charge, the Bark *Talbot*, was one selected. On Sunday, the 28th July, at night, about one of the clock, the enterprise was undertaken, which took effect, though not so good as was expected; for it drove two of their galleasses to be foul of one of the other, so that the one plucked away the other's rudder, which afterwards drove into Calais and went aground upon the sands. The next morning, by the dawning, we found all the fleet put from their anchors, with the loss, by report of some of them that were afterwards taken, of 100 or 120 anchors and cables.

Hundreds of people on the beach at Gravelines witnessed the fires raging among the Spanish fleet and saw the remainder of the ships hastily setting sail on what would prove to be a voyage to disaster. After sailing along the east coast of England, the invaders rounded the north of Scotland and headed for Ireland, battling terrible gales all the while. As history has recorded, few of their number escaped being sunk and the mission of the Armada ended in complete failure.

Fate had another twist in store for the port of Gravelines. July would again prove a time of great significance in the town's history and the 28th of the month the date of another invasion of England – both over three hundred and fifty years later.

On the morning of Wednesday, 11 September 1940, people in New York eating their breakfasts or on their way to work were startled by a banner headline on the front page of the *New York Sun*, the city's most popular tabloid. The report – marked 'exclusive' – brought the war on the other side of the Atlantic much closer to home for readers than at probably any time during the past year:

BRITISH FIRE HALTED INVASION AS NAZIS TRIED TO RUSH COAST

Sun's Informant Says Hand-propelled Barges Were Cut Off by Navy and Blasted by Land Batteries

The report began,

An attempted invasion of England by the Germans from occupied Europe has been confirmed to the *Sun* today by an unofficial British source. The *Sun*'s informant, who returned from England only a few days ago, based his belief that the Nazi forces had made a disastrous attempt to land on the south-east coast of England in the later part of August, probably the 25th, on stories told to him by friends who were on leave from the navy. They had taken part in the British action to repel the invaders, they told him, but had been cautioned to tell no one about it for the time being.

According to the *Sun*, the invasion had been attempted in barges and had almost certainly been doomed to failure from the start:

The barges were very light, of wood and metal, and obviously intended for a one way trip. They carried no artillery, probably because their only hope of getting across the British mine fields safely was their light draft, which would have been deepened by the weight of guns and ammunition. Because their draft was no more than six feet, the barges did negotiate the mine fields, but the withering fire from the land sank them as fast as they appeared. The extremely shallow draft of the craft probably explains why it is believed that an invasion could not be attempted except when the Channel lay quiet, and smooth.

Each barge contained 200 soldiers with full equipment. Evidently the Germans had counted on their airmen being able to silence the land batteries before they were able to annihilate the invaders, who were helpless because they did not carry artillery. The barges sank under a withering fire as soon as they appeared. Meanwhile, detachments of the British Fleet appeared to the rear cutting off the barges from France.

As with any good exclusive, the *Sun* followed it up later in the week with a still more sensational story. The paper informed its readers that, while many of the German soldiers were floundering in the sea, incendiary bombs had been dropped to set alight tanks of oil that were already in position in the Channel. The result was that thousands of men were literally burned to death, as the second report outlined under an even more sensational headline:

NAZI INVADERS 'CONSUMED BY FIRE'

DEAD ARE PUT AT 80,000

Barges Ran Into Flames When RAF Bombers Fired Tanks in Water, It Is Stated

The facts, the *Sun* said, had been gathered in France from 'workers in the occupied areas along the Channel coast and confirmed by nurses who worked in hospitals attending German soldiers who had escaped from the British flames'. The paper went on,

'We were caught like fish in a frying pan,' was the way a German soldier who escaped from the debacle described it to a French nurse. Only a few thousand Germans succeeded in reaching the French coast. The others perished in the sea or were burned to death. People in the occupied French ports estimate that perhaps as many as 80,000 German troops perished. The fact is that hospitals in occupied France are filled with Nazi soldiers, all of them suffering from severe burns. Thousands of German bodies have been washed ashore.

The British press, fettered of course by censorship, were unable to follow up these claims and had to content their readers with the briefest stories cherry-picked from the *Sun* or the US news agencies that also circulated details. A single paragraph in the *Daily Mirror* of Saturday, 15 September, under the heading RUMOUR DENIED, was typical of the majority: 'It was stated by the War Office yesterday that there was no foundation for the stories in circulation to the effect that an actual attempt at invading this country had been made by the Germans. These stories have been of a circumstantial kind.'

Even the Germans, when they got wind of how widely the story had been circulated on the other side of the Atlantic, issued their own statement relayed by AP on 25 September under the headline CHANNEL LOSSES DENIED:

Berlin – Authorised German sources said today that there was no truth in reports that many thousands of bodies of German soldiers were being washed ashore along the English Channel. Such accounts were declared to be an indication of a situation that compels the British 'to put out such silly lies'.

Just for once there was some truth in the Nazi statement and a full-blown mystery was soon in the making, as J M Spaight, the principal assistant secretary at the Air Ministry, was to write in his memoirs, *The Battle of Britain 1940*, published the following May:

In mid-September something happened which is still a mystery. There were persistent rumours then that an invasion was attempted and foiled by our naval forces. That was probably untrue, but it is fairly certain that some kind of disaster did overtake the 'invasion fleet' about that time. It is known that a large number of German soldiers had to be treated in hospital for burns, the result, it was reported, of a heavy raid by the RAF at that time. The raid caught the troops just when they were engaged in a 'dress rehearsal' for embarkation; the boats in which they were carried were sunk; and when they took to the water, the oil, set alight by the incendiary bombs, burned them severely before they could be rescued. For days after this incident bodies of dead soldiers were being washed up on the French, Belgian and Dutch coasts.

Spaight believed that a bad storm at the time had contributed to the German losses of men and boats. He also thought it no coincidence that the advance of Italian troops into Egypt had begun at the end of the first week of September and had reached Sidi Barrani just after the middle of the month. The man from the Air Ministry argued further:

The advance would have continued, one may surmise, to Mersah Matruth and beyond that to the Delta, *if* the German invasion had been launched and had succeeded. Resistance in the Middle East might then have collapsed. Mussolini was, in fact, acting again as Hitler's jackal. What spoilt the plan was the shattering blow that the Royal Air Force struck at the *Luftwaffe* on 15 September – a blow which was the culmination of a series of others delivered in the preceding five weeks. There is a good deal of evidence that 15 September was the date fixed, approximately, for Germany's attempt to smash our air defences and the projected invasion of this country by both airborne and seaborne forces.

Such reports and comments do not, though, resolve the question of what had happened in the English Channel. For there is also the evidence of people living on the French coast – and at Gravelines in particular – to be considered. *Their* stories point to an even greater mystery that began sweeping 'the Opal Coast'. Indeed, to some of those who lived beside the River Aa, the rumours and gossip that came their way about the defeat of an invasion force by fire seemed rather like history repeating itself.

Dr Paul Schiff was a general practitioner from Paris who owned a villa on the coast between Gravelines and Dunkirk. Shortly after the terrible events of the evacuation, he returned at the end of July to find out whether his holiday home was still standing. A few hundred yards from the beach, a German roadblock prevented him from seeing the villa, let alone getting close enough to see if it had been damaged. He recalled later in a personal letter to a relative (now in my possession):

> I went back into Dunkirk and spoke to a friend who was the manager of the Le Seur works. He told me the road to the beach was being guarded night and day by German soldiers with fixed bayonets who had orders to shoot anyone who tried to go any further. My friend said there were a lot of bodies that had been washed up onto the beach. They were all apparently blackened and burned. The Germans were burying them in the sand.

Horrified by this story, but still determined to discover the fate of his villa, Dr Schiff stayed overnight with another friend who kept a small café in the centre of the town close to the citadel. Here he learned more about the mysterious events on the beach.

> The landlord told me that his daughter had come home a couple of days earlier in a very distressed state. She had gone for a walk to the beach by way of a little creek that

she had known since she was a child. The Germans knew nothing about this creek. All of a sudden, the girl said she almost walked into a group of German soldiers organising a burial party. All over the beach were mounds of sand and bodies waiting to be buried. She did not wait around to see any more. As she hurried home she met a friend in the town who told her that the Germans were employing local men to get rid of the bodies and paying them 8 Francs an hour.

Mme Pauline Lozère, a shopkeeper who remained in Gravelines throughout the occupation, provided another – slightly different – version of events in a diary she kept throughout the occupation, a copy of which I have seen:

Some German officers told me and my friends – so that I had it from three different sources – that the Germans had made an attempt to land in England starting from Calais and Brest. They had used rubber canoes like those used for crossing streams and rivers, but the attempt failed. No one knows how many were killed. The soldiers could be seen being washed ashore upright. It was like an army of the drowned. Their heavy equipment had slipped to their feet so they were kept upright.

A third witness from the area was Charles Barbe, an ambulance driver, who lived in a small house about ten kilometres south of Dunkirk. In the aftermath of the French Armistice, he was kept busy driving between the coast and Paris. It was on his way back from Paris with a colleague that they 'saw something strange', as Barbe recounted in an interview.

'At a point on the coast quite near to Dieppe,' he said, 'we saw bodies on the shore like driftwood, something which could in some cases be identified as once having been human, while others looked like blackened tree stumps. I don't believe I shall ever get the stench out of my nose, not if I live to be a hundred years old. They were just burned beyond recognition. I had previously spoken to a couple of German soldiers just north of Paris who had told me they had been badly burned during the latter part of August. One of the boys said he would be shot if he spoke about it. He said he was out in a rowing boat "fishing" – that is the official word, "fishing" – when, in his words, the sea exploded in flames. I do not know what happened – I only know what the results were.'

There are stories that people living elsewhere in northern France also heard rumours of an 'invasion' of England and its apparently catastrophic outcome. Some estimated the casualties at between a few thousand and an outlandish hundred thousand. A retired naval officer, Philippe Niçois, in Boulogne, wrote to his sister in Saint-Tropez in August,

> The Germans have lost a big battle against the British. Apparently they attempted to land and the sea is now full of their corpses. The Germans have rounded up all the Frenchmen along the coast to collect the bodies, which will total about 35,000. The English gained their victory by spreading petrol on the sea and setting it on fire.

A month later, on 14 September, Dr Charles Bove, the former head surgeon of the American Hospital in Paris, returned to New York and was asked by an AP news agency reporter if he had heard the stories of 'hundreds of German bodies in the water near Cherbourg'. The doctor said that he assumed that, if the reports were true, the corpses must have been of men who had been taking part in an attempted invasion. He added, 'All along the French coast the Germans are constantly practising for invasion. They set out on ships and are made to leap overboard and swim considerable distances with all their equipment.'

Another American who heard about these 'rehearsals' was Robert Solberg, the vice-president of a steel company who also returned home that month. According to a report of his arrival on board a liner in New York in the *New York Times* of 21 September,

> Robert Solberg, returning with his wife and daughter after some 20 years of residence in France, said the Germans were holding invasion practice off the French coast. He asserted, as did other passengers, that the Dutch and the French were supplying the British with advance information of German exercises on self-propelled barges in the Channel and that British bombers had taken a heavy toll. Mr. Solberg added that he had definite information that the Germans have attempted no actual invasion of England. He said the British, tipped off by the Dutch and French, waited for the barges with planes and submarines and that 'thousands of Germans have been lost in this fashion.' He said he recently visited a French Channel port where bodies of German troops were being washed ashore daily.

A number of members of the medical profession still practising in occupied Europe added their contributions to the growing legend. A French medical orderly in Paris wrote to his mother in the Dordogne that same month of the 'terrible failure' of a German invasion:

> I can vouch for it, because I know a doctor who personally attended two German soldiers whose faces were burnt. It happened when they fell into the sea which the English had set on fire with fuel oil. I heard that badly burnt men had been sent to hospitals as far afield as Angouleme.

A GP, Doctor Armand, working in the capital, added to the allegations in another statement I have seen:

The Germans have tried to land in England. In Paris, all the hospitals have been requisitioned and they're all full. Trains keep on arriving packed with wounded still wearing their field dressings. My wife, who lives near the Rothschild hospital, swears it is full of burnt face and eye cases because the English set fire to the sea.

Undoubtedly, though, the most fascinating accounts of this mystery come from two American journalists, Lars Moen and William Shirer, who, as representatives of what was then still a neutral country, were allowed to travel throughout occupied Europe during the summer of 1940 and file reports home.

Lars Moen, who combined the professions of journalist and scientific researcher, worked in Belgium from 1939 until October 1940, when the uncertainty of life under the German occupation made him decide to pack up and return home. There he spent a year writing his memoirs and published *Under the Iron Heel* in 1941. His detailed account of the invasion story is worth quoting in full:

On or about September 16, a considerable force of towed triple-barges set out from a point along the Belgian coast, constituting the first wave of the attack, which was to occupy a strip on the English coast at which liners could put in and disembark the invasion troops. At a point probably not far from the Belgian coast, they were spotted by the British. Destroyers of the Royal Navy then managed to cut them off, and forced them well out into the North Sea. Here planes of the RAF dropped oil drums with great quantities of oil on and near the barges, then followed the incendiary bombs which turned the whole sea into a blazing inferno.

During the first weeks of October, the bodies of hundreds of German soldiers were being washed up ashore along the Belgian coast, especially in the vicinity of Ostend. Many of them were so badly burned as to be almost unrecognisable. Many of the invasion barges were missing, although the naval craft and merchant liners were still in the harbour, their numbers having been increased by fresh arrivals.

Moen admitted that none of the facts, taken alone, could be taken as proof of an attempted invasion – but collectively they did point in one direction:

I believe these facts to be exact. I first learned of the burned patients from a Belgian nurse working in an Antwerp hospital. Americans living near Ostend confirmed reports of the bodies being washed ashore. Later, I heard these stories scores of times which proves nothing – but it was extremely significant that reports from the most widely scattered sources were unanimous on one point: that a considerable number of German soldiers had been badly burned.

Lars Moen's conclusions were also supported by his fellow American journalist, William Shirer, who would later become acknowledged as one of the most distinguished historians of the war for his classic work of research, *The Rise and Fall of the Third Reich* (1960). Twenty years earlier he had begun to make his reputation with *Berlin Diary* (1941), which provided US readers with a graphic account of life under the Nazis in their early days of triumph. Shirer first heard the rumours while visiting Geneva on 16 September and wrote in his *Diary*:

The stories there were that either in attempted German raids with sizeable landing parties on the English coast or in rehearsals with boats and barges off the French coast, the British had given the Germans a bad pummelling. The reports reaching Switzerland from France were that many German barges and ships had been destroyed and a considerable number of German troops drowned; also that the British had used a new type of wireless-directed torpedo which spread ignited oil on the water and burned the barges.

Shirer admitted he was initially inclined to take these stories 'with a pinch of salt'. But he had cause to reflect on this verdict when he returned to the Potsdamer Bahnhof in Berlin two days later:

I noticed several lightly wounded soldiers, mostly airmen, getting off a special car which had been attached to our train. From their bandages their wounds looked like burns. I noticed also the longest Red Cross train I've ever seen. It stretched from the station for half a mile to beyond the bridge over the Landwehr Canal. Orderlies were swabbing it out, the wounded having been unloaded, probably during the night. The Germans usually unload their hospital trains after dark so that the populace will not be unduly disturbed by one of the grimmer sides of glorious war.

As I stood there, I wondered where so many wounded could have come from as the armies in the west had stopped fighting three months ago. As there were only a few porters I had to wait some time on the platform and picked up a conversation with a railway workman. He said most of the men taken from the hospital train were suffering from burns. Could it be that the tales I heard in Geneva had some truth in them after all?

It was not, in fact, until 1944 that the facts about the so-called invasion and the mysterious burned bodies began to come to light – and somewhat longer before a full explanation was forthcoming. The second part of the drama began – as did so many elements of this phase of the war – with the man who

Above: Steel scaffolding being erected on Clacton beach to prevent enemy tanks from landing.

Imperial War Museum H11545

Right: Pretty girls – and small boys – still managed to bathe on many of the beaches along the East Anglian coast during the summer of 1940.

SUGGESTED MEASURES FOR FOILING NAZI TROOP-CARRIER

ARTIST G. H. DAVIS.

IN RELATIVELY SMALL SPACES. THESE DRAWINGS SHOW THEIR CAPABILITIES, AND SUGGEST A NUMBER OF WA
OR STOPPED IN THIS COUNTRY.

down-wind and bumped and bounced over ploughed fields and similar rough surfaces, oftentimes throwing their inmates in a heap and breaking arms and legs. Yet as long as a certain percentage of the men reached the invaded soil unscathed the demands of the Nazi generals were satisfied. Such desperate tactics must, of course, also be anticipated in any attempted invasion of our own island. Everywhere over the English countryside—surpassingly beautiful just now in the full tide of summer—are open spaces, and each area of over two hundred square yards is a potential landing-field for Nazi troop-carriers, which,

with the use of air-brakes, can reduce their run on alighting to three hun yards and get off again in only a little more space after the troops have them. The need therefore appears to be vital to place obstructions in the of such possible landings, either through trenching or the raising of effec this end. In many areas, particularly around Greater London, the defenc open spaces was recently stated to be complete. Soldiers have been ploug up certain areas and trenches have been dug.

Above and opposite page: Practical suggestions to meet the threat of airborne invasion drawn by G H Davis, *Illustrated London News*, 15 June 1940.

EETING THE THREAT OF AIR-BORNE INVASION IN BRITAIN:

DRAWN BY OUR SPECIAL

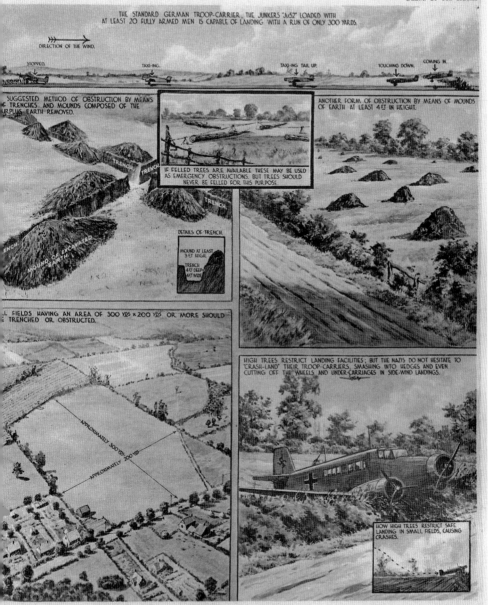

THE STANDARD GERMAN TROOP-CARRIER, THE JUNKERS "Ju52" LOADED WITH
AT LEAST 20 FULLY ARMED MEN IS CAPABLE OF LANDING WITH A RUN OF ONLY 300 YARDS.

DIRECTION OF THE WIND.

STOPPED. TAXI-ING. TAXI-ING TAIL UP. TOUCHING DOWN. COMING IN.

SUGGESTED METHOD OF OBSTRUCTION BY MEANS
F TRENCHES AND MOUNDS COMPOSED OF THE
UR-PLUS EARTH REMOVED.

ANOTHER FORM OF OBSTRUCTION BY MEANS OF MOUNDS
OF EARTH AT LEAST 4 FT IN HEIGHT.

TRENCH

IF FELLED TREES ARE AVAILABLE THESE MAY BE USED
AS EMERGENCY OBSTRUCTIONS. BUT TREES SHOULD
NEVER BE FELLED FOR THIS PURPOSE.

MOUND OF EXCAVATED EARTH

DETAILS OF TRENCH.

MOUND AT LEAST
3 FT HIGH.

TRENCH
4 FT DEEP
4 FT WIDE

L FIELDS HAVING AN AREA OF 300 YDS × 200 YDS OR MORE SHOULD
E TRENCHED OR OBSTRUCTED.

APPROXIMATELY 300 YDS

APPROXIMATELY 200 YDS

HIGH TREES RESTRICT LANDING FACILITIES; BUT THE NAZIS DO NOT HESITATE TO
"CRASH-LAND" THEIR TROOP-CARRIERS, SMASHING INTO HEDGES AND EVEN
CUTTING OFF THE WHEELS AND UNDER-CARRIAGES IN SIDE-WIND LANDINGS.

HOW HIGH TREES RESTRICT SAFE
LANDING IN SMALL FIELDS, CAUSING
CRASHES.

ZI TROOP-CARRIERS, WHICH PLAYED A VITAL PART IN THE INVASION OF NORWAY AND HOLLAND, CAN CRASH-LAND
BY WHICH THEY CAN BE HINDERED

he light of the aerial invasions which have so largely brought about the
missions successively of Poland, Norway, Holland and Belgium, the menace
ne troop-carrying aeroplane is a very real one to Britain. Various counter-
sures are possible which may have the effect of thwarting the enemy's plans
his direction, one being to obstruct open country where troop-carriers could
and also arterial roads and, finally, rivers so that the big aircraft, carrying
human loads of enemy soldiers, will be unable to alight without crashing.
these pages we illustrate various means of obstructing such fields as

might offer troop-carriers chances of emergency landings. Britain, with its wealth
of trees and ubiquitous hedges, provides many more natural obstacles than have
been offered by the countries successively invaded by the Nazis. On the other
hand, in the ruthless determination of the German High Command to carry out
its will, great risks are taken by the pilots of the troop-carriers and many
" crash " landings have been reported, when aircraft were brought down in very
restricted areas and smashed in ditches. Some even were brought down in side-
winds, and had their under-carriages wrenched off, while others were landed

To the Country People of Britain

YOU have a great duty — the duty of keeping the roads free for our troops, no matter what happens.

Should parachutists land, or should enemy forces push inland from our coasts, some less-brave people may be tempted to flee from threatened villages and towns.

Don't do it. Stay where you are. This is not just advice, it is an order from the Government. The greatest harm any man or woman could do to Britain at such a time would be to clutter up the roads, and so hinder our own troops advancing to drive the enemy out.

In France refugees crowding the roads made it impossible for the army to bring up reinforcements. So France was lost!

This must not happen here. Remember, you will be far safer from bombing and machine-gunning downstairs in your own home than you would be on the open roads.

Remember, too, the Home Guard will be defending your village, and the Army will be defending your country. They need the roads.

... that's why you must STAY PUT

ISSUED BY THE MINISTRY OF INFORMATION. SPACE PRESENTED TO THE NATION BY WHITBREAD & COMPAN

Above: While city mothers were urged to send their children to the countryside, country dwellers were instructed to stay where they were even if the Germans invaded in the summer of 1940.

Right: The threat of German paratroops landing was a serious matter to the Ministry of Information.

What do I do...

if I hear news that Germans are trying to land, or have landed?

I remember that this is the moment to act like a soldier. I do *not* get panicky. I *stay put*. I say to myself: Our chaps will deal with them. I do *not* say: "I must get out of here." I remember that fighting men must have clear roads. I do *not* go on to the road on bicycle, in car or on foot. Whether I am at work or at home, I just *stay put*.

Cut this out—and keep it!

Issued by The Ministry of Information.
Space presented to the Nation by The Brewers' Society.

IMMOBILISATION OF VEHICLES

IN THE EVENT OF INVASION

Every owner of a motor vehicle should be ready, in the event of invasion, to immobilise his car, cycle or lorry the moment the order is given. Failure to act promptly would give the enemy the chance to provide himself with transport.

It is important that owners of vehicles should understand now what they have to do, and satisfy themselves that they can carry out the order at any time without delay.

With a view to helping them, the Ministry of Transport gives the following information and advice on what they must do when informed by the Police or through the Civil Defence services that immobilisation of vehicles has been ordered in their area:

Petrol Vehicles
Remove distributor head and leads, and empty the tank or remove the carburettor.

Diesel-Engined Vehicles
Remove the injection pump and connection.

HIDE THE PARTS REMOVED WELL AWAY FROM THE VEHICLE

Making sure invaders could not use cars became a vital issue – although getting around the countryside was no easy matter for those who still had vehicles!

The fear of Poison Gas being used by the Germans prompted posters like this one, seen all over Eastern England in the summer of 1940. Imperial War Museum D2376

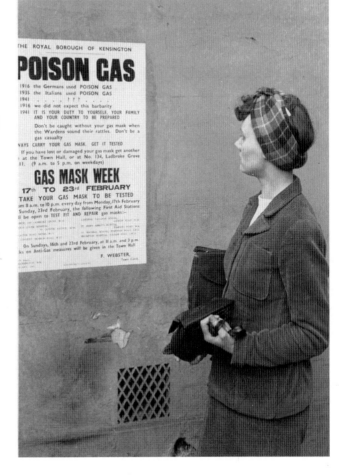

Admiral Raeder inspects the shipping being prepared for Operation Sea Lion.

German troops practising landing manoeuvres for the planned invasion. © Corbis

'Setting the Sea on Fire', an experiment off the East Anglian coast that helped to inspire sensational headlines in the *New York Times*.

The infamous 'Wroxham Roaster' developed by the group of scientists known as the 'Wheezers and Dodgers' at the Admiralty.

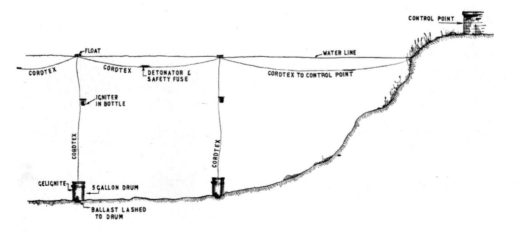

WIR FAHREN GEGEN ENGELLAND

DER KLEINE INVASIONS-DOLMETSCHER	PETIT MANUEL DE CONVERSATION POUR L'INVASION	TAALCURSUS ZONDER LEERMEESTER VOOR DUITSCHE SOLDATEN

I. Vor der Invasion

1. Die See ist gross — kalt — stürmisch.
2. Wie oft müssen wir noch Landungsmanöver üben!
3. Ob wir wohl in England ankommen werden?
4. Ob wir heil zurückkommen werden?
5. Wann ist der nächste englische Luftangriff? Heute morgens; mittags; nachmittags; abends; nachts.
6. Warum fährt der Führer nicht mit?
7. Unser Benzinlager brennt noch immer!
8. Euer Benzinlager brennt schon wieder!
9. Wer hat schon wieder das Telefonkabel durchgeschnitten!
10. Haben Sie meinen Kameraden in den Kanal geworfen?
11. Können Sie mir eine Schwimmweste — einen Rettungsring — leihen?
12. Was kosten bei Ihnen Schwimmstunden?
13. Wie viele Invasionsfahrten brauch' ich für das E.K.I?
14. Sieben — acht — neun.
15. Wir werden gegen Engelland fahren!

I. Avant l'invasion

1. La mer est vaste — froide — houleuse.
2. Combien de fois encore devrons-nous faire des exercises de débarquement?
3. Pensez-vous que nous arriverons jamais en Angleterre?
4. Pensez-vous que nous reviendrons jamais d'Angleterre?
5. Quand le prochain raid anglais aura-t-il lieu? — Aujourd'hui, dans la matinée, à midi, dans l'après-midi, dans la soirée, dans la nuit.
6. Pourquoi est-ce que le Fuehrer ne vient pas avec nous?
7. Notre dépôt d'essence continue de brûler!
8. Votre dépôt d'essence a recommencé à brûler!
9. Qui a encore coupé notre ligne téléphonique?
10. Avez-vous jeté mon camarade dans le canal?
11. Pouvez-vous me prêter une ceinture, — une bouée de sauvetage?
12. Quel prix prenez-vous pour les leçons de natation?
13. Combien d'invasions dois-je faire pour recevoir la Croix de Fer de 1ère classe?
14. Sept — huit — neuf.
15. Nous partirons pour l'Angleterre! (Qu'ils disent.)

I. Vóór de invasie

1. De zee is groot — koud — stormachtig.
2. Hoe vaak nog moeten w'exerceeren om 't landen op een kust te leeren?
3. Zullen we ooit in Engeland komen?
4. Zullen we heelhuids wéerom komen?
5. Wanneer komt de volgende Britsche luchtaanval? Heden — morgen, middag, namiddag, avond, nacht.
6. Waarom reist de Führer niet met ons mee?
7. Ons benzinedepot staat nog steeds in lichter laaie!
8. Uw benzinedepot staat alweer in lichter laaie!
9. Wie heeft onze telefoonleiding nou weer doorgeknipt?
10. Heeft U mijn kameraad in de gracht gesmeten?
11. Kunt U mij een zwemvest — een reddinggordel leenen?
12. Hoeveel kost het om bij U zwemmen te leeren?
13. Hoe dikwijls moet ik aan een invasietocht meedoen om het Ijzeren Kruis te winnen?
14. Zeven — acht — negen keer.
15. Wij zullen gauw naar Engeland varen! (Plons! Plons! Plons!)

II. Während der Invasion

1. Der Seegang — Der Sturm. — Der Nebel. Die Windstärke.
2. Wir sind seekrank. Wo ist der Kübel?
3. Ist das eine Bombe — ein Torpedo — eine Granate — eine Mine?

II. Pendant l'invasion

1. Le gros temps — la tempête — le brouillard — la violence de l'ouragan.
2. Nous avons le mal de mer. Où est la cuvette?
3. Est-ce une bombe — une torpille — un obus — une mine?

II. Tijdens de invasie

1. De deining — de storm — de mist — de orkaan.
2. Wij zijn zeeziek. Waar is de kwispedoor?
3. Is dat een bom — een torpedo — een granaat — een mijn?

The 'Anti-Invasion' propaganda that was distributed over France in the summer of 1940, aimed specifically at troops training along the Channel coast.

Right: *Leutnant zur See* Bernd Klug, 'The Eagle Who Landed'.

GERMAN "PEACE"

This jackboot tramples on the lives of men, of women and of children in all the countries over which the Nazis rule to-day.

A German "peace" does not just mean a change of government. It would mean that everybody's daily life, whether poor or rich, would be run the Nazi way—everybody slaves to German masters! Their spies everywhere. Their guns and rubber truncheons bossing people, from morning until night. Those who do not please them imprisoned, tortured or shot.

Remember what has happened wherever Germans rule.

A German girl—she might have been your daughter—was sent to prison for 18 months for dancing with a Polish prisoner. A shopkeeper got 6 years' imprisonment for selling cloth without a ration card. A whole

British propaganda leaflet issued by the Ministry of Information in July 1940.

THE ILLUSTRATED LONDON NEWS

The World Copyright of all the Editorial Matter, both Illustrations and Letterpress, is Strictly Reserved in Great Britain, the British Dominions and Colonies, Europe, and the United States of America.

SATURDAY, JUNE 29, 1940.

"THE BATTLE OF BRITAIN" BEGINS WITH LITTLE BUT LOSS TO THE GERMANS: ONE OF THE SEVEN ENEMY BOMBERS BROUGHT DOWN IN THE FIRST MASS RAID CRASHES IN ESSEX.

The first German air raids on Britain were probably in the nature of rehearsals to accustom the crews of German night bombers to flying over the country; to explore the effectiveness of air and ground defences; to placate German public opinion, and, finally, to destroy British aeroplanes at their home stations and shipping at the docks. In the June 18 raid, in which about a hundred German aircraft took part, twelve people were killed and thirty injured, but little material damage was done. An eye-witness who described the scene to our artist said: "The night was beautiful, with a full moon. Presently a big aeroplane flying high was picked out, other searchlights quickly converging upon the machine, which was surrounded by bursting shells. Suddenly it lurched, then shot downwards in a trail of black smoke, twisting and turning in a spinning dive right into the ground, where it remained upright for a moment before collapsing in flames."

DRAWING BY C. E. TURNER.

Nazi fighter brought down over Essex during one of the first German Mass Air Raids on 18 June 1940, as pictured by war artist C E Turner.

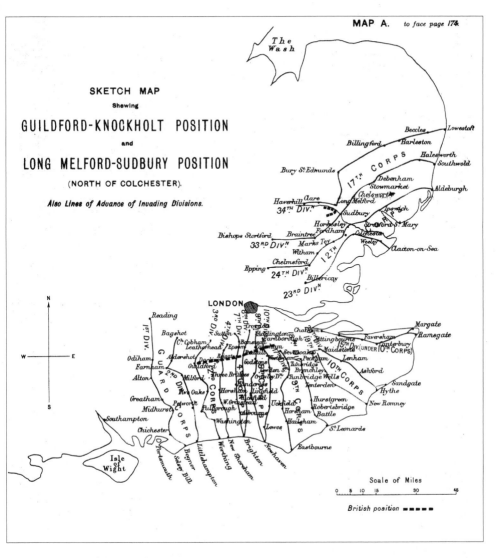

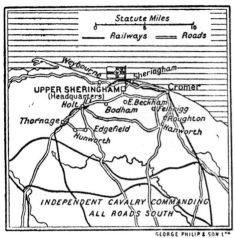

Above: Fictional Prediction of Invasion 1, from *The Writing on the Wall* by 'General Staff', 1906.

Left: Fictional Prediction of Invasion 2, from *The Invasion of 1910* by William Le Queux, 1910.

Colonel Wolfgang Martini who spied on England from a Zeppelin in August 1939 – but completely missed the secret radar base at Bawdsey.

Hitler and Admiral Erich Raeder at one of their first meetings in May 1940 to discuss the invasion of England.

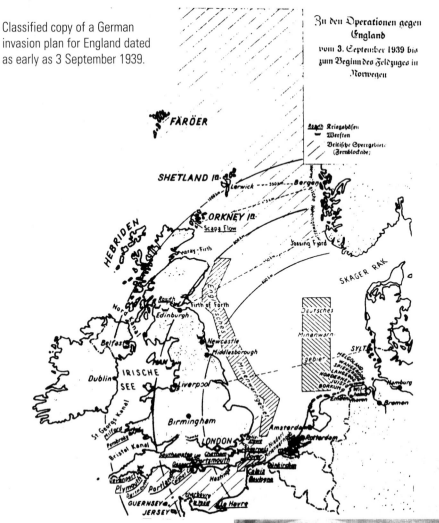

Classified copy of a German invasion plan for England dated as early as 3 September 1939.

Zu den Operationen gegen England

vom 3. September 1939 bis zum Beginn des Feldzuges in Norwegen

Kriegshäfen
Werften
Britische Sperrgebiet (Fernblockade)

FÄRÖER

SHETLAND In.

Lerwick — 350 km — Bergen

ORKNEY In.
Scapa Flow

HEBRIDEN

Moray-Firth

Jössing Fjord

SKAGER RAK

Rosyth

Firth of Forth

Edinburgh

Deutsches

Minenwarn-

gebiet

SYLT

Belfast

Newcastle
Middlesborough

HELGOLAND
WANGER
SPIEKEROOG
LANGEOOG
NORDERNEY
JUIST
BORKUM

Hamburg

MAN

Dublin

IRISCHE
SEE

Liverpool

Enden

Bremen

St Georgs Kanal

Birmingham

Amsterdam

Pembroke

LONDON

Rotterdam

Bristol Kanal

Southampton

Portsmouth

Dünkirchen

Hastings

Calais

Boulogne

Plymouth

Portland

Cherbourg

Le Havre

GUERNSEY

JERSEY

Suffolk milkman enjoying one of the German propaganda leaflets dropped across the country with details of Hitler's Reichstag speech of 19 July.

LAST APPEAL TO REASON
BY
ADOLF HITLER
Speech before the Reichstag, 19th July, 1940

The Daily Telegraph

and Morning Post

B

No. 26,355

LONDON, MONDAY, JULY 15, 1940

LONDON
LATE
EDTN.

ONE PENNY

BROADCASTING—Page Three

MR. CHURCHILL AND AN INVASION

READY, UNDISMAYED, TO MEET IT

"WE SEEK NO TERMS & ASK NO MERCY"

LONDON IN RUINS BETTER THAN ENSLAVEMENT

Mr. Churchill, in a broadcast to British, Empire and American listeners last night, reaffirmed his confidence in the determination and ability of this country to resist invasion and, when the time comes, to lift the dark curse of Hitler from our age. He declared:

"Be the ordeal sharp or long, or both, we shall seek no terms, we shall tolerate no parley. We may show mercy, but we shall ask none."

Never before had Britain had an army comparable in quality, equipment or numbers with to-day's. London itself, fought street by street, could easily devour an entire hostile army, and we would rather see London laid in ruins and ashes than that it should be abjectly enslaved.

Looking to the future, Mr. Churchill declared that we must prepare not only for 1941 but for 1942, "when the war will, I trust, take a different form from the defensive in which it has hitherto been bound."

The Prime Minister said that in a week the Royal Air Force and Fighter Command had shot down more than five of the German aircraft which tried to attack convoys in the Channel.

FRANCE WILL BE LIBERATED

Mr. Churchill began his foster the trade and help the the of

U.S. DEMOCRATS MEET TO-DAY

THIRD TERM TAKEN FOR GRANTED

From Our SPECIAL CORRESPONDENT
CHICAGO, Sunday.

Delegates to the Democratic National Convention, which gets off to a slow-motion start to-morrow, have gathered here with three views uppermost in their minds.

The first is that it would be a grave mistake to under-estimate the strength of the Republican candidate. Mr. Wendell Willkie.

The second, arising from this, is that Mr. Roosevelt must be nominated for a third term if the party is to win; and the third, following on from that, that Mr. James Farley, Postmaster-General, must manage the

Mr. Farley has been national chairman since Mr. Roosevelt's first nomination eight years ago. He still holds himself aloof from the New Dealers, headed by Mr. Harry Hopkins, Secretary for Commerce, who are now running the Roosevelt candidacy.

Mr. Farley's opposition to a third term has frequently been expressed in the past, and he has also objected to interference by New Deal organisation and strategy.

The President's acceptance of nomination is now taken for granted by a majority of Democrats.

NAMES ON THURSDAY

The actual work of the Convention, in all its phases, takes two days. But delegates must be given an opportunity to spend money for an opportunity to... If the strategists, no the Presidential nominations will not take place until Thursday.

Mr. Roosevelt will, according to present plans, be offered the party's nomination for the Vice-Presidency also. Mr. John Garner, Vice-President, will, according to present plans, be out and he is expected to retire to private life although he has organised opposition in the Senate to many of the President's policies.

LUXURY TAX EXPECTED

NEW BUDGET PLANS

By Our Political Correspondent
Sir Kingsley Wood, Chancellor of the Exchequer, may make no

EIRE WARNED BY MINISTER

May Soon Be In A Tight Corner

WAR-TIME ADVICE TO PEOPLE

FROM OUR OWN CORRESPONDENT
DUBLIN, Sunday.

Mr. F. Aiken, Minister for Co-ordination of Defence, in Eire, speaking at a recruiting meeting yesterday, said that Eire may be in a rather tight corner soon, but that is nothing new to us, and with God's help and the pull of our people, we will pull the old land through.

He added that every civilian must realise that his district might become the scene of military operations at any time. In such a case, they should observe the following rules:

Do not hinder the Army by crowding the roads or do anything which hampers the enemy.

Do not co-operate with or assist the enemy in any way.

Obey all orders issued by the Army authorities or local security

FRENCH NATIONAL DAY IN LONDON

Gen. de Gaulle inspecting a French guard of honour in Whitehall before he placed a wreath on the Cenotaph in celebration of the French national holiday yesterday—the anniversary of the fall of the Bastille. (Adml. Muselier is on the left. (Another picture on Page 6.)

60-MINUTE AIR BATTLE OFF DOVER

7 NAZIS DOWN: DIRECT A.A. HIT

Pilots of the R.A.F. Fighter Command and anti-aircraft gunners yesterday combined to shoot down seven enemy aircraft in air fights off the South-East Coast. Other enemy planes were hit and may also have been destroyed.

About 40 Ju. 87 dive bombers were engaged as well as a number of escorting Me. 109 fighters.

The anti-aircraft guns were firing almost continuously for more than half-an-hour. In the air the fight continued for a full hour, many of the Junkers being chased back across the English Channel. Each the dive

BRITISH ATTACK AFTER FOUR-DAY SIEGE

ADVANCE OVER RIVER BED AGAINST ITALIANS

From Our Special Correspondent, ALEXANDER CLIFFORD
CAIRO, Sunday.

Deep in the heart of Africa a little British garrison is holding out heroically against a spectacular Italian offensive.

This is at British Moyale, on the Kenya-Abyssinia border, where the defenders are repulsing attacks on a scale out of all proportion to the place's value. The garrison has been holding out for four days and heavy fighting continues.

In the western desert, whence I have just returned, I learned how the difficulties of Marshal Graziani, the Italian Commander-in-Chief in Libya, caused Mussolini to push this Kenya outpost as his No. I objective.

He has ordered artillery fire of great intensity, while bombers and fighters have been trying to flatten out the British defences and pave the way for the final capture.

But the undaunted defenders are not giving up their positions yet. They have even launched a counter-attack of two series against the Italians entrenched in their own fort

Our planes have been helping to beat off the first convoys, which are continually bringing up supplies of ammunition. It seems impossible for the attack to continue. Even if the Italians occupy the British positions there is no telling if the... continued. So far...

PEACE MOVE IN FAR EAST

BRITISH EFFORT AT MEDIATION

SINGAPORE, Sunday.

Efforts by the British Government to bring peace between China and Japan were disclosed in a broadcast to-night by Mr. S. W. Jones, Acting Governor of Malaya.

At the moment, he stated, the British Government was discussing with the Japanese Government certain proposals affecting the war in the Far East, he continued.

"Believing that an honourable peace is the real desire of the Chinese people to whom at great length continued" has stated His Majesty's Government will give to the greatest length forward every effort it can afford to end it What the result will be no one knows.

In the time-battle she was fighting against heavy odds Britain offered and make every sacrifice to gain a victory against Germany, which was the sole hope of civilisation.

CHEAP SUCCESS SOUGHT

This offensive is a sequel to the message which Graziani is reported to have received from Rome ordering him to follow up the British patrol news that the British patrol were in possession of an outpost to the south of Sollum, in Egypt, the message continued. The war into Egypt and gain a cheap success by the capture of Sollum.

Accordingly Italian propaganda started to build up this miserable... mortal combat... and...

Opposite page: *Daily Telegraph* front-page story on Churchill's 'Invasion Broadcast' of 14 July 1940.

Left and below: Bestselling novelist Dennis Wheatley and his concept of a German invasion plan.

1st day { 1		EMF	16.200	Air-borne troops
2		WMF	22.600	" "
2nd day { 3		NEF	16.200	" "
4		NWF	22.600	" "
3rd day { 5		SF	10.000	" "
5		SF	95.000	Sea-borne troops
4th day 6		NF	90.750	" "
5th day { →	TEN FEINTS		20.000	" "
7	MAIN FORCE		12.100	Air-borne troops
			301.700	Sea-borne troops

Highly populated areas shaded in

No. 22812
AIR MINISTRY
3 JUL 1940
TIME 1110 HOURS

SUMMER ON THE EAST COAST—1940:
MANNING THE "CHURCHILL LINE."

INSTEAD OF HOLIDAY-MAKERS ENJOYING THE VIEW FROM THE BENCH ON THE LEFT, ROYAL SCOTS FUSILIERS, WITH BAYONETS DRAWN, GUARD THE CLIFFS.

EXERCISES IN HOME DEFENCE: TROOPS RUSHING FROM THE BASE OF A GUN-TOWER TO DEFEND THE FORESHORE.

WATCHING FOR HOSTILE 'PLANES: WITH A BREN GUN (MOUNTED AS AN A.-A. GUN) ON TOP OF A PILL-BOX.

ANOTHER VIEW OF THE MOUNTED BREN GUN, SHOWING THE "STEPPED" DESIGN AND ELABORATE CAMOUFLAGE OF THE LATEST TYPE OF PILL-BOX.

AN ANTI-TANK GUN-CREW ON GUARD ON THE FORESHORE, SOMEWHERE ON THE EAST COAST OF ENGLAND.

BLACK SMOKE AGAINST THE SUMMER SKY, CAUSED BY A SALVO FROM THESE GUN-TOWERS, SOMEWHAT SIMILAR TO THOSE DEPICTED BY OUR ARTIST ON PAGES 106-107.

On a double-page in this issue appears a drawing by Captain Bryan de Grineau of gun-emplacements in what a "Times" correspondent aptly called the "Churchill Line." The photographs on this page afford further glimpses of the various defences embodied in this coastal line. Every day our shores and cliffs bristle more and more effectively with men and arms. When happier times return, there will be substantial memorials of this grim time to interest seaside holiday-makers. Every hour the defensive belt is being deepened, and the tank obstacles guarding the roads are of a far more solid type than the lanes of rails that turned out to be such an ineffective device against armoured columns in France. Camouflage has been greatly developed and improved, most of the correspondents who toured the defences remarking on this and on the great solidity of all the defence works. The implication of total warfare was never so clearly defined in France, it was said, where a distinct gulf seemed to separate the mentality of the soldier and the civilian, who unconsciously at times were pulling different ways. Britain might well be called an island fortress; we are happily reaching a point at which every individual in it knows his place in a state of siege. (British Official Photographs; P.N.A.)

'Summer on the East Coast', a series of evocative photographs taken for the *Illustrated London News*, 27 July 1940.

surely knew the facts: Winston Churchill. Indeed it was on 20 June of that year that he was directly questioned about the matter in the House of Commons. According to the evidence of the report of Prime Minister's Question Time in Hansard, Churchill was at his most elusive and tantalising when replying to Major Vyvyan Adams, the Conservative MP for Leeds West:

Major Adams: May I ask my right honourable friend if he cannot tell at this interval of time, as a matter of historical interest, whether the enemy ever set in motion the apparatus of a sea-borne invasion?

Mr. Churchill: Well, sir, it is a matter on which I should not like to take people off other current jobs in order to use their time today. I do not know what my honourable and gallant friend means by 'set in motion'. 'Set in motion' in the sense of crossing the Channel, no. 'Set in motion' in the sense of making very heavy concentrations, both of troops and ships, to cross the Channel, yes.

No sooner had the prime minister sat down, however, than another member joined the fray. He was Emanuel Shinwell, the tough and resourceful former national organiser of the Marine Workers' Union, Labour MP for the Easington Division of Durham, and destined to become a secretary of state for war himself in 1947.

Mr. Shinwell: Can the right honourable gentleman say that if such an attempt was made, at any rate, it was unsuccessful?

Mr. Churchill: Yes sir.

Clearly still not satisfied, Major Adams again stood up waving his question paper.

Major Adams: Can my honourable friend answer this –
Did any of that shipping emerge from the ports across
the Channel?

Mr. Churchill: Not to my belief. A great deal of it was
smashed in the ports and then they changed their minds.

There was evidence to support Churchill's statement, too.
Photographs taken by RAF pilots skirting the French coast had
identified 1,004 barges between Flushing and Boulogne on 18
September. Only 691 could be seen at the end of the month and
the count was down to 448 before October was over.

These facts, though, only seemed to confirm for those
who still felt an invasion might have been attempted that there
could be some truth in the stories of a 'coast white with dead
bodies', to quote Egbert Kieser. Indeed, despite efforts to
disprove the story, a number of bodies – 36 in all – *had* been
washed up on beaches between Land's End and Yarmouth over
a period from August to October, 1940. Details were to be found
not in the national newspapers, but in the local press, such as
in this short account in the *Dover Express* of 25 October:

A German soldier believed to be one of the thousands who
perished in Hitler's rehearsal attempt to invade Britain last
month was washed ashore at Littlestone on the south-east
coast on Monday. He was wearing the field-grey uniform
of a German infantry regiment and was apparently a non-
commissioned officer between 25 and 30. He had been in the
sea for several weeks and death is believed to be by drowning.

The following day, the *Express*'s neighbouring newspaper, *The
Folkestone, Hythe & District Herald*, added further information:

The body had been in the sea possibly as long as six weeks
and such a period fits in with the report recently published

that the RAF inflicted severe losses on the German invasion troops on the other side of the Channel at about that time. There were no signs of injury externally. Arrangements were made to bury the dead man at New Romney.

Subsequent research has established the identity of the dead German. He was Heinrich Poncke of the Anti-Tank Reserve Company 19 and his death certificate is bereft of any personal details of his birth, parentage or occupation. The cause of death is given as 'Due to war operations'.

Gunner William Robinson, a British soldier serving in the 333 Coastal Artillery Battery at this time, had to deal with the recovery of a number of German bodies like that of the unfortunate Poncke and never forgot the experience. Robinson spent several weeks in the autumn as a member of a detail of six soldiers looking for corpses washed up along the coast between Hythe and Hastings. It was not until 1957, however, that he spoke about his gruesome task in a television interview: 'I was among a party of soldiers sent to search for bodies. The first day we found two soldiers. They had no badges. We took them back in a lorry to a field at the back of New Romney. We left them there behind a canvas screen and carried on. During the course of the next few days we found seven or eight more. I was told – and I believe it – that they were caught by the RAF during a pre-invasion manoeuvre in the Channel.'

Later, Gunner Robinson retold his story to the *Folkestone & Hythe Gazette*. He was sure the bodies were German, because they were all dressed in field-grey uniforms. As far as he knew, any identification discs or paybooks had been removed by an officer, and the bodies were all later buried in a mass grave. Robinson admitted to the local paper: 'They gave us a special inducement for the job. We got 20 Woodbines [cigarettes] which we collected each day and an extra two shillings [10p] a day on our pay.'

All of these stories are consistent in having no mention of the bodies being burned or scorched – for a solution to this element of the mystery it is necessary to turn to a book published in 1946 entitled *Flame Over Britain: A Personal Narrative of Petroleum Warfare* by Sir Donald Banks, the head of another clandestine organisation similar to the DMWD. Banks was appointed to the Petroleum Warfare Department in 1940 by Geoffrey Lloyd, the secretary of petroleum, with a brief to find the best use for the nation's petrol supplies and – in particular – how to destroy these resources if the Germans invaded. Lloyd asked Banks, 'Could we swamp the invader in a sea of flame? Flame all across Britain – ringing the coasts, spurting from the hedges and rolling down the hills to burn the invader into the sea?'

According to his account, Banks and his men carried out a whole series of experiments to establish the practicality of using smoke to screen vital factories from enemy attack, to see if roads could be flooded with burning petrol, and whether 'flame traps' laid as burning trails astern of oil tankers were feasible. The results were a mixture of successes – such as the 'Cliff Hopper', barrels of oil to be set rolling downhill onto any invader; the 'Flame Fougasse', a forty-gallon drum containing a mixture of oil and gas, which, when ignited, sent out a tongue of flame thirty yards long; 'Flame Chariots' to be driven into the enemy – and more ambitious schemes, which regularly generated huge billows of black smoke that were visible for miles along the east coast near Shoeburyness, where Banks's team regularly worked. Therein lay the first clue to the burned corpses, as *Flame Over Britain* reveals:

There were many schemes for flame warfare under the stress of threatened invasion and British inventiveness blossomed with new ideas. They played an important part in the summer and autumn of 1940, not least in the effect which they had on the minds of the German commanders and troops. The stories that were allowed to spread on the Continent, and the reports of strange sights seen by German pilots of reconnaissance, were calculated to daunt the stoutest heart among the victorious soldiery assembled on the shore facing England. Besides the known dangers of earth, water and air, they were threatened by the unknown horrors of the Fourth Element, fire on the cliffs and fire even on the sea.

In his book, Sir Donald allowed himself a wry recollection of the way some of his more visible experiments were later referred to on German radio broadcasts as Luftwaffe bombing triumphs, and how the old adage of 'no smoke without a flame' was turned on its head by a British propaganda leaflet, 'Wir Fahren Gegen England', which was dropped by the RAF on the other side of the Channel. It was printed in German, French and Dutch and written in the style of a tourist's vade-mecum, enquiring of its readers:

Do you think we shall ever get to England?

Do you think we shall ever get back from England?

Why is the Führer not coming with us?

What is the charge for swimming lessons?

Is our boat capsizing – sinking – burning – blowing up?

Where is our fleet – our air force?

What is that strong smell of petroleum?

What is setting the sea on fire?

Does not the Captain burn beautifully?

Karl, Willi, Fritz – all incinerated? Drowned? Sliced up by propellers?

Wir fahren gegen Engelland (worse luck!)

In fact, the simple truth about the sea-of-burned-corpses story was just that – it was a story. A combination of the English flame experiments and the problems the Germans were having with their invasion plans mixed in with some half-truths, a lot of gossip and some clever propaganda – as one of the men closest to the deception, John Baker White, admitted fifteen years afterwards in his book, *The Big Lie* (1955). White, who was a major in the Directorate of Military Intelligence in 1940 and later became Conservative MP for Canterbury, describes the lengths to which his agency went to present a fictitious picture of the British defences with new weapons of terribly destructive power and what Hitler would have to face if he launched an invasion against England. He was particularly proud of the burning-sea story:

> I am convinced that one rumour, one deception, above all others, discouraged the Germans from launching their invasion attempt in 1940. It is true that other factors compelled Hitler's decision to abandon the attempt. The failure to destroy the RAF, fear of his generals to embark upon the operation without complete air cover and certain fine weather. All played their part, but one rumour created the psychological conditions that breed nervous-ness, reluctance, uncertainty and even real fear. It consisted of eight words. *The British can set the sea on fire.*
> This rumour was fed into the 'pipe-line' that ran to the bar of the Grand Hotel in Stockholm, the Avida in Lisbon, the Ritz in Madrid and other places in Cairo, Istanbul,

Ankara and elsewhere, not forgetting New York. It had to be technically watertight so that the German chemical warfare specialists could not shoot it down as impossible. Once our experts told us that it was a perfectly feasible but extravagant and expensive operation, it was just a matter of getting it past the committee that had to study all rumours before they were launched. It was passed back, approved, with the pungent remark, 'No objection, but we think it a pretty poor effort.'

It was a little while before the rumours began to spread, Baker White says, but then they were soon springing up like mushrooms all over the place:

A Luftwaffe pilot shot down over Charing in Kent and taken to the Cockfosters reception centre for interrogation, said that in his *Geschwader* [Wing] they knew of the 'English burning sea defences'. Three days later another Luftwaffe man volunteered the same information – and he came from a different airfield. It had been our first large-scale attempt at the Big Lie and it proved amazingly successful.

Another man who helped in disseminating the rumour was Sefton Delmer, the legendary *Daily Express* journalist, who also provided his services to the Political Welfare Executive, making regular propaganda broadcasts for the BBC aimed at German listeners. In his autobiography, *Black Boomerang* (1962), he describes giving a taunting speech in which he warned the Germans against invading and suggested that all troops should learn the declension of the verb *brennen* – to burn. Writing about this he says,

Crude stuff, but excellent in one important respect. The line about burning in the Channel fitted in perfectly – as, of course, it was intended to – with the information which our deception services had planted on Hitler's espionage service. Our rumour agencies, too, had been busy spreading it everywhere. The mean, murderous British, it was said, had apparatus in readiness with which they were going to set the Channel and the beaches on fire at such time as Hitler launched his boats. This was a lie. But it went over so well that it is believed by many Germans to this day.

Even Winston Churchill himself finally came clean about the events in the second volume of his war memoirs, *Their Finest Hour* (1949), when he admitted that the corpses of 'about forty German soldiers' had been washed up on our shores in the autumn of 1940:

> The Germans had been practising embarkations in barges along the French coast. Some of these barges put out to sea in order to escape British bombing and were sunk, either by bombing or bad weather. This was the source of a widespread rumour that the Germans had attempted an invasion and had suffered heavy losses either by drowning or by being burnt in patches of sea covered with flaming oil. We took no steps to contradict such tales, which spread freely throughout the occupied countries in wildly exaggerated form and gave much encouragement to the oppressed populations.

But, as with all the best mysteries, there are often unexpected sequels – as John Baker White confessed in *The Big Lie*:

> One of the mysteries of the whole operation I have not been able to solve to this day; nor, I think, has anyone else. That is how the rumour got back to Britain and had such a wide circulation. It was put out only through very

carefully chosen channels and the few of us who were in the secret preserved absolute silence. But it was soon all over Britain and it took on many guises. Men in German uniforms being brought ashore at Harwich, Newhaven and Dover with their faces and hands covered in bandages. A convoy of ambulances arriving in the dead of night at a hospital outside Norwich and an SOS sent to other hospitals in the area for anti-burn dressings. A great pillar of smoke rising from Sandwich Bay and the secret burial in the sand dunes of hideously charred bodies. These were but a few of the forms the rumour took, and there are plenty of people in Britain who to this day remain convinced that there was an invasion attempt in 1940 and that it was defeated by setting the sea on fire.

Indeed there are – but what the barrage of rumour and gossip has done is effectively to obscure the *real* story. It is time, now, to begin examining the facts, which begin with a local tradition that has endured for over sixty years of a landing at the tiny Suffolk coastal village with the apt name of Shingle Street.

Chapter 9

The Legend of Shingle Street

In the uneasy days of summer 1940, rumours of invasion proliferated across the British Isles. Stories could be heard about supposed landings of German forces at places as far apart as the coast of Cornwall and Scotland. Anxiety fuelled most of them, while word of mouth spread them with alarming speed and many were a long time dying, despite the evidence to the contrary in the newspapers or broadcasts on the radio. Undoubtedly, though, the most extraordinary – and enduring – of these reports concerns the remote little community of Shingle Street on the Suffolk coast. Only now, though, after half a century, is it possible to resolve this particular World War Two legend, which is inextricably linked to the mystery of where the German eagle landed.

A few of the 'false alarm' stories from this period of time will suffice to convey the general state of mind in the country and serve to represent other similar incidents. On the morning of 14 August, for instance, people in the rural areas of Derbyshire, Yorkshire and lowland Scotland awoke to find German parachutes spread across the countryside. They were speedily reported to the police and Home Guard, who reasonably assessed that they must have been discarded by parachutists and an invasion alert was called.

The following morning further parachutes were found in other parts of England and Scotland along with more alarming items. These included wireless transmitters, quantities of high explosives and bags of maps, photographs and even lists of the names and addresses of prominent people. More sinister still were 'orders' to 'secret agents' giving them instructions for the coming invasion, which appeared to be targeted at the east coast.

Within hours of these discoveries, German radio was busy transmitting to England the news that parachutists in British uniforms and civilian clothes had landed and were making for Birmingham, Manchester, Glasgow and other major cities. There, after getting in touch with contacts, these men were hiding themselves among the rest of the population to await the next phase of the invasion plan.

Some of those who found the parachutes convinced themselves they could *see* footprints on the ground beating a hasty departure; while others thought they had actually *heard* the radios being used for transmissions. There were even reports of explosions and gunfire from certain localities.

Once military experts had collected the items and examined them, they told a very different story, however. The whole operation had been a German ruse – an *Abwurfaktion* (dropping operation) – a piece of psychological warfare similar to the earlier scattering of propaganda leaflets. Every item had been dropped from German aircraft with the intention of unsettling people, trying to convince them invasion was imminent, and that the country was full of fifth-columnists. It was clear the planners in Berlin believed no one would actually be able to *prove* that parachutists had not landed.

Certainly, this two-day 'invasion' prompted front-page newspaper stories and there is no doubt that in a number of remote areas rumours persisted for days that Germans *had* landed. But the truth was that not a single 'invader' had been sighted and the official line from the Ministry of Information was that it had all been a hoax. As John Baker White has written:

It might have been a very ingenious and effective operation, but in the inimitable way the Nazis had, they overdid it. There was reasonable presumption that the items were discarded equipment of parachute troops for an invasion alert. A wide search was instituted, but not one was found. The operation orders had been clumsily written and were intended to fall into the hands of the military authorities. They were too amateurish to mislead anyone.

In another instance, the accidental transmission of the anti-invasion codeword 'Cromwell' on Saturday, 7 September, following a particularly heavy aerial bombardment on London, coupled with the news of the massing of a large number of German craft near Boulogne, also generated more curious stories. The codeword, prepared by the Joint Chiefs of Staff, was a warning to the civilian authorities and the Eastern and Southern Commands of the army to be on 'instant readiness'.

In some areas of the region it was therefore assumed that the invasion *had* actually started – and in Lincolnshire, for example, a number of bridges were demolished and live mines laid along the road. In towns and villages from Kent to the Cotswolds, men and women prepared to defend themselves and their homes with anything to hand – their armoury ranging from kitchen knives to garden implements!

The following Monday, *The Times* reported another typical scare story under the headline: A MISTAKEN ALARM OF INVASION:

A false alarm caused military and civil forces throughout the West Country to stand to arms just before midnight last night. It was about 11 o'clock at a coastal town that boats were seen coming inshore through the mist – boats that could not be accounted for.

There were air-raids in the neighbourhood and the circumstances were regarded as so suspicious in the light of warnings that had been received that it was decided that the threatened invasion was at hand. Some of the boatmen rushed to the parish church and soon the bells were sounding the alarm. Neighbouring villages took up the warning signal and soon it was passed from Cornwall until it reached the outskirts of Bristol.

It is suggested that the false alarm may have been due to a fishing fleet returning to harbour through the mist earlier than expected after making a lucky catch.

One more embarrassing scare story from later that same month deserves a mention here – if only because it occurred near Epping, where I began my career as a journalist in the fifties and was still being told with relish by former members of the Home Guard who were involved. As one participant explained, 'We received this police message that fifty enemy parachutists had landed at High Beech in Epping Forest. Most of our men were at their jobs and we only had half a dozen men – and half an hour – to deal with the situation. In fact, we had no time to get anything organised before we got another message from the police.'

He continued, 'They told us that their information was wrong. It was actually puffs of smoke from AA shells that had been mistaken for German parachutists!'

There was, however, nothing amusing about the story of the discovery on 29 October of a badly decomposed body of a German airman on an isolated beach at Shingle Street on Hollesley Bay in Suffolk. The facts of this discovery and its sequel have a special place in the history of the invasion scare of 1940.

At almost any time of the year, Shingle Street is a dramatic and windswept place. Situated about six miles from Orford Ness, the island of military secrets, and two miles from Bawdsey, the 'Home of Radar', it consists of two dozen bungalows and houses and a row of whitewashed coastguard cottages. Behind are water meadows and in front the North Sea with its blustering cold winds.

The ever-moving shingle that gives the hamlet its name dips steeply from the front doors of these properties down to the waves breaking on the vast, curving foreshore, which it constantly reshapes into great humps of brown pebbles. Hollows amid these shimmering piles of shingle have created shallow lagoons left by the high tides. Alongside them lie the upturned hulks of small fishing boats beached just beyond the reach of the ocean.

The rolling, dark sea constantly breaks in grey surf on a reef inhabited by the occasional gull and numerous terns who swoop like falcons to strike the water with a splash in search of fish. Oyster catchers, too, circle the shingle making their distinctive, ringing cry. The sombre mass of a Martello tower just to the south, in which some of the birds nest, bears witness to that time two hundred years ago when the invader feared was Napoleon.

On late autumn days like the one when the body was discovered on the beach, Shingle Street is often covered in sea mist and lives up to its reputation of being 'the British equivalent of Siberia', as residents claim, pointing out that the winds here come straight from the Arctic. The discovery of the corpse was an immediate reminder of another time almost forty years previously when tragedy had struck the little hamlet.

Then, early on the morning of 1 May 1914, seven coast-guards had taken a small boat and made the voyage up to Aldeburgh for a day out. As evening fell, they embarked to return to their station on Shingle Street. Just off Orford Ness, though, their vessel was struck by a freak wave that overturned it, causing five of the seven to drown. The facts of the drama – complete with the names of the men who lost their lives – are related in a poem by W S Montgomerie, 'The Blind Organ Grinder of Westleton', a copy of which still hangs in the bar of the Jolly Sailor at Orford.

In October 1940, Shingle Street was, once again, a place of lowering clouds and silence. Gone was any sign of the fishing industry that had flourished in the hamlet for over two hundred years, and a profusion of the sea poppies and sea peas that had saved the people from starvation in Tudor times were growing rank everywhere. The Lifeboat Inn, the only substantial, two-storey building in the hamlet, stood barred and shuttered, as did the little wooden church that had resounded to singing for generations and now only contributed to an oppressive silence, broken only by the hissing of the waves on the shingle.

Nor was there any sign of life in the row of dwellings with their wistful names such as Veronica Cottage, Old Ned's Cabin and Marine Villa. Dumb-Boy Cottage, too, famous in Shingle Street's long association with smuggling, was as silent as the grave, abandoned like Hollesley road, featured in the classic tale, *The History of Margaret Catchpole* by Richard Cobbald (1845), as the place where the smuggler Will Laud was shot by customs men while trying to escape to sea with his lover.

Life in the village had, in fact, begun to change soon after the outbreak of the war. In November 1939, soldiers of the 2/4th Battalion of the Essex Regiment had been posted to guard the vulnerable coast. A group of them patrolling Shingle Street contributed the first wartime mystery surrounding the hamlet, reported by local historian, Derek Johnson, in his book, *East Anglia at War 1939–1945* (1992).

According to Johnson's information, six men were out on the beach one bleak winter night keeping watch. They carried wireless equipment and every hour were required to put in a call to HQ. After several hours, however, the men failed to report. The next morning a search party was sent out and although this was extended well beyond the normal patrol boundaries all that was found was a rifle and a steel helmet near the water's edge. The author continues:

No trace was ever found of the men and the affair was hushed up. The general feeling was that the men had been taken by a patrolling submarine or E-boat in the hope that they could give valuable information on some of the secret radar installations and defences along the coastline. If this was the case, what happened to them afterwards? Were they taken to a POW Camp in Europe? Or, more likely, were they dropped over the side into the freezing waters of the North Sea once the Germans discovered that these ordinary rank and file infantrymen knew very little about such matters? Another theory was that the ship or E-boat carrying the men was sunk by a patrolling British vessel.

There is, however, very little concrete evidence to substantiate this curious story. What is indisputable is that the Essex Regiment were removed from the area in April 1940, to be replaced by the 1st Battalion of the Liverpool Scottish Regiment. For the next two months, the local people went about their business as usual and got on quite well with the feisty northerners.

Then, on 22 June, a bombshell fell on Shingle Street. It was to be evacuated of every man, woman and child.

The process of creating a defensive area around the east coast had, of course, started immediately after Dunkirk. But the order for the complete evacuation of Shingle Street had waited for ten months before being issued under Regulation 16(a) of the Defence Regulations, 1939, signed by the regional commissioner, Will Spens. It was to come into effect on 25 June – allowing the inhabitants just three days to pack up and leave. Most had to make do with the bare essentials, leaving behind furniture and other large items in their locked and shuttered homes by the seashore.

It says much for the character and sense of duty of the people that they left their homes 'with very little fuss', to quote one contemporary report, realising the danger they and their children might well be in if they stayed. Fortunately, none had any difficulty finding alternative accommodation inland in the villages of Hollesley, Bawdsey or Alderton, where most had relatives or friends.

As the last lorry load of people and chattels pulled out of Shingle Street on that bright, sunlit Tuesday morning, the hamlet was left in the care of four coastguards, responsible for patrolling the shore to Bawdsey, and a working party from the Royal Engineers, already busy laying minefields along the road down to the shingle. Several little streams were also widened to create antitank traps.

After the sappers had finished their work, a platoon of the Liverpool Scottish settled down in tents pitched beside a pillbox. The Martello tower was commandeered by the coastguards, whose long night watches were regularly relieved by members of the Home Guard.

The summer of 1940 passed peacefully enough for all these men in Shingle Street. Occasionally, they would hear a lone German bomber passing overhead and, later, the sound of explosions inland towards Ipswich or further up the coast at Aldeburgh and Southwold. Nothing fell in their vicinity, however, and, as summer turned into autumn, the likelihood of invasion seemed ever more remote. *That* feeling was rudely shaken on the morning of 29 October.

Private Tom Abram, who had served in the Liverpool Scottish since the outbreak of the war and was one of those based at Shingle Street, recalled the moment in a letter to the *Sunday Telegraph* in April 1992. He was responding to an article, DID THE EAGLE REALLY LAND?, by its defence correspondent Christy Campbell:

From June on, we had to 'Stand To' from sunset to dawn with orders to hold out at all costs. The pillbox was stocked with enough iron rations – and toilet paper – to last 48-hours. Although there were constant warnings about imminent invasion, the only German we saw was a dead airman who was fished out of the sea and carried back to camp on a hurdle.

According to Russell Edwards in another article, 'What happened at Shingle Street?' published in *Norfolk Life* in its February–March issue of 1993, the body was immediately whisked away in a van.

The following day, two more German corpses were washed ashore on the same bit of coast – the first at Bawdsey and the second near Hollesley. The evidence suggests that all three men had belonged to the crew of the same aircraft and had been in the water for at least ten days. In all, five bodies were picked up on the shore, according to Ministry of Defence records. [The others were found south of Walton Pier on 1 November and at Languard Point, Felixstowe, on 5 December.] Was this the beginning of the Shingle Street mystery?

It certainly seems like it if we accept his evidence, that of Private Abram and a small group of investigators. Put together, their reports help finally to unravel this strange affair.

What happened in Shingle Street in the years after the discovery of the unidentifiable airman's corpse is also an important element in the development of the legend. Such, though, was the secrecy that surrounded these events and the fact that no one was living there permanently that it was not until after the end of the war that the details became known.

For two years, as the events of the conflict with Germany swirled along on various fronts in Europe and North Africa, the remote Suffolk hamlet seemed locked in a time warp. Then, because of a 'profound lack of action', as Tom Abram referred to it, the Liverpool Scottish battalion were withdrawn and the coastguards left to make the occasional foray along the beach.

On 28 March 1943, a team of experts from the Chemical Defence Research Establishment (CDRE) at Porton Down arrived at Shingle Street to test a new bomb. Among their number – according to one account – was Barnes Wallis, the aeronautical engineer who was then working on his famous bouncing bombs that would be used later by the RAF's 617 Squadron in the famous Dam Busters raid on the Mohne and Eder dams. There is, however, no confirmation of this in Wallis's diaries or his biography by J E Morpurgo.

In any event, the scientists moved in with a minimum of fuss, their presence known only to the local police inspector, John Bird, and some members of the Auxiliary Fire Service from Woodbridge who were put on standby for the tests. After a study of the locality, the Lifeboat Inn, at the very centre of the community, was selected as the unlucky target for the test.

There is some doubt as to precisely *what* was tested, though it seems most likely to have been a 250lb high-explosive bomb of a type that could be used in conjunction with chemicals to combine both damage and contamination. Although charged with explosives for the trial at Shingle Street, it almost certainly contained nothing more sinister than a quantity of innocuous oil of wintergreen.

The pub was painted with yellow markers on its front and veranda and left to its fate. According to a subsequent RAF report, a twin-engined Bristol Blenheim made several trial runs over the beach before finally releasing its payload. The missile struck the Lifeboat Inn head on, blasting the pub out of recognition and seriously damaging the surrounding cottages.

The wholesale destruction seemingly told the scientists all they wished to know. Taking just enough time to thank the police and firemen for their cooperation, the men hurried back to their headquarters at the CDRE at Porton Down. Whether any of them ever gave a second thought to having changed the face of Shingle Street for ever is not on record.

It was not long after this, however, that new rumours began to circulate about the area to join with those of the dead bodies on the beach. Derek Johnson has again recorded the facts of one story such as they are:

> One semi-official source – a member of MI9 – has suggested that it was on the cards that early atomic missiles had been tested around the Orford Beach area. Interviewing former wartime officers of the local police and coastguard revealed that they knew something, but refused to divulge any information knowing that they were bound by the Official Secrets Act.

An equally alarming rumour was that actual chemical weapons – in particular mustard gas – had been tested at Shingle Street. This suggestion has since been meticulously investigated by a local historian, James Hayward, for his fascinating booklet, *Shingle Street: Flame, Chemical and Psychological Warfare in 1940* (1994). In it he reveals that the Chemical Defence Research Establishment certainly *did* propose that biological weapons might be tested in the village. The trials were to last for up to ten days and would require accurate bombing from 500 to 1,000 feet. When the army were contacted for their cooperation, little enthusiasm was shown for 'experimental gas bombing', but Lieutenant Colonel Douglas Meynell gave the go-ahead.

Hayward believes any suggestion that a mustard gas bomb was tested at Shingle Street is ridiculous and it is 'unlikely a new means of delivering mustard gas would have attracted such high-profile attention as late as 1943'. The CDRE may well have intended to use Shingle Street for tests similar to those that did take place on the Scottish island of Gruinard in the summer of 1942 and on a beach in Wales the following year, but no such thing occurred in Suffolk. The empty village, though, remained as a suitable target site long after the scientists had gone elsewhere.

The author does not believe, either, that an early atomic weapon might have been exploded at Shingle Street – or that there is any truth that people in the vicinity were injured by the tests. He writes,

> Others have suggested that the bombing resulted in civilian casualties after stubborn locals refused to leave their homes. The charge that Shingle Street was designated a free-strike zone by the station commander at Martlesham Heath is somewhat fanciful. Both former coastguard Ronald Harris and Suffolk historian Norman Scarfe, himself a resident in the village for many years, have flatly denied that anyone was murdered in cold blood by the RAF. Added Mr. Scarfe, 'When the war was over they all came back. Some of the houses were badly knocked about, but I never heard of anyone grousing about what happened.'

Several more events – all less controversial – did occur in Shingle Street before the end of the war. In early 1944, the area was used for invasion training, with specially adapted Churchill tanks of the 79th Armoured Division being put through their paces on the constantly shifting pebbles. Later that year, the hamlet found itself on the track of the V-1 'flying bombs' being aimed at Britain from northwestern Germany and two Bofors guns and a large antiaircraft weapon were set up on the edge of the beach to try to shoot the mechanical raiders down.

When peace finally came in 1945, Shingle Street was a truly desolate place, many of its houses wrecked by the experiments or the fury of the elements with no one to carry out necessary repairs. The large numbers of mines buried in the vicinity also made it seem to Ministry of Home Security inspector W R Philipson, who visited in 1945, like a place that 'cannot be looked upon as a potential habitable hamlet, but as an extremely dangerous and awkward minefield'.

It would take almost five years for the mines to be cleared and for those inhabitants who wished to return to obtain compensation from the government for their wrecked homes. Only a few were still fit to repair; the remainder required demolition and complete rebuilding. No replacement for the Lifeboat Inn was ever attempted and any thoughts of restarting the fishing industry were also dashed.

Shingle Street in the fifties was a completely different place from its days prewar – if anything even more isolated and remote. What, though, continued to haunt the little community was the story that it had also been the location of an abortive invasion attempt.

During the years in which I have lived in East Anglia since moving there with my family in the mid-seventies, I have visited Shingle Street on a number of occasions. I had heard of the bodies washed up on the coast and was naturally curious about the suggestion that they might have been Germans who were part of an invasion force. Even after I had met the man who told me Shingle Street was *not* where this incursion had occurred, the various conflicting opinions I encountered continued to run through my mind until the Saturday morning in March 1992 when the local newspaper, the *East Anglian Daily Times* (*EADT*), arrived on my breakfast table. It carried a front-page story that brought the whole legend back into focus – and would ultimately lead to solving the mystery.

This report, datelined 7 March, appeared under the headline DOZENS OF SOLDIERS KILLED IN NAZI INVASION BLUNDER, and was written by Henry Creagh. I quote it in full because of the protracted saga that followed its publication:

Dozens of British soldiers were burnt to death by one of their own men in a wartime exercise on the Suffolk coast which went wrong, it was claimed yesterday. New information has come to the *EADT* about the secret of Shingle Street, an isolated coastal hamlet which was evacuated in 1940 for use by the armed forces. The incident allegedly occurred during a training exercise near the radar installation at Bawdsey, just south of Shingle Street.

Part of the base's defences was a system known as PLUTO (Pipe Line Under the Ocean) in which drums of petrol were chained to concrete blocks under the sea and wired to detonators. In case of an enemy assault from the sea, the drums would be blown and the petrol would rise to the surface, where it could be set alight using tracer rounds.

The Army had decided to carry out a mock assault on Bawdsey and contacted the base to say it would be doing so, but somehow the message was not passed on. Later that night, a sentry saw rubber dinghies approaching the base and, assuming it was the enemy, detonated the charges. The petrol was set alight by the tracer bullets from a machine gun post. Many soldiers died in the inferno and their bodies were carried out on the tide, only to be washed up on Shingle Street.

Mr. Ron Harris, one of the few residents to remain in Shingle Street after the evacuation, was a coastguard at the site throughout the war. He can remember being given an order to look for charred bodies, but cannot recall the date or any incident where the sea was set on fire. A file on the mystery has lain in the Public Records Office since the Second World War under a 75-year embargo lasting until 2014. Such an embargo can only be ordered by the Lord Chancellor and would be granted for reasons of national security to protect confidential information supplied by the public, or where publication of records would distress or embarrass any living person. The Ministry of Defence could not comment on the claims.

It would be true to say that the story opened a Pandora's Box of theories and heated discussion – not to mention a stream of correspondence to the newspaper's offices in Ipswich. The journalist Henry Creagh also found himself a centre of attention, being interviewed by the press, radio and television. When asked to name his source for the report he would admit only that it was 'a man close to the Ministry of Defence who had come across the classified papers by chance'.

It was, though, soon pointed out to Creagh that he had confused PLUTO with the experiments made in the summer of 1940 by the Petroleum Warfare Department (PWD). The PLUTO pipes had successfully carried petrol direct to the beachhead in France after the Allied invasion in June 1944, unlike the PWD experimental 'flame barrage', which had, of course, already long been ruled out.

Despite such discrepancies, the *EADT* was kept busy with telephone calls and letters to the editor during the following days. On Tuesday, 10 March, another three-column story claimed that more evidence of the affair had come to light. A British Naval Intelligence officer, John Edgar Burton, had apparently actually seen the beach at Shingle Street 'strewn with bodies in the aftermath of the 1940 tragedy', according to his grandson, John Rux-Burton of Long Melford. He told the newspaper,

At the outbreak of the war my grandfather handed over a thriving chartered accountancy business in Piccadilly to his partner in order to travel the country allegedly procuring wood. It was ideal cover for intelligence work and he was often in Suffolk. One day he was told a German force had attempted to invade Suffolk and was sent to Shingle Street to find out what had happened. When he arrived the beach was covered with dozens of charred bodies which the defenders believed were Germans dressed as British soldiers.

Then a senior officer arrived on the scene and said that they were British troops on a training exercise. My grandfather was absolutely devastated by it all. Imagine the horror and despair of finding what you thought were the hated enemy were really your own men.

The belief that the tragedy had been a 'friendly-fire' incident haunted John Edgar Burton until his death in 1985. His grandson said he was also convinced there had been a cover-up by the government because of the speed with which the bodies had been removed and all records of the incident destroyed. He was suspicious, too, that one of the dinghies he saw on the beach had *German* markings. John Rux-Burton added in his statement to the newspaper,

If it really was an invasion, they might not have wanted it publicised. It was an age when people's ideas of what was acceptable in warfare were different from today. The government might not have wanted to admit that scores of German soldiers had been fried alive and the popular reaction to news of an invasion attempt might not have been satisfactory. An announcement would also have told the Germans we had that kind of secret defence weapon, so one can see why they might not have wanted the details to come out.

The following weeks brought a bumper set of communications to the *EADT*. One correspondent pointed out that if there had been a friendly-fire incident, there would have been a court martial. Unfortunately, the records of courts martial remained sealed for a hundred years, he said, so there would be a long time to wait.

In general, the responses were split between those who believed it was German invaders who had been burned alive and those who thought the victims were British troops killed in an accident. Their accounts are a graphic illustration of how the Shingle Street legend captured the imagination – and stirred the memories – of men and women all along the Suffolk coast.

Typical of these was sixty-year-old Terry Banham of Great Barton near Bury St Edmunds, who said he could always remember his uncle, Hector Ransome, a civilian lorry driver, telling him of the time when he collected the bodies of German soldiers from the Felixstowe area, as Banham wrote to the *EADT*:

I remember it as if it was only yesterday, although I was just seven years old at the time. He told me the sea had been set alight and that it was German soldiers who had tried to land. He and a group of civilians had to spend two days in the area helping to clear bodies from the shoreline. It is something that has stayed in my memory.

Gerald Wallis from Woolpit was a teenager living not far from Shingle Street when he heard of a failed invasion attempt:

At the time a group of infantry soldiers were based near our home for the purpose of coastal defence. On the night in question, the commanding officer visited my parents and said there was an invasion warning. He said if it did go off we would have to go into the dug-out with him. Later, I remember seeing a battle going on out to sea. The sky was all red and looked like it was alight. It went on for several hours. Some days later my uncle, Edward Bye, who was a regimental sergeant major in Felixstowe, visited the family. He said the Germans had tried to invade – about 50,000 of them – but they set light to the sea and burned a lot of them in their boats. I don't remember seeing any bodies washed up on the shore at Shingle Street, but there were certainly rumours that Germans wearing British uniforms had been washed on to the beach.

One person who was in no doubt about the nationality of the bodies was an 85-year-old widow, Rose Aldous, from Ipswich, whose husband, Claude, had been responsible for collecting some of them from Shingle Street. The couple had been planning a rare night out, she said in an interview in July 1992, when her husband was instructed by his employers, the Ipswich Co-operative Society, to go and retrieve some bodies which had been swept ashore. She explained,

Claude was not fit enough to enlist in the armed forces and so he worked for the Co-op. We were going out that night, but he called me to say he had to go to Shingle Street. He went out there with some colleagues – who are all now dead. When he returned he said he had picked up dead bodies – Germans. He had to sling them in boxes. They were in a horrible state.

Mrs Aldous said she was convinced a cover-up had been ordered by the government after it was discovered that the Germans had nearly succeeded in invading Britain. 'I think they kept it quiet – they did not want us to know that the Germans were that close.'

Another driver also ordered to Shingle Street added his contribution to the mystery. Arthur Smith of Somersham near Ipswich had worked for Carters of Bromeswell until the outbreak of the war, when he was commissioned to drive for the War Department. In October 1940 he was given instructions to collect a load of eight tons of sand from Bealing and deliver it to a 'training area' on the coast that he remembered looked 'just like a ghost town'. He told the newspaper:

The orders told me that on approaching Shingle Street I would be met by a warden who would tell me where to unload the sand and then I was to come straight back the way I came. I told the warden I heard Germans had tried to land, but he said, 'I never saw any Germans, but I know British soldiers were killed. They were a terrible sight and the flesh was burnt off their bones.' The warden said there had been no end of experiments, but this was one that went wrong, but was quickly covered up. He even pointed to a spot where one soldier had been found on the ground near to where I had to unload the sand. He then helped me to shovel the sand out of the lorry before I drove away.

I believe the sand was to be used to douse a chemical experiment on the site that had gone terribly wrong. No one knew how many soldiers were killed, but the whole operation, which was believed to be a raid by German troops, was covered up. Later I made other trips to Shingle Street to collect shingle for coastal gun emplacements. I think I may have collected contaminated materials, because a few weeks later two huge holes formed on the back of my neck. None of the doctors or nurses knew how they came about and they've left me scarred for life.

Ken Jarmin was serving with the Royal Marines off the east coast and saw the events from a different perspective. A Suffolk man from Boxford, he told the *EADT*:

I was on a landing craft rehearsing for D-Day and the locals used to tell us the RAF had spotted landing barges full of Germans and set the sea alight around them. The boats were roped together as if in distress – they probably were adrift after RAF attacks on the German invasion fleet – and to me they should have been rescued, not set on fire. It's just my opinion, but they may have hushed it up to safeguard British prisoners of war in Germany.

Perhaps, though, the most vivid account of all is by Ronald Ashford, who has created his own website (www.shford.fslife. co.uk/ShingleSt/) to investigate the mystery. He was eighteen years old at the time and a volunteer in the Local Defence Volunteers (LDV) serving under the World War One veteran, Sir Basil Eddis. After drilling for some months without weapons, he and the other thirty men in the platoon were issued with .303 rifles and four clips of ammunition. The events that were to stay rooted in his mind occurred on 'a Saturday night late in August, 1940', as he has stated on his website:

Not long after we were issued with these rifles, and before we had been properly instructed in their use, a red alert was declared along the East Suffolk coast and we found ourselves dug in behind a long brick wall facing the Aldeburgh marshes . . . We knocked out firing slits at intervals of a few feet. It was a clear, dark evening. About 9 pm the heavens appeared to open up south of Orford Lighthouse – in the Shingle Street area. We heard a tremendous amount of gunfire and explosions and the night sky was lit up with a red glow.

Ronald Ashford says that sporadic gunfire went on for several hours. In the trench on the marshes the group of men began to wonder what on earth had happened. They were not long in finding out:

We received word that a German landing had taken place. This was later confirmed by eyewitness accounts of a shoreline littered with burned bodies. It appeared that this landing had been expected and that we had been laying in wait. The sea bed had been laid with piping from the shore at intervals with flammable liquid. I am uncertain about the exact number of German E-boats and the number of men that the regiment had laying in wait, but without doubt the target would have been the newly completed Radar station at Bawdsey Manor – vital to our defence at the time.

Apart from these five testimonies, the press, radio and television were deluged with any number of theories of increasing strangeness during the five months from March to July, as James Hayward has neatly summarised in his book *Shingle Street* (2002):

> Beside endless variations of the main theories, it was claimed that a skeleton found by a party from the Hollesley borstal in June 1985 was that of a Nazi; Germans landed in Suffolk on motorbikes and lobbed grenades at coastal gun batteries; the dead men at Shingle Street in British uniforms were German Brandenburg commandos and the RAF later bombed civilians there; German POW's were used as guinea pigs in a chemical warfare trial; Lord Mountbatten was responsible for the Texel disaster [two destroyers, HMS *Esk* and *Ivanhoe*, were sunk when they inadvertently entered a newly laid minefield on 31 August], the action being an attempt by the Navy to thwart a German invasion from Holland.

To these I can add stories that I have been told: how disaster struck Allied troops while they were on an exercise for the invasion of Europe; the more curious idea that the doomed men were German commandos planning to attack Bawdsey; alternately, they were Nazi secret agents on a mission to discover whether rumours that the British were testing a *Todesstreifen* (death ray) were true.

None of this, of course, satisfactorily answered what had occurred at Shingle Street. If there was to be a definitive answer it surely lay in the embargoed secret file in the Public

Record Office that Henry Creagh had referred to in his original article. This, however, proved singularly elusive.

The first request to see the file on 16 May prompted a response from the archives' PRO that it 'could not be found' on the ninety miles of shelving. The conspiracy theorists were at once alerted and began claiming that the dossier must contain sensitive information and 'had been lost by someone with a vested interest'.

The truth was actually far simpler: it was the reference number that was missing. Once this was located – as it was a week later by the *EADT*'s resourceful political correspondent, David Weisbloom – it was just a matter of getting the 75-year ban on File HO 207/1175 rescinded. Two local MPs, the Conservative agricultural minister, John Gummer, in whose Suffolk Coastal constituency Shingle Street lay, and the Labour backbencher Jamie Cann of Ipswich, were recruited to the cause in June and agreed to raise the matter with the home secretary, Kenneth Clarke. After more lobbying and further newspaper stories, Clarke announced in a written reply to Jamie Cann on 7 July, 'I have decided all the files will be opened to access in the Public Record Office as soon as possible.'

After all the waiting, the speculation and the rumours, the brown cardboard file entitled 'Evacuation of the Civil Population from the Village of Shingle Street, East Suffolk', carefully marked 'PRESERVE – Not To Be Destroyed', proved to be anything but sensational. Inside were a total of 130 letters between the War Department, the Ministry of Home Security, government and army officials, civil servants, landowners and a number of residents of Shingle Street. The 'top-secret information' told of the measures taken to requisition all the dwellings in the hamlet in order that it could be used as a minefield and for testing new weapons.

There was no mention at all of any attempted German invasion or a friendly-fire accident with British troops. No details of charred bodies being washed up on the shore. The only surprise amid the yellowing, typed sheets of foolscap paper was a bland statement that mustard gas had been tested in Shingle Street during March 1943 – a statement that would be challenged within days.

All the talk of the need to keep the file closed until 2021 because it might contain something damaging to the government or cause embarrassment or distress to any living person was patently absurd. Certainly, some of the letters from residents turned from their homes arguing for compensation were sad, while reports of the ransacking of some of the homes by soldiers in the vicinity did not make for very edifying reading. One letter in particular from a Mrs K Burwood stood out from all the others:

I am a widow getting ten shillings [50p] a week and lived in my own home. Now I am turned out and having to pay six shillings [30p] a week rent. Since our evacuation my house has been broken into by the soldiers, windows smashed and doors broken from hinges and also goods taken from house. Can you help and give me advice what steps to take?

The conspiracy theorists were again eager to seize on the story, suggesting the file had been censored before being made public. The Ministry of Defence was charged with having orchestrated a cover-up by removing any references to an attempted invasion. The frustration felt by everyone interested in the legend of Shingle Street intensified and finally, on 18 July, the MOD issued a five-point statement it maintained was based on records kept by Eastern Command and the diaries of government scientists and army units based in Suffolk during World War Two.

This stated there had been *no* flame defence trials on the Suffolk coast and – contrary to the Home Office file released the previous week – *no* tests using mustard gas. The army records also revealed *nothing* to support claims that any accidents had occurred during training in the area that had resulted in the loss of a large number of servicemen. A *single* corpse of a German national had been found on the beach.

The statement then addressed the case of the charred bodies: 'There is no record of any large number of bodies being recovered from the beaches in the area in the summer, autumn or winter of 1940. It is believed this theory emanated from the erroneous reports that flame defences were used.'

Finally, came their answer to the $64,000 question about an enemy invasion at Shingle Street. The MOD said unequivocally,

Records show that a British Army paper exercise on 29 July 1940 mentioned Shingle Street as a German invasion target. The relevant passage from the 11 Corps exercise states: '14.50 Enemy troops landing in Dovercourt Bay . . . 15.10 Confused fighting at Woodbridge . . . 15.22 Frinton and Mersea captured . . . 15.23 Ipswich heavily damaged and many casualties. Strong enemy force arrived on outskirts of town from Harwich . . . 15.47 Sniped en-route at Ashbocking and Otley . . . 16.00 Enemy landing one mile south of Shingle Street.' There is no evidence to support claims that British troops dressed in German uniform landed at Shingle Street during a mock invasion.

Equally there is no evidence of any German invasion attempt or even German commando-style raids by sea or air. Indeed, there is no evidence in either the most highly classified contemporary British records, or apparently in the contemporary German records, of an actual attempt by the Germans to land in Britain, apart from the Channel Islands, which were occupied by the Germans after the fall of France.

While I am prepared to accept the first four points of the Ministry of Defence statement – although the statements of those who saw or heard strange events at Shingle Street are of such a number and conviction that the feeling does persist that *something* unexplained happened there – they are definitely wrong in stating that no Germans landed on British soil. In fact, by a curious coincidence, the real thing occurred on the same weekend as the theoretical event at Shingle Street and the moment has arrived in our story to reveal exactly *where*.

Chapter 10

A Discovery on Smuggler's Beach

In the aftermath of the release in July 1992 of File HO 207/1175, one of the first people whose reactions were sought by the media was Jack Higgins, author of *The Eagle Has Landed*, whose novel had been inspired by several mysterious wartime incidents in East Anglia, including that at Shingle Street. Higgins, who was then living on Jersey, which Hitler had invaded and occupied from 2 July 1940 to 8 May 1945, was disappointed with the 'revelations' – or lack of them. After reading the reports, he told Alan Hamilton of *The Times*,

> There is a great deal more to it than this. You must realise that not everything is written down in documents, and that not all documents are necessarily released. I have grave doubts that the Hess documents tell the whole story, and the Shingle Street papers certainly don't. I'm convinced that some big accident did occur, either with British troops on exercise or German soldiers on invasion. The key question is, that if that is all there was to it, what has all the fuss been about for 52 years? I do not believe for a moment that this is the whole story.

As I shall demonstrate, Jack Higgins is right – though not in quite the way he thinks.

It seems evident now that the legend of Shingle Street arose from the admixture of two incidents in the summer of 1940: the tales of a sea of burned corpses and the experiments on the evacuated beach of Hollesley Bay. However, though the accounts by the people in occupied France and the reports of the good people of Suffolk make compelling reading, there is no doubt that the Germans *never* attempted an invasion at Shingle Street.

The bodies of enemy soldiers were certainly washed up on the east coast and the speed and secrecy with which they were removed leaves a number of questions unanswered. But there can now be no question that the British government encouraged stories of invading German forces being incinerated while still at sea as a propaganda coup. New scientific developments – however merciless – would seem to the rest of the world to make the island that bit less vulnerable.

But, as Jack Higgins and several historians agree, the Shingle Street story did not grow entirely from rumour and hearsay. If it involved a tragic accident with British soldiers – or was perhaps a case of 'friendly fire' – then the secrecy surrounding the deaths is not surprising. Either way, the facts would certainly be categorised top secret to spare the feelings of living relatives and embargoed for much longer than File HO 207/1175.

None of this, though, deflects from the fact that a German raiding party *did* land on the east coast of England in that pressurised summer of the Battle of Britain – and the facts make for an even more intriguing and dramatic story than the legend of Shingle Street.

The story returns to that July morning in the summer of 1940, when young Jeff Fisher stumbled across pieces of wrapping paper, scraps of food, cigarette butts and a German officer's cap on the Suffolk coast. The location was, in fact, Sizewell Gap, some fifteen miles up the coast from Shingle Street, and the date of his find was Sunday, 28 July. It is his story and the evidence of several other investigators, which confirms that a small party of enemy troops did land on this picturesque sweep of sands in an exercise designed to discover whether it would make a suitable invasion point.

I first met Jeff, a friendly, ruddy-cheeked man with crinkly grey hair, in Essex in the seventies. He was an engineer by profession, specialising in central-heating boilers, and had moved from his native Suffolk following his marriage. His work took him all over a large part of East Anglia and – occasionally – back to the scenes of his youth.

It was after one particular trip to Sizewell – now the location of a huge nuclear-power station – that we enjoyed a drink together in a pub near Colchester and he first told me about his wartime experience. To say I sat there dumbfounded as this self-effacing, good-humoured and essentially modest man told me about his brush with some of Hitler's crack seamen over thirty years before is an understatement.

Because I knew little about his early life – or where he lived at the time – I asked Jeff to fill me in on his background. He told me he was born in 1924 in Leiston, a Suffolk town best known for the Garrett Engineering Works, where his father was employed. The family lived on Sizewell Road within walking distance of the factory. It was only walking distance, too, for Jeff to get to school or the beach at Sizewell Gap, where he spent many a happy summer day until the outbreak of the war.

The development of Leiston owed much to Richard Garrett, a local blacksmith who, in 1778, had begun manufacturing steam-driven traction engines, rollers and steam wagons and created what would become an engineering empire during the Victorian era. The sons of the founder added the manufacture of agricultural machines, stationary engines and railway equipment to the company's range, while all around the works on Station Road a flourishing town of houses and shops grew up across the flat Suffolk coastal region.

The outbreak of World War One saw Garrett's change their manufacturing to making twelve-pounder shell cases and, briefly, in the winter of 1917–18, an aircraft, the FE2B biplane. The twenties, however, marked a slow decline in the company's fortunes as the internal-combustion engine rapidly replaced steam, with the result that the workforce was put on short time or laid off. On Monday, 15 February 1932, the now bankrupt family had no option but to close the factory, and Jeff, then eight years old, remembered when his father had come home distraught that he had lost his job.

The closure of Garrett's hit Leiston hard. Almost three-quarters of the male population of the town were made redundant and a feeling of desolation and isolation settled over the whole community. This was followed by very real fears that the town itself could die like the engineering works that had been its heartbeat for over 150 years.

Once the receivers, Price, Waterhouse & Co., were in place, however, 130 men were re-employed to complete the existing orders – and Jeff's dad was one of the lucky ones. The accountants also set about finding a new owner for the business. A local consortium of businessmen tried unsuccessfully to raise the finance, but they were outbid by Beyer Peacock & Company, a Manchester firm of railway locomotive builders, headed by an ebullient septuagenarian, Sir Sam Fay. R A Whitehead, the biographer of the company, believes that the new boss had an ulterior motive behind the purchase, as he has written in *Garrett 200: A Bicentenary History of Garrett's of Leiston 1778–1978* (1978):

It is reputed that Sir Sam's interest in the works stemmed from the fact that a lady who had caught his attention resided at Aldeburgh and that a works at Leiston afforded ample excuse for frequent visits. Be that as it may – and it was by no means out of character – his wish to own it did not deter him from driving a hard bargain.

A hard bargain the old man may have struck, but, by the time war was declared in September 1939, Garrett's was thriving once more as an engineering business. The war threw fresh orders the company's way to produce armaments. However, the location of the works put them in a tricky situation, as Whitehead has also explained:

By this time, with the whole of the Continental Channel and North Sea coasts in German hands, Leiston and the East Coast had become a front line area. With Admiralty consent the firm had, at its own expense, placed six 12-pounder guns, manned by the Home Guard, at what were considered to be strategic points around the town. It must be admitted, in retrospect, that though the manning and use of these guns against an invasion would have been a brave act of defiance, neither they nor the Home Guard could have long delayed a determined invader supported in force by the sea, although against a small group landed by air the odds might have been different.

Jeff Fisher, then in his teens, remembered the guns being put in place and the pleasure they gave to young children who were constantly having to be shooed away whenever they tried to play games of 'Killing the Jerries' – having picked up the colloquialism used by their fathers about the enemy. When, much later, I showed Jeff the account by R A Whitehead, he allowed himself a chuckle at the prophetic mention of a 'determined invader' in the vicinity.

Memories of life in Leiston in the opening year of the war remained firmly fixed in Jeff's mind. He was in his last year at school and had already decided that he wanted to follow his father into engineering and hoped to get an apprenticeship at Garrett's on his sixteenth birthday the following July.

Already the Nazi threat had led to a revival of recruitment into the Territorial Army with the Works Hall at the factory

187

being used for evening training sessions. Because of the war, the Ministry of Supply had declared Garrett's a 'protected place' that prevented the call-up of men involved in munitions work.

Jeff recalled that his father and some of his workmates felt that, because Garrett's parent company was in Manchester, the security of the factory was being underestimated. As a result, in June 1940, a request was made to the Ministry of Supply for permission to arm seventeen full-time security patrolmen. A month later this scheme was given the go-ahead and the recruits were armed with rifles, mostly American Remington .200s, and a plentiful supply of ammunition.

However, still not entirely sure of their security, a group of representatives met the director of Naval Ordnance on 4 July to set up a plan for moving the shell manufacture and the gun mounting work in the event of an invasion. A building at the Coventry Ordnance Works was earmarked and a number of assembly parts were actually dispatched the following month. Ironically, though, when the invasion threat had lessened, the return of these parts to Leiston was hindered by the German air raids on Coventry!

On 7 July – Jeff was to hear later – at just before ten o'clock in the evening, Frank Andrews, the commander of the local Home Guard, received a message: 'Invasion expected tonight. Man all guns.' It was certainly a heart-stopping moment in the town and ever after my friend was to wonder just how a group of men who had hardly been in training for a month might have dealt with an attack by the all-conquering German Army.

Leiston was a resourceful place, though, as was evident all over the town in that uneasy summer. Jeff never forgot the formidable figure of Mrs Sylvester, who answered Lord Beaverbrook's appeal for 'Saucepans for Spitfires' and organised the town's appeal. A large lady in a floral print dress and tall hat, she swept through the streets gathering up scrap wherever it could be found. She was never slow at badgering those who were hesitant in answering the call and one of her great successes was to collect the remains of the girder work of the Zeppelin L48 that had been brought down 23 years earlier in nearby Theberton, killing its crew of sixteen Germans, who were buried in the local churchyard. The aluminium struts may have been a piece of history, but to Mrs Sylvester the past had to give way to the demands of the present.

All the time, aircraft passed overhead regularly, while military detachments rumbled through the streets. After a brief glance, though, the people of Leiston went about their jobs in the factory, the offices, the shops or out in the fields. At home, families like the Fishers would sit around the radio to hear the latest BBC news bulletins and make a choice between the aristocratic Lord Swinton giving his view of current events and the rantings of Lord Haw-Haw.

Rumours and hearsay flourished in Leiston as they did everywhere else, of course. Two investigators from the Mass Observation Unit who visited the town in June reported several pieces of overheard conversation, including one pessimistic comment from a woman:

Everybody round here has it in their minds about what we shall do if we're invaded. A lot of people expect it. Most of them have very wild ideas about what we ought to do. Should we stay put or hop it if they land? I've had my handbag ready, with banknotes in it, since the day war was declared!

The majority of people, though, were filled with a kind of bravado – like the worker from Garrett's who was heard calling out to an ARP warden, 'Let me know if you see any of them para fellows about, Harry – I don't want them to be distressing my pullets now they've just come to lay.'

Shortage of food was an everyday fact of life to mothers like Jeff's. Green vegetables were in short supply as a result of the terrible winter, the quality of meat was poor and since 3 June rationing had reduced the amount of sugar from twelve to eight ounces per person and the amount of butter to only four ounces. Jeff had helped out his father in the garden growing potatoes as he waited for his sixteenth birthday and the possibility of a job at Garrett's.

There was no immediate question of his being called up into the forces like some of his older friends. The National Services Act had originally made young men *liable* to be called up when they were eighteen, but during the early months of the war they were not in fact being enlisted until they were twenty. This figure was later reduced to nineteen and it was not until January 1942 that eighteen-year-olds started to receive their call-up papers. That same year, however, the minimum was dramatically lowered to seventeen and shortly afterwards to sixteen years of age.

Freed at last from the classroom, Jeff Fisher spent happy days down on Sizewell Beach. As well as his swimming trunks and towel, he remembered his mother insisted he always carried his gas mask. And, despite the fact the coast had become a front-line area with various sea defences, there were still places a lad could find for a swim and a sunbathe. In fact, Sizewell was situated at about the only gap in an almost solid line of pillboxes and other fortifications that ran down the coast from Lowestoft to Aldeburgh.

The first bombing raid on Leiston occurred in May 1940 after the town had been bypassed for months by the Luftwaffe looking for bigger targets in East Anglia. The Germans appeared to have learned about munitions being manufactured at Garrett's and, in the months that followed to the end of the year, more than fifty air-raid warnings would be sounded, keeping those manning the twelve-pounders on their toes. In the interim, the factory buildings had been camouflaged by blacking out the roof lights and windows, while underground shelters had been constructed for the men.

On 21 August, a communiqué broadcast by the German High Command claimed that 'effective bomb attacks were made on a munitions factory near Aldeburgh in Suffolk'. As Garrett's was the only such factory in the vicinity, local people were understandably puzzled by the fact that no bombs at all had fallen within a quarter of a mile of the works! But Leiston was not always so lucky, as R A Whitehead has noted:

> The number of alerts rose to crescendo in April 1941. Ten bombs fell on the machine shop in one raid in February 1941, fortunately without any of them exploding. On a second occasion in May the bombs missed the works, but killed a lad nearby. The roofs of the shops suffered damage, but only one shift was lost while temporary repairs were made.

In fact, such was the demand for armaments, that the factory that had so recently been forced to close introduced round-the-clock shift work. As Jeff's sixteenth birthday approached, he grew quietly confident that he would be taken on as an apprentice. Before that fateful day, however, he was to have an experience that would remain with him for the rest of his life.

'I remember it so well because it was Sunday, 28 July, the day before my birthday,' he said as we sat drinking in the Colchester pub. 'The following day, I was going to Garrett's to sign on as an apprentice. Despite the war, I was excited about starting work and hoped that I might be put in the same section as my father.'

The Sunday morning dawned bright and hot and Jeff decided to make the most of it by going down to the beach at Sizewell Gap. He loved the place with its straggle of fishermen's cottages, and images of its fascinating history often slipped into his mind as he lay on the sands. For Sizewell had been famous for centuries as a smugglers' haunt.

The stories told about the area were colourful and violent and many had been handed down by word of mouth until a local author, Louis Chandler, collected them together and wrote *Smuggling at Sizewell Gap* in 1922. The Fishers had a copy and Jeff remembered that it was quite unequivocal about the village's reputation.

'Sizewell Gap was the most notorious place for smuggling on this coast,' Chandler wrote. 'It was the headquarters of the smuggling gang of the district. The common of large extent which lay between Leiston and the Gap was as desolate as the African veldt. Vaults for storing casks of spirit were dug in the common, the sandy soil facilitating the operation of concealment. These vaults or holes were covered with stout planks, the turf was replaced, together with odd pieces of whin [furze] and gorse to divert attention. One of the smugglers' houses at Leiston had near the ridge of the roof a small wicker window, which commanded a view of the sea, and from this signals were made when a landing was desired.'

From the early years of the eighteenth century, Sizewell had all the attributes required to make it a perfect spot for illegal landfalls. According to Chandler, the inhabitants would on occasions see anything up to a hundred carts gathered on the beach along with three hundred horses that would make the normally deserted foreshore look like 'a representation of a horse fair' when the smugglers gathered to await their contraband.

The poorly staffed and financed Revenue Service fought a losing battle from the start. Their cutters were easily eluded by the local seamen who knew how to pick their way through the maze of tidal creeks and channels in the broad estuaries along the low-lying, isolated coast. Smugglers from other points along the east coast sometimes landed their booty at Sizewell, as is revealed in a fascinating document held at the Suffolk Records Office at Ipswich entitled 'An Exact Account of the Quantity of Goods Smuggled into the County of Suffolk Alone from the First of May 1745 to First of January 1746 Being So Much as Came to the Knowledge of the Officers of the Customs and Transmitted by Them to the Honourable Commissioners'.

Three typical extracts will serve to demonstrate the importance of Sizewell Gap in this nefarious business:

> May 20. Seventy horses with dry goods landed at Sizewell out of Colbys by the Hadleigh gang well armed . . .

> June 16. Eighty horses mostly with tea landed out of Colbys Cutter about two miles from Sizewell; and 20 next morning out of the same at Sizewell . . .

> July 22. 300 half ankers [four-gallon tubs] of wet goods carried off by people unknown with one cart and about 100 horses landed at Sizewell out of the *May Flower* cutter . . .

The document also gives an indication of the huge range of dutiable luxuries that were being smuggled: geneva (gin), rum, silks, laces, coffee, playing cards, golden guineas and – occasionally – spies from the Continent. Records such as this demonstrate what a huge industry smuggling was in its heyday, often involving whole communities such as Sizewell Gap and alarmingly accounting for a quarter of all England's overseas trade.

A number of notable Sizewell incidents are recorded by Stan Jarvis in his later book, *Smuggling in East Anglia 1700–1840* (1987), which further underlines how ideal the locality was for landing undetected. In April 1745, for example, he says the Hadleigh gang worked with two other well-known organisations from Yarmouth and Norwich to make 'a huge landing under armed protection of military proportions'. The Revenue cutters might well have been in a position to challenge such a barefaced incursion, Jarvis says, if they had not already been called away to strengthen the British fleet about to go to war with France and Spain.

The author also reveals that the smugglers had invented their own special 'tub-boats' for carrying the contraband –

deep, flat-bottomed vessels very full fore and aft and built of small, thin timbers bound by iron – which were ideally suited for landing on the east coast. They were generally referred to as 'luggage boats', but their real purpose fooled no one.

The smugglers were not always successful in their nefarious activities, however. In 1726, Richard Clement, the captain of the Revenue smack, *Prince of Wales*, received a report that several suspicious-looking French ships had crept into Sizewell Bay. A contemporary account reports what happened next:

> The Captain set sail, found two of the ships at anchor and one of their boats on shore and a great number of horsemen which he supposed ready to receive their cargoes. As the Captain came to them there was a boat stood away from one of the French vessels. He made after them upon which the Frenchman stood in again for their own vessel, but the Captain cut them off from boarding. Upon which both the French vessels fired upon the Captain to such a degree both their great guns and small arms were used up till they were forced to quit. However the Captain secured five of the men, took ten half anker casks of brandy, four rowles of chocolate and about four dozen packs of cards. The five persons above-mentioned are now secured in gaol.

Before the law finally brought the heyday of smuggling on this stretch of the east coast to an end in the early years of the nineteenth century, there were to be many more such incidents. As late as 4 August 1810, the *Suffolk Chronicle* reported to its readers,

> On the 28th ult. The Sitter and Boatmen belonging to the Customs of Southwold seized an open Lugger on Sizewell beach with 187 half ankers of Geneva Gin on board. And on the 29th ult. Messrs J. Easey and R. Gildersleeves,

riding officers, seized 42 half ankers of Geneva, which they found concealed in a vault in a barnyard in the parish of Leiston.

The English poet and scholar Edward Fitzgerald, who was born at Bredfield House in Suffolk and is famous for his translation (1859) of the *Rubáiyát of Omar Khayyam*, was a keen sailor and wrote on one occasion in a letter to his friend, the illustrator Charles Keene, about the reputation of the area:

I have, like you, always have, and from a child have had, a mysterious feeling about the Sizewell Gap. There were reports of kegs of Hollans found under the Altar Cloth of Theberton Church nearby, and we children looked with awe on the Revenue Cutters which passed Aldeburgh, especially remembering one that went down with all hands, the *Ranger*.

In fact, for years the authorities seriously wondered whether they would ever beat the trade in contraband. Lord Pembroke was probably voicing a long-held opinion when he spoke about the iniquity of the country being hard-pressed by the mounting debts of fighting the War of Independence in America and losing huge sums in unpaid duty to the smugglers. 'Will Washington take America,' he was heard to say wearily, 'or the smugglers England first?'

Sizewell Gap continued to be the location of dramatic incursions in the twentieth century. During World War One, in December 1916, two German U-boats surfaced near the Gap planning to 'blow' their air tanks and take in much-needed fresh oxygen. When the first of these, U-176, surfaced in the grey light of dawn, she was spotted by a keen-eyed sentry in an army camp on the shore. At once the soldiers in the camp were roused and began to fire on the submarine. Before it could dive, one of the marksmen had succeeded in hitting a member of the crew standing in the conning tower, causing the man to tumble into the water. The vessel successfully escaped, however – according to John Suffolk in his account of the events, 'Grey Water', in the *East Anglian Magazine* of February 1937 – but the body of the unfortunate seaman was later washed ashore and buried in Leiston churchyard. A disc around his neck named him as Heinz Vogel.

Three days later, U-177, clearly unaware of what had happened to its predecessor, also rose into the night air off Sizewell Gap at around 2 a.m. Because of the previous incursion, a close watch was being kept on the bay and the beam of a searchlight suddenly broke the darkness and bathed the intruder in a glaring white light. Moments later this was followed by a volley of shots. John Suffolk takes up the drama:

> The gunners presented the newcomer with a welcome that was as enthusiastic as it was deadly. In a few seconds it was all over. Her conning tower a wreck and her hull a charnel house, U-177 rolled over and slid below the waves to come to rest at the bottom of the North Sea off Sizewell Gap. There were no survivors, though there were some people who declared that they saw a man wading in the sea who then disappeared. Obviously he must have collapsed and drowned in the process.
>
> No one thought any more of the incident until a Government diver came to Sizewell and went down to U-177. He groped about under the water for a couple of days and then emerged with the identification discs for the German authorities and with quite a mass of information about the craft itself for the British.

German submarines were again reported off Sizewell right at the start of World War Two, according to the logbook of Number 18 Observer Corps, who were based in the vicinity:

29 December 1939, 15.15 hrs. H2 (Orford) reports submarine close to land in (map ref) M8765 (Hollesley Bay) and two small boats had left the submarine.

21 February 1940, 3.25 hrs. H2 post reports sounds at sea off Sizewell. Could be a submarine charging batteries.

Derek Johnson has recorded several strange happenings during the early months of the war on the east coast, including the story of a character named Old Smokey Joe, who ran a tea shop near Sizewell and 'may even have played host to a U-boat crew'! The local historian writes:

Smokey Joe's shack was a Dickensian shanty, shrouded with canvas and a thick coating of black tar. Come the war, he enjoyed a brief period of prosperity catering to the shore patrols – later banned from using his facilities after several outbreaks of food poisoning. According to Joe, a submarine was beached in a backwater creek during the first winter of the war. Some of the crewmembers took to calling at his hut for food and water. They told the old man that they were Dutch. Seeing no reason to disbelieve them, he didn't tell anyone about his 'visitors' until well after the event!

Jeff Fisher was blissfully unaware of these recent events as he walked from Leiston to Sizewell Gap. Nor had he seen the story in his father's *Daily Sketch* the previous day that restrictions were about to be placed on the east coast. Headlined CURFEW FROM THE WASH TO SOUTHEND, it explained that the regulations would come into effect from Monday:

The Regional Commissioner of the No. 4 Eastern Region, Sir Will Spens, has issued a directive imposing a curfew from one hour after sunset to one hour before sunrise on the coastal fringe of the Eastern Defence Area which extends from the Wash to Southend-on-Sea to a depth of approximately five miles. The confines of towns, villages and hamlets and vehicular traffic on the A and B classified roads are exempt from this restriction. The Commissioner has issued a further direction prohibiting access to beaches on the same coast, except to the extent permitted from time to time by local military commandants.

It was just the weather that concerned Jeff. Dawn had broken at 5 a.m. and the sun was due to set at 9 p.m. The radio had said the forecast was good until Tuesday, after which it would become overcast and rainy. That alone seemed to him all the more reason to make the most of the day, as he strode towards the beach just after 9.30 a.m.

Apart from the line of the defences stretching along the shoreline, the sands were deserted in either direction as far as Jeff could see. He walked a short distance and then sat down, putting his gas mask on the sand beside his towel.

'I was just about to lie down in the sun when I saw out of the corner of my eye these little objects on the sand,' he said. 'They appeared to have just been thrown down – rather like the sort of things careless picnickers leave behind them. I could see what appeared to be a cap, several pieces of wrapping paper and some cigarette ends. There were also footmarks in the sand that went straight down through a gap in the defences to the sea.'

Jeff got up and went to examine his find more carefully. As he knelt down, he experienced one of the biggest surprises of his life.

'The cap looked a bit like one of those worn by officers in the Royal Navy. But there was a golden eagle on top of a swastika on the peak. The bits of paper were obviously the wrappers from bars of chocolate and pieces of food. I couldn't read the printing on the paper, but I was pretty sure I knew what the words *Schokolade* and *Wurst* meant. They had to be German.'

Jeff got to his feet, the significance of what he had stumbled across beginning to dawn on him. Everyone knew the Nazis were only a few miles away in Holland and France. German submarines and E-boats were in the North Sea and Luftwaffe planes were constantly flying overhead. Had some of the enemy actually landed on Sizewell Gap just as the smugglers used to do?

Though he hardly realised why, a story that his father had told him sprang into his mind at that moment. 'Dad said that at Christmas someone had broken into Sizewell Hall while everyone was celebrating. The thieves had stolen a petty-cash box from the office of Lieutenant Commander Lord Edward Hay, the commander of the local Territorial Army battalion. The rumour was that the cash box also contained secret plans of all the defences and minefields on the coast around Sizewell.

'No one had been able to find out who stole the box and its contents, he said. Apparently, several of the NCOs who had been on guard duty that night were reduced to the ranks. The TA tried to keep the whole thing hush-hush, but one of the civilian staff at the Hall heard about it and before long it was all over Leiston. One story said it might even have been Germans who had landed at Sizewell and stolen the plans while everyone was too busy having a good time.'

The incident had occurred six months before and the suggestion still seemed to most people to be ridiculous. But as Jeff stood there on the beach with the naval officer's cap in one hand and bits of wrapping paper in the other, he was not so sure. Certainly, the items could not have been there since Christmas – they were quite dry – and the small bits of food on the sand were still fresh. All of them were too far up the beach from the last tide to have been washed ashore.

'I knew there were patrols along the beach every day,' said Jeff, 'so those things could only have been there a short time. A day at the most, I reckoned. The thought made me shiver even in the heat of the morning sun. I had to be the first person to be at the spot since the Germans had landed.

'I wondered what they had been doing. They couldn't have been part of an invasion or we would have known about it by then. Perhaps they were checking out the area. That seemed to me the most likely explanation then – and it still does now. People say the Germans never landed in England, but I *know* they did.'

Jeff did not stay long on the beach after that. He wrapped up the naval cap and two of the pieces of paper in his towel and brushed sand over the rest. He supposed he should report his 'find' to the Home Guard, but did not really want to give up his prize souvenirs. If he told his mother he knew it would upset her – and his dad would probably be angry that he had gone so far onto the beach.

So my friend decided to say nothing to anyone. He smuggled the cap and the wrapping papers into his room and they remained his secret long after he started work for Garrett's on Monday, 29 July. Even after the end of the war, they stayed in the attic. Nor were they moved when he left home, married and later settled near Colchester.

It was not, in fact, until after the death of his mother in 1969 – his father had passed away two years earlier – that Jeff looked out his German souvenirs once more. He was clearing out the house prior to selling it.

'I suppose I was a bit surprised to find they were still there,' he said with a wry smile. 'My mother had got rid of a lot of my old stuff – old comics and toys and that sort of thing. But I decided I didn't want to keep the cap. I had read about the market for Nazi memorabilia and decided to put it in an auction and see what I could get.'

Jeff took the hat to Reeman, Dansie and Howe, one of the oldest-established auction houses in Colchester, who had a good reputation for their 'collectables sales'. There he discovered rather more about his 'find' from one of the firm's experts.

The hat had belonged to a *Leutnant zur See* (lieutenant first class), the seaman's rank indicated by three symbols: the gold cap badge of the eagle with spread wings standing on a swastika inside a wreath; the bullion cockade with its blue, white and red circles surrounded by a halo of gilded oak leaves; and, thirdly, the single line of gold brocade around the peak of the cap.

The expert told Jeff that such caps were usually worn by men serving on destroyers. But to have landed on Sizewell Gap – and departed just as easily – was not something any destroyer would have attempted. It was more likely the lieutenant had been on a *Schnellboot* ('fast boat', known in Britain as an E-boat). Jeff's adviser found support for this conclusion in the records of the *Kriegsmarine*.

In July 1940 when the teenager had picked up the cap on the beach, the E-boats had been operational for just a few months. Indeed, it would not be until May of the following year that a badge for this branch of the service would be produced. Until then, E-boat crews wore the same badge as the seamen on destroyers – a handsome silver medallion depicting one of the big vessels ploughing through a rough sea – which had been instituted on 4 June 1940 by Admiral Raeder. The later *Schnellboot* variation, also in silver, showed one of the much smaller torpedo craft slicing through the waves at speed.

Work prevented Jeff from attending the auction, but he was very happy with the 'couple of hundred pounds' he got from the sale, which he used as part of the deposit on a new car. He never gave a thought that by keeping the cap he would retain the best proof of his experience on Sizewell Gap.

Jeff died in 1980 with the question of the German landing on the east coast still unresolved. I had, though, made a firm promise before moving to Suffolk to investigate his fascinating tale further. He would be pleased to know that others also share his conviction that the incident *did* occur – not in August or September as all previous accounts have suggested, but on that auspicious date of 28 July 1940.

Chapter 11

Incident on 'E-boat Alley'

At first sight, Sizewell does not look like the kind of place to find the answer to one of the most enduring mysteries of World War Two. The huge nuclear-power station that dominates the Suffolk skyline somehow compounds the feeling. Yet it was here that I came first when I began investigating Jeff's story with one thought uppermost in my mind: was it feasible the Germans could – or, for that matter, would – have landed at Sizewell?

The vast grey hulk of the nuclear plant can be seen from miles away and it is not hard to appreciate why for a number of years it was the cause of bitter controversy and attracted large groups of protestors. Standing on a 245-acre site, it supplies electricity through a network of enormous pylons striding across the countryside to the Midlands. It uses 27 million gallons of seawater per hour to cool the reactors, and, when this water is returned to the sea through two large offshore structures that resemble oil rigs, it raises the temperature of the sea by ten degrees. Fish, attracted to the warmth, gather in shoals making Sizewell a popular spot with anglers.

The nuclear plant was erected some twenty years after the war, when the threat of a Nazi invasion was history. There is, though, no doubt that the Germans devoted considerable time and energy to studying this part of East Anglia and its coastline, with typical attention to detail. The maps and historical documents the Nazis gathered were later found largely intact in Berlin and help to explain how the Luftwaffe's bombing in the region was often so accurate.

The best example of this Teutonic thoroughness is probably the devastating air raids on Norwich in April 1942, when 230 men, women and children were killed, 700 injured, thousands made homeless, and whole tracts of housing, business and industrial buildings were laid to waste. The attack was one of a number ordered by Hitler as *Vergeltungsangriffe* – 'retaliation raids' – against targets whose destruction would have 'the greatest effect on civilian life', to use the Führer's words. A popular prewar English guidebook provided a crucial source of information for the attacks, as Baron Gustav von Stum, the deputy of the German Foreign Office Foreign Press Department, revealed in a boastful media briefing on 24 April: 'We shall go all out to bomb every building in Britain marked with three stars in the *Baedeker Guide.*'

Curiously, while there is no question that the Germans had copies of Karl Baedeker's famous series of guidebooks to the countries of Europe, he actually *never* marked any building with more than two stars!

There is also no doubt that German intelligence had learned about the armaments being manufactured at Leiston and duly set about trying to destroy the factory – thankfully with less success than at Norwich. They were equally suspicious that some kind of secret work was going on at Bawdsey and Orford Ness, so it is unlikely that nearby Sizewell would have escaped their meticulous attention.

Similarly, the Nazis had good reason – and in some cases painful memories – to remember the locality from World War One. Then, a navigation beacon standing near the Gap in 1918 had been used to aid the British warships bombarding occupied Zeebrugge in Belgium to deadly effect.

Careful study of local maps along with history and geography books about East Anglia would have revealed that here was a

203

region of isolated estuaries and sheltered coves. The impudent successes of generations of smugglers would have further confirmed the impression that this was a spot where surprise landfalls could be carried out with a minimum of risk.

Was Sizewell, then, an ideal locality for a first wave of German troops to land? The answer is certainly in the positive – and the fact that there was a factory making armaments within a mile made it a target worth securing at the earliest opportunity.

Jeff Fisher's conviction that the landing occurred on a Saturday night also fits in with careful planning. At the end of a busy working week, the local people would certainly be looking for some relaxation at home or perhaps in the pubs or the local cinema. It would be the one night of the week, too, when the army and the Home Guard might reasonably be expected to be less watchful.

But what other proof is there to support this theory? A substantial amount, in fact, which dates back as far as I am concerned to the interview with Dennis Wheatley in 1974. His story about an enemy incursion near Sizewell flashed back into my thoughts when Jeff was giving me his version of events in the locality.

Of course, I could not be sure after all this time whether Wheatley was being *specific* about Sizewell, or just referring to the stretch of coast in general. Back in the seventies, the story of Shingle Street was fairly common knowledge and his information might well have been based on that legend. It was, though, still a piece of evidence not to be ignored.

All his life Wheatley had been fascinated by stories of spies and spying. Certainly during the first year of the war there had been a number of well-documented instances of German secret agents landed successfully on the English coastline, albeit that precious few succeeded in their missions. Among the many reports from that dangerous summer of 1940 was one of two men put ashore from a rowing boat on Romney Marsh near Kent who answered a challenge from a suspicious soldier by declaring 'they did not know the codeword', according to a subsequent report in *The Times*.

An equally inept pair were landed near Dungeness and swiftly arrested after knocking on the door of a pub during closing hours and asking for bottles of cider. These two were following specific orders to travel northeast and report on the movement of British troops in the area between London and Ipswich. In the men's knapsacks the arresting police officers found tinned meat, chocolates and cigarettes – all marked with their German origin!

Julian Foynes, the author of the definitive history of *The Battle of the East Coast 1939–1945* (1992), which he based on official wartime records, is in no doubt that the region was a major German target, as his chapter entitled 'Invasion Imminent' makes very clear:

The overrunning of Holland in May 1940 first raised the spectre of invasion on the East Coast. With British forces still tied up in Belgium and Norway there were very understandable fears that the enemy might sidestep France and rush Eastern England with parachutists and light naval craft. Mile after mile of shore lay quite open and unguarded and even the 'strong points' – for instance Harwich and Felixstowe – were weak.

Bombing only added to the public's fear of invasion, Foynes says, along with large-scale army manoeuvres in East Anglia such as the one ostensibly in response to a landing by five German divisions on the coast.

'The report luridly describes the imaginary devastation of Lowestoft and Great Yarmouth,' says Foynes. 'Churchill was rather peeved by this "Operation Victor" since he disliked the Army's assumption that the Navy and RAF might not be able to stop an invasion happening in the first place.'

Practical jokers such as the two men of the Queen's Regiment stationed at Shrublands camp near Ipswich did not help the mood, either. The pair, who had been given German uniforms to dress up in for a training exercise, sneaked out of their camp one night in the Nazi regalia and 'swaggered around until troops from another unit arrested them', according to a subsequent report. Taken to Ipswich Police Station, the two men kept up their act and pretended not to understand English. Just how annoyed the local security forces were – or what punishment the pair of clowns received – is not recorded.

Julian Foynes is convinced there is no truth in the tales of an invasion attempt at Shingle Street because he has been unable to find any mention in the war diaries of the three services based on the Suffolk coast that he has painstakingly examined. He did, though, find documented evidence of German naval activity at this time that provides another vital clue in substantiating Jeff Fisher's story.

It *may*, however, be the case that an E-Boat or E-Boats carried out closed reconnaissance of Orford Ness and the nearby Bawdsey RDF Station on the night of 2 December 1940 and the following misty morning. A motorboat was spotted flashing a light only five hundred yards off North Weir Point and then heard and seen near Bawdsey and off the Naze. Engines could still be heard at daybreak, by which time it had been established that no British craft were in the area, but the search mounted was blocked by mist and when this cleared nothing was to be seen. This we know from Nore Command (Royal Navy) and Army Record. No landing or bombardment is mentioned. Could it be the incident behind the invasion story?

Not the Shingle Street story, perhaps, but it certainly bears similarities to the Sizewell story – and Julian Foynes is not the only writer to believe that E-boats were the most likely vessels to have come inshore while the Germans contemplated invasion.

The first author to make this suggestion was Richard Baxter, a London journalist, in his now extremely rare little work, *Hitler's Darkest Secret: What He Has in Store for Britain*, published in 1941. The book, poorly printed on the grainy, yellowing paper enforced by wartime economies, is a diatribe about the horrors Baxter predicts the Nazis will inflict on the country after an invasion. He writes of the Gestapo terror machine, a plan to stamp out Christianity and the Führer's intention of setting up concentration camps.

All that prevents Hitler coming is his knowledge that invasion will not be a simple matter. He knows that coasts are mined and the channels through these mined areas are unknown. However, Nazi airmen have been keeping observation by day to mark the course being followed by shipping. E-Boats have ventured out at night to fathom the secret, coming ashore in some instances, but they have failed, too.

Unfortunately, Baxter provides no more evidence for his statement that the E-boats landed, but he is convinced such missions were conducted by the *Kriegsmarine* to prove to Hitler that a landing was possible – and that entry via the Suffolk coast was the most likely to be successful.

Half a century later, Michael Glover shares this view in his thoughtful and detailed study, *Invasion Scare 1940* (1990), a book that has also become hard to find. The only copy I was able to obtain for my research came from, of all places, the public library at Leiston! Glover, of course, had the advantage when writing his book of using captured German documents, including a report prepared for Admiral Raeder by one of his lieutenants, Rear Admiral Karl Fricke.

Fricke headed his memo dated 27 May 1940, 'Studie England', and suggested there would be 'a very obstinate defence since the ancient fear of invasion has again manifested itself and has grown into an almost hysterical anxiety in England'. The rear admiral believed a very powerful assault wave of troops would be required and proposed a landing area near Yarmouth. Glover writes:

[This] was preferable since the crossing would be shorter, air cover more easily available, the flanks more easily sealed with mines and, for part of the front, artillery support would be available from heavy guns mounted in the Pas de Calais. Fricke also pointed out reasons for preferring the area because the landing beaches were easier and more numerous, where the country behind them was less heavily populated and less easy to defend. Moreover an invasion fleet aiming for the east coast of Britain could be prepared in harbours between Denmark and the Scheldt where it would have more security from British bombing and aerial reconnaissance.

Glover also quotes Rear Admiral Fricke's telling final paragraph in 'Studie England':

Our small fleet cannot and will not achieve much. Nevertheless, as in the case of Norway, it should be possible to put personnel ashore quickly. The remaining naval vessels, with auxiliaries in the form of merchant ships, fishing boats and E-Boats, will be able to carry out the landing over short distances.

It is evident from this conclusion just how important a role the E-boat would play in the invasion of England. Fricke's opinion was clearly based on the vessel's already growing operational reputation and the evidence I have also gathered more than substantiates this fact. It also reveals the E-boat to have been a far superior craft that summer of 1940 than the Royal Navy's scant fleet of motor torpedo boats (MTBs) that were attempting to keep them at bay on the stretch of sea along the coast of East Anglia from Harwich to Yarmouth known colourfully as 'E-boat Alley'.

Lieutenant Commander Robert Hichens, who won both a DSO and DSC for his exploits in MTBs, liked to tell the story of how the Royal Navy could have had its own craft to match the E-boat at the very start of the war if someone had taken the trouble to look at the current edition of *Jane's Fighting Ships*. Formerly a solicitor in Falmouth whose exploits would earn him the sobriquet of 'the Nelson of the Navy's Little Ships', Hichens recounted the story in *We Fought Them in Gunboats* (1944):

One day in 1942 I was in the C.-in-C.'s secretary's office in Plymouth waiting to see the Old Man. I was idly turning over the pages of a 1938 edition of *Jane's Fighting Ships*. Suddenly my attention was riveted. There before my incredulous eyes was an admirable photo of an E-Boat, exactly in every detail like the one we had captured the year before. The raised fore deck, the bridge, the four torpedoes, two of them re-loads, the let-in torpedo tubes, the large after compass, the low side rails, and the smoke apparatus. Only the two Oerlikon guns were missing.

I collected my scattered wits and read the paragraph beneath. It was the advertisement of a German shipbuilding yard, proclaiming their wares and inviting all and sundry to come and buy! Here was the world's fastest diesel-driven torpedo boat, 36.5 knots. Exactly the speed we had arrived at after poring over the captured logs and comparing notes with all who had taken part in E-Boat hunts.

The whole thing seemed too fantastic. The reiterated instructions to bring one back alive at all costs. The intense interest in all the details we could remember of our short hour on the captured boat. The continual bombardment of questions on every point, even as to whether the engines were diesels, carried on for weeks. The tremendous discussions and controversies as to maximum speeds. And here it was all laid out for us in *Jane's*. The Admiralty, who would have given untold sums to have an E-Boat, could have bought as many as they wished but one short year before the outbreak of war!

Such knowledge gained in hindsight was, of course, of no use to Hichens and the other Royal Navy men brought together in the aftermath of the fall of the Low Countries to combat the E-boats rampaging in the North Sea shipping lanes, laying mines and attacking merchant shipping. As was evident, these boats were no mean fighters.

The first type of *Schnellboot* was powered by three Daimler Benz MB 501 high-performance diesel engines. Built by Lurssen Shipbuilders in Bremen, it was 32 metres long with a displacement of 78 tonnes. The vessel could reach a speed of over 36 knots and was equipped to carry a crew of 18 men plus a fearsome armoury.

This armament consisted of two G7a torpedo tubes carrying a maximum of four torpedoes: two in the tubes and two as reloads – a demanding task for the crew in high seas – as well as two 20mm flak weapons mounted in the stern. Completing the boat's arsenal were six EMC contact mines stored on the stern deck until required for action.

The second version of the *Schnellboot* that operated in the German navy's 1st Flotilla preying on the east coast shipping lanes from May 1940 was slightly longer at 34 metres, with a displacement tonnage of 92 tonnes and capable of speeds in excess of 40 knots. The armoury had also been upgraded to a 40mm Flak 28 Bofors. Initially, these boats were based at the Hook of Holland, but soon they would have bases in Belgium (Ostend) and France (Cherbourg), as Bryan Cooper has explained in *The Battle of the Torpedo Boats* (1970):

Within a comparatively few weeks of their possession of the Dutch harbours, the Germans had installed these weapons in concrete covered shelters, with doors, easy slipping facilities, and steam heat ready to connect to the engine rooms. An achievement doubtless made easier by the use of slave labour. The ravages these boats began to inflict upon our large east coast convoys proved serious.

After an auspicious start on 9 May torpedoing Lord Mountbatten's flagship, HMS *Kelly*, which had to be towed back to the Tyne, the E-boats launched a series of strikes during the month on ships off Dover and Harwich, and by early June were ranging as far north as Cromer. On 10 June a group of *Schnellboots* clashed with a destroyer, *Vivien*, off Lowestoft and the following day sank a merchantman, *Togston*.

All of these operations were carried out under the cover of darkness, as Julian Foynes has reported: 'Night after night destroyers shot at these craft. Auxiliary Patrol vessels were vigilant for their approach and motorboats hunted them right over to the Dutch coast. But for long the speed and elusiveness of the E-Boat made her an almost invulnerable phantom.'

The choice of the word 'phantom' is very apt. The E-boats were rarely audible to the ear because they approached their victims with their two main diesel engines switched off, using only a special, quiet-running motor. Sometimes they would stop just ahead of a moving British convoy with none of their engines running, switching these into life at the last moment and setting about their victims like ravenous sharks.

Such was the threat posed by the *Schnellboot* that, after frantic research by the Admiralty, the highest priority was given to the building of motor torpedo boats to match the Germans at their own game. Within the ranks of the Royal Navy, these new MTBs were categorised as a 'secret weapon', but, once the first were in service, they proved rather less of a match for their rivals than had been hoped, as Lieutenant

Commander Hichens admitted in his account, *We Fought Them in Gunboats*:

> Our boats were 70 foot long and could barely do 40 knots. If they tried to do more, or even this speed, for any length of time, the engines invariably blew up. Although they were gunboats, they carried no guns worthy of the name. How proud I was of my .303 Browning guns, but they were hardly the weapons to kill a 110-foot E-Boat armed with two 20 millimetre .8 guns and many of .303 calibre as well. But above all, they were not secret – nothing could be less secret. A small unit of three of these boats with their nine petrol-driven Rolls-Royce Merlin 1,100 h.p. engines blasting away, could generally be heard a good 10 to 15 miles off, and in quiet weather considerably further.

The racket an MTB made enabled the captain of any lurking E-boat to distance himself long before his presence was known. The low, sleek lines of the *Schnellboot* made it ideally suited for cruising the shallow east coast waters and close-to-shore missions were undertaken only on moonless nights. Painted in matt-silver night camouflage – which appeared like a 'dirty white colour' in the darkness – with its S-number just a shade darker on the bows, the *Schnellboot* was impossible to see when more than 500 yards away.

The German naval officers who captained the E-boats proved to be as audacious, quick-witted and elusive as their vessels. The log report of Lieutenant Clive Hamilton of HMS *Exmoor* patrolling 'E-boat Alley' is typical of many similar accounts from the heyday of the *Schnellboot*:

> There was no indication of E-Boats. The best Asdic operator was on watch, but he heard nothing. There was an explosion aft. I have no idea what caused it, but I am certain it was not the ammunition. Whatever it was that

hit the ship, it probably hit the pom-pom deck, which blazed at once and the whole thing was a twisted wreck. The pom-pom ammunition started going off and the ship listed over to port at about 20 degrees with the whole of the after ship ablaze. She blazed from aft as far as the searchlight platform and then took a list to port.

As luck would have it, a British corvette was close enough in the vicinity to rescue 32 survivors from the sinking destroyer. In the subsequent enquiry, the insistent reports of crew-members that they had heard the 'rushing' or 'slushing' noise of a torpedo just prior to their ship's demise convinced the navy the *Exmoor* must have been sunk by an E-boat.

A British merchant navy captain who was on one of a small group of auxiliary ships operating on the Suffolk coast at this time has also reported in naval records a terrifying ambush he and his crew endured one night within sight of Lowestoft.

We knew the Germans had E-Boats in the area and they let our boats almost reach harbour. Then all hell broke loose. The E-Boats made a half-circle around us and opened fire. As soon as our MTBs hove into view, the Germans turned and made off at a terrific speed. Our chaps just could not keep pace.

The hapless MTBs were in all probability part of the 6th Motor Gun Boat Flotilla, one of the two groups set up to cover the east coast convoy route. Their duties included combating the German raiders and air-sea rescue missions. But, as E-boat hunters, they were usually left floundering in the wake of their enemy, and it would not be until 1941, with improvements in the speed of the Rolls-Royce engines and the introduction of a 20mm gun and two .5s in twin power-operated turrets on either side of the bridge – or 'dustbin', as it was called by the crew – that the odds between the two combatants were evened.

Lieutenant Commander Hichens's time on the east coast left him in no doubt that the skill and daring of the E-boat captains would make carrying out a landing on the shore perfectly feasible: 'Many rumours circulated as they always do on these occasions. The E-Boats were swarming and we began to think there was some truth in the whisperings of an invasion.'

Hichens does not refer to this possibility again in his book, which describes how the MTBs, operating from bases at Felixstowe, Lowestoft and Yarmouth, gradually turned the tide on their enemy. The assistance of radar and the development of 'star shells' that could light up areas two miles in diameter helped in the pursuit of the German wraiths. So, equally, did the first 'Headache' operators – German-speaking Wrens who listened in to the E-boats' radio conversations and relayed the details of their whereabouts to the MTBs.

Tragically, though, after taking part in 148 operations, Hichens was killed by a stray shell off the Dutch coast on 13 April 1943. His unfinished manuscript of life on the MTBs was later prepared for publication by David James, a member of his flotilla, as a tribute to the man who – James wrote in *We Fought Them in Gunboats* – ultimately helped to 'burn the Germans' "unsinkable" E-Boats within sight of their own harbours'.

The tide of war for the E-boats was, of course, still running very much in their favour on the night of 28 July 1940, when one of their crews audaciously landed on Sizewell beach. The final piece of evidence of a German landfall is provided by a man who was actually on the east coast the night in question and who subsequently told his story to the distinguished researcher, W O G Lofts.

'Bill' Lofts, as he was known to his friends, was a former Royal Artillery soldier who served against the Japanese in the jungles of Malaya. While a prisoner of war, he came across a paperback edition of a Sexton Blake detective novel, which inspired in him a fascination with juvenile fiction and its usually unaccredited authors. After the war, his dedicated research in the major libraries and the archives of the leading publishers, Amalgamated Press and Fleetway House, enabled him to unearth the identities of almost 2,000 anonymous writers who were *The Men Behind Boys' Fiction*, to quote the title of his pioneer work co-written with his friend, Derek Adley, which appeared in 1970. The duo also published highly regarded bibliographies of Edgar Wallace, Leslie Charteris, creator of the Saint, and Charles Hamilton (a.k.a. Frank Richards), inventor of the immortal 'fat boy' Billy Bunter.

This work – and other equally extensive research into topics that fascinated him, especially unusual aspects of World War Two – earned Lofts the reputation of 'one of the great researchers of the century', to quote his obituary in the *Independent* on 12 July 1997. It was Bill's bequest to me of his rich archive of research material, including newspaper cuttings, documents and notes, that has enabled me to complete the investigation into the landing of the German eagle on English soil.

Born in Marylebone, London, he had a rudimentary education before becoming an apprentice engineer in 1940 at the age of seventeen. Three years later he was on active service with the Royal Artillery in India and subsequently in Malaya, where his interest in boys' fiction was ignited by Sexton Blake, the more physical crime-busting rival to Sherlock Holmes, both of whom live on Baker Street. Later, combining a job with a London PR firm for whom he conducted numerous private investigations, Lofts also began to explore the main sources of information in England at a time long before the Internet made such tasks far easier. His indefatigable enquiries found him spending days in the reading room of the British Museum or, alternately, the births-and-deaths ledgers in Somerset House, the Public Record Office, Companies House, the Imperial War Museum and the essential British Newspaper Archive at Colindale.

The information Bill Lofts unearthed was often startling, particularly where World War Two was concerned. These 'finds' were as varied as identifying an Englishman whose father had been a Nazi war criminal and unearthing an unknown short story, 'Man Overboard', by Winston Churchill. His one romantic attachment – to a German woman to whom he was briefly engaged – also motivated his interest in untold episodes of the conflict. It was in his capacity as 'official researcher' to Fleetway House – the successor to Amalgamated Press, for decades one of the principal publishers of boys' comics – that he was enabled to make the connection that secured the last piece of the puzzle in the mystery of the Nazi landing in 1940.

In the years following the publication of *The Men Behind Boys' Fiction*, Lofts continued assiduously to track down any other writers who had not been included, as well as revising and updating existing entries. Among these was one for Clifford Gates, a member of the staff of Amalgamated Press 'for a short period before the last war' who had worked for Hedley O'Mant, the editor of the boys' adventure magazines, *Ranger* and *Pilot*. What had excited Lofts's continued interest in Gates was the knowledge he had written a complete issue of *The Sexton Blake Library*, number 735 (2nd Series) published in January 1941. The rest of Gates's entry read, 'During the Second World War he was in the Royal Navy *and was killed in action.*'

In Lofts's master copy of the bibliography, which he was annotating for a new edition – now in my possession – he ringed the words I have put in italics and wrote in the margin 'No record that this is true.' With the resourcefulness that he had once brought to proving that George Orwell was right in insisting that Charles Hamilton could not have written as much as he claimed, he used the archives of Amalgamated Press and the facilities of Fleetway House to track down his man. He soon became convinced the previous assumption had been wrong. And, finally, he located Gates, still hale and hearty, in Norfolk in the summer of 1986, and soon discovered he had stumbled across a much bigger story than he could have imagined.

216

Gates, then in his late sixties, was living in retirement in his hometown, Yarmouth. He had developed a passion for boating in his youth, and later bought a yacht that he sailed whenever he could on the nearby Norfolk Broads. While working for the Amalgamated Press before the war, he told Lofts, he had written a number of nautical stories for both *Ranger* and *Pilot*. He had become known as 'Skipper' or 'Skip' and had signed up eagerly for the Royal Navy when he became old enough in the year after war broke out. Bill Lofts takes up the story in a handwritten account of his enquiries:

Cliff Gates joined up on 22 June, 1940. He told the Navy he had some experience in small boats and so they immediately made him a petty officer. He was given command of a 42-foot motor cruiser based at Lowestoft. The boat had a crew of three and they were armed with a Lewis gun, a rifle and a pistol. Gates told me he never forgot his first orders, which were to look out for any Germans trying to invade. If they did try, the cruiser was to get out to sea with any other ships in port and just use their wits to make as much trouble for the Jerries as possible.

Lofts discussed with Gates his experiences as a writer for boys' comics as well as swapping stories about the war. In the middle of a pause as the two men were looking out from a window of the author's house towards the North Sea, Gates made an extraordinary admission to his interviewer:

He told me that while he was out on patrol one summer night in 1940 he had unexpectedly come across some Germans who had just landed on the coast at Sizewell. It was an area he knew well and had sailed past many times. His cruiser was making its usual night run down the coast when he saw a dinghy being hastily rowed out to a silvery-white boat at anchor about a hundred or so

217

yards from the beach. Gates said he knew at once that it must be an E-Boat.

As he raced towards the German vessel, Gates said he saw about half a dozen figures in the dinghy scramble up onto the deck. The boat was already revving its engines and the men did not stop to pull the dinghy aboard, but roared away, leaving a wake of churning foam. The cruiser loosed off a couple of rounds from its Lewis gun, but the E-Boat was too quick. Gates said they followed in its wake going south for several miles, but soon lost contact.

As a man fascinated by curious episodes of the war, the story naturally excited Lofts's interest. He had heard rumours of a German invasion on the east coast – but here was someone who had actually seen enemy seamen making a landfall. How long they had been there – or what their purpose might be – Gates could only guess at the time. That night he filed a report that simply stated he had 'engaged an E-Boat off Sizewell', fired off two rounds but been unable to hit the enemy. He had briefly glanced at the boat's number on its bow and noted it down: 21.

Under further questioning from Lofts, Gates said the date of his encounter had been a Saturday night, 27 July. He remembered this because, during the cruiser's return to Lowestoft, the engine had begun to falter because of the speed at which it had been driven in pursuit of the E-boat. This required repairs that lasted the following week – the only period he was nonoperational in 1940. Clifford Gates's final remark to his guest on the subject was that he would 'love to know who the Germans were who landed at Sizewell'.

It was just the sort of challenge Bill Lofts relished. In the weeks that followed he set about checking wartime records of action on the east coast at the Public Record Office in London. He eventually found the information he required in the Admiralty files coded ADM covering navy lists (179), operational records (199) and 'Red Lists' (208), giving the locations of minor warships and landing craft. The Imperial War Museum also provided him with details about the E-boats, their officers and operations off the coast of East Anglia. Gates's recollection of the E-boat's number provided the final clue to the mystery.

The Admiralty navy lists indicated that, during the last few days of July, E-boats had been observed 'laying a destructive contact minefield off Harwich'. In most cases, though, all that had been seen were white wakes disappearing on the horizon; tiny, fleeting black silhouettes against the glares of exploding shells; or the faintest flicker on antisubmarine-warfare (ASW) scopes.

The Royal Navy command knew that the one way to frustrate the 'night crawlers on E-Boat Alley' would be for the convoys of merchant ships to sail in daylight. But this would have meant leaving or arriving at the Thames Estuary in darkness when the glow of the navigation and signal lights would have been an invitation to the E-boats or passing Luftwaffe bombers. Their records revealed that in July 1940 there was only one group of E-boats operational off the east coast – the 1st Flotilla based at Ijmuiden, the outpost of Amsterdam, just 120 miles east of Lowestoft. There were six boats in the group under the command of a wily veteran, *Kapitänleutnant* Heinz Birnbacher.

A master tactician with exceptional qualities of leadership, Birnbacher was conducting a dual mission for the *Kriegsmarine* – to perpetrate all the damage he could on the enemy's shipping and scout possible landing points for an invasion. His reports were to be forwarded directly to Admiral Raeder for incorporation into Operation Sea Lion. To further his objectives, the *Kapitänleutnant* occasionally allowed his handpicked lieutenants to operate independently around the East Anglian coast as they roamed the North Sea from Felixstowe to as far north as Cromer. Although there are no specific details of his success on record, Birnbacher was later awarded a *Ritterkreuz* (Knight's Cross), a higher order of the Iron Cross.

The *Kapitänleutnant* had three of his E-boats on patrol on the night of 28 July. They were the S 18, commanded by *Leutnant zur See* Georg Christiansen, who stalked a convoy near Yarmouth; S 22 captained by *Leutnant zur See* Ludwig Grund patrolling the vicinity of Lowestoft; and, a little to the south, S 21 with *Leutnant zur See* Bernd Klug at the helm. The three younger officers were reckoned to be his best men and together legend says the quartet were known as 'the Four Horsemen of the Apocalypse'.

E-boat S 21 was, it seems clear, the one that Clifford Gates had disturbed making a landfall at Sizewell. So who was the audacious Captain Klug, who had hastily left his cap and evidence of a picnic shared with some of his men on the beach? The evidence from German navy records is not extensive, but still revealing.

Bernd Klug was born in Wuppertal on 12 December 1914. After training as a naval officer he took part from 1936 in the Spanish Civil War. After the outbreak of World War Two, he was assigned to the first E-boat flotilla and was a key figure in a series of successful operations during the German campaign against Norway, before being transferred to the North Sea under the command of *Kapitänleutnant* Birnbacher. Taking part in more than a hundred operations during the first year of the conflict, Klug displayed a streak of daring, sense of adventure and all-round efficiency that earned him an impressive reputation among his men. It was said they would follow him anywhere.

The Admiralty records credit Klug with sinking three ships in the summer of 1940 – the SS *Corbrook* and SS *New Lambton* near Haisborough Sands at Yarmouth and the SS *Loch Inver* off Aldeburgh. In December, he took command of a new, bigger vessel, the S 28, a boat nearly 35 metres long, with a displacement of 93 tonnes and a maximum speed of 42 knots. It also carried a larger crew of 24 men. On Christmas Eve, Klug's elusive new E-boat made her first kill, a Dutch merchantman, the *Stad Maastricht*, which sank off Orford Ness.

The S 28 achieved another notable strike off Winterton on 7 March, when Klug displayed another side to his character. After hitting the SS *Corduff* with a salvo of torpedoes, he did not disappear but pulled up alongside the stricken boat, according to an account of the incident by Julian Foynes:

> Seven of her crew were killed, two were left injured on the sinking ship, and 14 – including Captain D. E. Rees – fled in a lifeboat. This was intercepted by Klug who asked if any of the occupants were officers – fearing capture, they replied there were none. Klug replied that the two wounded men had been taken prisoner, and after giving them a bearing to the coast, sped away into the night. At dawn, Rees and his men were rescued by the inimitable Cromer lifeboat.

That March day was to prove the most successful of the entire war for the German raiders. Apart from Klug's contribution, a total of seven merchant ships were sunk or destroyed in two convoys that had the misfortune to be sailing in 'E-boat Alley' that night. The *Leutnant* soon after joined his commanding officer in being awarded a *Ritterkreuz*.

The attacks of the E-boats were to continue for the next two years as the MTBs gradually gained the upper hand in their home waters. Klug was promoted to a *Korvettenkapitän* in 1941 and for the next three years commanded the 5th E-boat flotilla, his successes earning him a further commendation – an *Eichenlaub* (oak leaf) in 1944. From June 1944 until the end of the war he was an *Admiralstabsoffizier* in charge of the rapidly declining E-boat operations primarily in the Baltic Sea off the coasts of Russia and Germany. Klug was briefly imprisoned in a POW camp from 1945 to 1946, and his postwar career consisted of several years as a naval attaché at the German Embassy in Paris and finally as *Kommander* of the Flensburg Marine School. He died in Kiel in 1975.

*

On a bright summer morning in 1995, Bill Lofts and I stood on the coast at Sizewell and tried to imagine ourselves back over half a century. I had told him how the version of events as described by Dennis Wheatley and Jeff Fisher tallied perfectly with Clifford Gates's account and we asked ourselves the same question. We both came to the same conclusion.

The bold *Leutnant* Bernd Klug *had* landed on Sizewell beach. It was a feat his mission that July day gave him the opportunity and expertise to carry out. It was certainly something he was capable of – and very much in keeping with his particular character. It was also very much in character that he would never have boasted or even talked about such a risky operation that could have endangered the lives of his men and threatened his career. Indeed, there is no evidence from any German source that he did so.

Bill Lofts and I felt the evidence was incontrovertible: Klug and his party deserve a footnote in history as the eagles who achieved what no other German managed during the entire Second World War. They *landed* on English soil on the night of 28 July 1940.

Epilogue

The roar of dozens of Stukas shatter the calm over the sun-dappled waves of the English Channel as they scream in low across the Straits of Dover, their guns blazing. Above the fighters, the engines of hundreds of bombers drone in a crescendo of noise as they near the coast; while behind both groups of attackers the churning of countless marine engines indicates a huge armada of ships on the move.

Where, moments before, there had been tranquillity all along the south coast of England, there is now only bedlam. Soldiers lolling behind beach defences and members of the Home Guard strolling along the headlands – all evidently expecting another undisturbed day – are suddenly confronted by the might of Germany sweeping out of the haze of the French coast towards them.

Before these men have time to gather their wits and their weapons, the Stukas are upon them, catching scores of terrified servicemen in their withering fire. Moments later, bombs begin to rain down from the sky and, as the explosives rip terrible holes in the earth, the first of the flotilla of speedboats begin spilling infantrymen onto the beaches. Soon, too, the larger, flat-bottomed landing craft packed with troops and ferries loaded with tanks and ammunition are grinding onto the beaches and pouring their fighting men and peerless armour onto the golden sands.

In the chaos that follows, the English military presence along the Kent and Sussex coast is swept aside by the sheer speed and ruthless efficiency of the German troops. Despite the fire that is returned from defensive positions and hidden mines exploding along the beach, there is no stopping the invaders from conquering the nation that had been threatened for almost a thousand years, but never fallen until now.

At this moment, the voice of an unseen commentator rises to a crescendo of excitement. The screen fills with pictures of dozens of bodies spread-eagled across the sands and men with their hands held high being rounded up by elated troops. Further along the beach, a group of the invaders are raising a swastika against the backdrop of the towering White Cliffs of Dover.

These scenes are, of course, imaginary. They were part of a film especially created by Goebbels's Propaganda Ministry in 1940 that lay hidden for over half a century, gathering dust, in the Deutsche Filmarchiv in Berlin until rediscovered in 1970 by some British researchers. The film is, indeed, an extraordinary mélange of genuine war footage and specially acted sequences that were made in the first week of September 1940 for the *Wochenschau* ('News of the Week') in readiness for screening at cinemas throughout Germany and the rest of occupied Europe. It was intended to show to Hitler's millions his greatest triumph.

Subsequent research has established that the 'newsreel' was largely shot in the vicinity of the occupied Belgian city of Antwerp. The 'beach' sequences were filmed at the popular excursion spot, St Anne, on the River Scheldt, directly opposite the city's waterfront, using fully equipped German troops who had been trained for the invasion of England. Their stylised manoeuvres – nothing like the real thing if the invasion had actually taken place – were then to be intercut with footage of German aircraft on the attack in the Spanish Civil War, in Poland and in other parts of Western Europe. There were also a few minutes of genuine tragedy: footage of dazed and bewildered British troops who had been captured at Dunkirk.

The American journalist Lars Moen, who was present at the filming, had the opportunity to ask one of the film crew the point of making the picture before the event and quotes the man's reply in his book, *Under The Iron Heel*:

> 'You see,' he said, 'when we invade England it will be at night, or very early in the morning, and there won't be enough light to photograph it. Since this will be the decisive event of the war, it must be covered for the newsreel – so we're staging it here, exactly as it will be done later on the English coast.'

It is a fact of which to be grateful that the utter conviction of Goebbels and his filmmakers of an ultimate victory was not matched by Hitler and his subordinates who planned 'Operation Sea Lion'. In fact, once the Führer had decided on his suicidal mission to attack Russia to obtain more *Lebensraum* (living space) for his people in the east, the likelihood of an invasion of England declined with each passing month – though the anxiety about it remained with the English for several years to follow.

On 31 July, just a couple of days after the audacious *Leutnant* Bernd Klug had landed with his men at Sizewell Gap, Admiral Raeder was meeting with Hitler yet again to tell him that the *Kriegsmarine*'s preparations for a landing would not be ready until 15 September. In the interim – the navy C-in-C appealed – could the Luftwaffe please drive the RAF from the skies? Hitler, of course, knew how essential this objective was and agreed that his final decision would not be made until about eight to fourteen days following the start of the 'great air campaign against Britain' scheduled to begin on 5 August.

In fact, bad weather (England's old ally) delayed the start of the German battle for air supremacy – codenamed *Adlertag* (Eagle Day) by Goering – until 13 August. Very soon, too, the

Luftwaffe discovered that – despite their favourable geographical position for operations against England – their lack of an overall plan and the carefully orchestrated British defence system ranged against them combined to prove a recipe for disaster. All the while they struggled for supremacy in the air, divisions from the Ninth and Sixteenth Armies continued to gather along the French coast between Dunkirk and Étaples, waiting for the off.

On 4 September, Hitler, probably to keep his people happy about the delay and certainly with the hope of alarming the enemy across the Channel, made what would prove to be his last public pronouncement on the subject in a ranting speech at the *Sportspalast* in Berlin. He told his cheering audience, 'In England people are very curious and keep asking, "Yes, but why doesn't he come?" We reply, "Calm yourselves. Calm yourselves. He is coming! *He is coming!*" '

Yet, despite this show of bombast, on 14 September Hitler prevaricated once again. Goering had told him of 'enormous successes' by the Luftwaffe, but the prerequisite of aerial supremacy was still not in place. Raeder quickly recommended an alternative date, 8 October. The Führer, though, compromised on 27 September, stating that he would issue the order to embark on 17 September.

Still bad weather continued to collude in making it difficult for Goering and Raeder to keep their plans on track – and both were clearly beginning to believe Operation Sea Lion might never take place, as the German historian Klaus A Maier has written:

Goering's remark on 16 September that *Seelöwe* must not disturb the operations of the Luftwaffe and his reference to 'subsequent attacks spread all over Britain' show that he, like Raeder, no longer expected the landing operation to be carried out. In view of the first dispersal order by the Wehrmacht High Command of

19 September for the *Seelöwe* transport fleet to avoid further losses as a result of British air attacks, and the instructions to halt further development of the transport ships, any serious preparations by the Luftwaffe for the invasion had become superfluous.

The last rites for Hitler's grand plan of invading England were not long in coming. On 2 October, the losses inflicted by the RAF air attacks on German planes and shipping caused the Führer to order that all measures in conjunction with Operation Sea Lion were to be 'largely dismantled'. The following month, on 21 November, he issued another directive – No. 18 – in which he stated that changes in the nation's economic situation 'might make it possible, or necessary, to revert to the plan in the Spring of 1941'.

Economic problems or not, Hitler now had his sights firmly set on crushing Russia as a result of his 'revelation' in July. The outline of this ill-fated campaign, codenamed 'Barbarossa', was announced in Directive No. 21 dated 18 December and its outcome in the snow-covered wastes of that forbidding country is now a matter of record.

In Britain, however, where nothing of Hitler's change of mind was known, the spectre of invasion would be a long time in disappearing. Churchill, in particular, would not let his guard drop for a moment and the following year warned that a new 'invasion season' could begin on 1 September, and he encouraged the local Invasion Committees to continue training exercises. The people of the east coast, in particular, needed no additional prompting, as the *Eastern Daily Press* reported on 8 October:

The greatest and most comprehensive manoeuvres ever held in this country in peace or war time have just been concluded and thousands of soldiers and armoured vehicles are now back in their war stations. For the purpose of this exercise, it was supposed that the Germans had forced a landing in East Anglia and were attacking in the direction of London.

In 1942, the reports of the German plight in Russia still did not completely ease the fears of invasion and action was taken after another terse note from Churchill to the members of his War Cabinet: 'A scheme must be prepared for the evacuation of civilians from the coastal areas from the Wash to the Isle of Wight and also of Nodal Points [regional control centres for communications, food, petrol and other essentials] like Colchester, Ipswich and Canterbury.'

Plans were also brought up to date for evacuation, operations against the enemy if he gained a foothold, and even the confinement of captured German soldiers in 'command cages' in Newmarket and Dunstable. Despite the fact that the consensus of opinion was that any Nazi invasion would land on the Kent coast, the East Anglian regional commissioner, Sir Will Spens, was not going to allow any complacency to creep into his area, and circulated a public warning:

> Do not persuade yourselves, and do not allow others to persuade you, that invasion is improbable. It is very much more probable than not, that at some point before the end of the war, Hitler will see fit to order invasion. When invasion does take place, it is practically certain that there will be a heavy attack in East Anglia.

In fact, rumours of German landings did still occur from time to time on the east coast. Bob Niblett of Halesworth near Southwold had an experience in 1943 that was almost a reprise of the landing by *Leutnant* Klug – but is without the same evidence to substantiate it. Niblett was involved in the erection and running of a radar station on the beach at Benacre near Kessingland. The station's main job was to provide details of all ship movements to the Naval Plotting Station at Yarmouth.

228

That summer, E-boats were still causing problems along the shore, as Niblett recalled in an interview with the *East Anglian Daily Times* in April 2003:

It appears that some cheeky E-boats had moved close to the shore. The shore batteries along the coast were unable to depress sufficiently to fire on these rapidly moving gunboats and, as it happened, our radar could not see them on the screen. The next morning I went down to the beach, gingerly stepping through the minefield, and found to my surprise some evidence that some Germans had landed and, as it were, left calling cards to show how cheeky they had been. It was mostly rubbish and food wrappings that were definitely German and they were well above the high-water mark, so they could not have been washed ashore. I wish I had picked it all up now, but you never think of such a thing at the time.

In the main, rumours of German incursions had their origin in the well-organised 'invasion exercises' staged in Norfolk and Suffolk in which some of the soldiers were dressed in captured Nazi uniforms to provide greater authenticity. In these manoeuvres, the army, the Home Guard, all branches of the Civil Defence, the police and various public services, including transport, communications and hospitals, combined to prevent the 'Germans' from seizing key installations. The operations were assessed by 'umpires', who would decide the probable consequences in terms of damage, the numbers of casualties and how many prisoners had been taken.

Soon, however, the tide of war in Europe began to shift the emphasis away from repelling an invasion of England to plans for invading Europe. The beaches, which had for years been considered possible landing spots, were now used by English troops preparing to return the threat to Hitler. Throughout the summer months the sands of Yarmouth, Lowestoft, Southwold and Harwich resounded to the noise of mock attacks, while the River Orwell and the estuaries of the Colne and the Blackwater were busy with well-manned flotillas of 'landing craft' under training. Unlike the German Sea Lion, of course, the Allies' counterblast, Overlord, which would open the 'Second Front', was destined for success.

The reasons for the German failure in the war are varied and have been widely discussed by a great many historians. One that is little mentioned is that witchcraft helped defeat the Nazis. This extraordinary claim was made by a former leader of Britain's witches, Gerald Brosseau Gardner, a one-time customs officer turned folklore expert, who had followers spread all the way from the Wash to the Kent Coast. According to Gardner's book, *Witchcraft Today* (1955), the covens of witches conducted a number of ceremonies around the coast, with extraordinary effect:

> Witches cast spells to stop Hitler landing after France fell. They met, raised the great cone of power and directed the thought at Hitler's brain: 'You cannot cross the sea.' 'You cannot cross the sea.' 'Not able to come.' 'Not able to come.' I am not saying that they stopped Hitler. All I say is that I saw a very interesting ceremony performed with the intention of putting a certain idea into his mind and this was repeated several times afterwards; and though all the invasion barges were ready, the fact was that Hitler never even tried to come. The witches told me that their great-grandfathers had tried to project the same idea into Napoleon Bonaparte's mind.

One less bizarre, but still very curious, footnote about the 'Invasion That Never Was' remains to be told. In 1994, Ulrike Jordan, a research student working at the Public Record Office in London, discovered a file of documents that revealed that several ministers in Churchill's cabinet had become concerned in 1941 that the Germans might try invading by a *tunnel* built between Cap Gris-Nez and the Kent coast.

The papers consist of a series of memos written in 1941–2, primarily between Lord Hankey, the chairman of a scientific committee advising the Chiefs of Staff, a scientist named R B Bourdillon, and one of the leading members of the Cabinet, R A 'Rab' Butler. The first of these documents, dated March 1941, is by Lord Hankey, who begins cautiously, 'I do not pretend to consider it more than a remote possibility, but a Channel Tunnel would be a very fine secret weapon for Hitler.' He then recommends that the Chiefs of Staff put the idea to various committees for a feasibility study.

Subsequent papers show that the idea was dismissed by the Royal Society; was considered very unlikely by the Institute of Civil Engineers – who believed such a project would take at least twelve years to complete; but given credence by Bourdillon, then working for the Medical Research Council. His report, prepared that autumn, makes fascinating reading – especially in the light of the successful building of the Channel Tunnel half a century later.

Bourdillon argues that such an idea is possible by using new rotary drilling technology. And, if a system of disposing of the extracted materials underwater could be devised, then the job could be done speedily and with less chance of detection. He estimates the tunnel could be built in about sixteen months and adds three points that he believes show that the idea is more than just Lord Hankey's pipe dream:

1. The suspiciously easy abandonment of the 1940 invasion plans. The Germans do not usually abandon major strategic objectives after one failure.

2. The statements recently made in Germany that when invasion comes it will be by a method that the English do not expect.

3. The insistence on engineering degrees for the higher ranks of the German army officers.

He also felt that the tunnel might already *be* in place – but would probably have more than one entrance. Indeed, it could have as many as twenty branches, all ready to open onto different parts of the coast between the Isle of Sheppey and Hastings. A vertical lift shaft would exit each of these branches, he thought, between 200 and 250 feet high. Bourdillon continued,

Each lift shaft would end in a short T-chamber cut out about 100 feet below the crest of a downland ridge. A series of short horizontal openings would lead towards the side of the ridge, but stop short of the surface until after dark on the first evening of invasion, when they would be blown open by powder charges.

The scientist had even gone to the trouble of calculating the potential size of the Germans' 'Channel Tunnel Invasion Army':

Under peacetime conditions each tube of the Anglo-French Tunnel that was proposed in 1930 was estimated to be capable of carrying 30,000 passengers and 30,000 tons of goods in 20 hours. Under wartime conditions, this rate could probably be increased for a limited period. With regard to the lift-shafts, I assume each to be capable of taking one heavy tank or 25 men with a transit time of two minutes, and loading and unloading time of two minutes each. This gives a six-minute cycle with a capacity for 500 lifts – if everything went without hitch – of 12,000 tanks a day or 300,000 men.

Far-fetched as this may all have seemed at the time, both Lord Hankey and Rab Butler agreed that some action must be taken. British Intelligence was asked to investigate and the

RAF given instructions to photograph the possible tunnel head at Sangatte – where, of course, the modern tunnel emerges. Neither group found any positive evidence.

Then, in May 1942, just to make quite sure German mining engineers were not busy burrowing away under the Channel, sound-monitoring devices were set up at Abbot's Cliff near Dover by a small group of scientists from the department of the director of torpedoes and mining. At the same time, some experiments were also carried out with digging equipment in an old tunnel shaft just below the cliffs – but everything remained still and quiet beneath the experts' feet.

If there *was* anything to be heard, it was nothing more than the distant echo of leaden German feet trudging away across the vastness of Russia, where another of Hitler's dreams of invasion was about to die.

Bibliography

Agar, Herbert, *Britain Alone: June 1940–June 1941* (Bodley Head, 1972).

Ansel, Walter, *Hitler Confronts England* (Duke University Press, 1960).

Banks, Donald, *Flame Over Britain* (Sampson Low, Marston & Co Ltd, 1946).

Bentley, James, *Gateway to France* (Viking, 1991).

Bonaparte, Marie, *Myths of War* (Imago Publishing Co Ltd, 1947).

Bowyer, Michael, *Action Stations* (Patrick Stephens, 1979).

Brophy, John, *Britain's Home Guard* (Harrap, 1945).

Brown, Louis, *A Radar History of World War II* (Institute of Physics, 1999).

Brown, R Douglas, *East Anglia at War 1939–1945* (Terence Dalton, 1981).

Buckley, Christopher, *The Commandos: Norway–Dieppe* (HMSO, 1951).

Calder, Angus, *The People's War: Britain 1939–1945* (Jonathan Cape, 1969).

Churchill, Winston, *The Gathering Storm* (Cassell, 1948).

Collier, Basil, *The Defence of the United Kingdom* (HMSO, 1960).

Collier, Richard, *Eagle Day: The Battle of Britain* (Dutton, 1966).

Cooper, Bryan, *The Battle of the Torpedo Boats* (Macdonald, 1970).

Cooper, Bryan, *The E-Boat Threat* (Macdonald & Jane's, 1976).

Cox, Richard, *Sea Lion* (Thornton Cox, 1974).

Cruikshank, C, *Deception in World War II* (Oxford University Press, 1980).

Fleming, Peter, *Invasion 1940* (Rupert Hart-Davis, 1957).

Glover, Michael, *Invasion Scare 1940* (Leo Cooper, 1999).

Graves, Charles, *The Home Guard of Britain* (Hutchinson, 1943).

Grinnel-Milne, Duncan, *The Silent Victory, September 1940* (Bodley Head, 1958).

Hayward, James, *The Bodies on the Beach* (CD41 Publishing, 2001).

Hayward, James, *Shingle Street* (CD41 Publishing, 2002).

Hichens, Lieutenant Commander Robert, *We Fought Them in Gunboats* (Michael Joseph, 1944).

Jarvis, Stan, *Smuggling in East Anglia* (Jarrold Publishing, 1987).

Johnson, Derek E, *East Anglia at War* (Jarrold Publishing, 1992).

Jones, R V, *Most Secret War* (Hamish Hamilton, 1978).

Jowett, Earl, *Some Were Spies* (Hodder & Stoughton, 1954).

Kieser, Egbert, *Hitler on the Doorstep: Operation 'Sea Lion': The German Plan to Invade Britain, 1940*, trans. Helmut Bögler (Arms & Armour, 1999); German edition *Unternehmen Seelöwe* (Bechtle Verlag, 1987).

Kinsey, Gordon, *Flight Over the Eastern Counties* (Terence Dalton, 1977).

Klee, Karl, *Das Unternehmen Seeloewe* (Musterschmidt, 1958).

Lampe, David, *The Last Ditch* (Cassell, 1968).

Longmate, Norman, *How We Lived Then* (Hutchinson, 1971).

Longmate, Norman, *If Britain Had Fallen* (Hutchinson, 1972).

Martiensson, Anthony, *Hitler and His Admirals* (Secker & Warburg, 1948).

Moen, Lars, *Under the Iron Heel* (Robert Hale Ltd, 1941).

Mosley, Leonard, *Backs to the Wall* (Weidenfeld & Nicolson, 1975).

O'Brien, Terence, *Civil Defence* (HMSO, 1955).

Parker, John, *Commandos* (Headline, 2000).

Pawle, Gerald, *The Secret War 1939–1945* (Companion Book Club, 1958).

Raeder, Erich, *Struggle For the Sea* (William Kimber, 1959).

Roskill, Captain S W, *The War at Sea 1939–1945* (HMSO, 1954).

Richmond, Admiral, *The Invasion of Britain* (Methuen, 1941).

Scott, Lieutenant Commander Peter, *The Battle of the Narrow Seas* (Country Life, 1945).

Shirer, William A, *Berlin Diary* (Hamish Hamilton, 1941).

Taylor, Telford, *The Breaking Wave* (Weidenfeld & Nicolson, 1967).

Turner, E S, *The Phoney War on the Home Front* (Michael Joseph, 1961).

Warlimont, Walter, *Inside Hitler's Headquarters 1939–1945* (Praeger, 1964).

Werner, Jack, *We Laughed at Boney* (W H Allen & Co, 1943).

Wheatley, Dennis, *Stranger Than Fiction* (Hutchinson, 1959).

Wheatley, Ronald, *Operation Sea Lion* (Oxford University Press, 1958).

White, John Baker, *The Big Lie* (Evans Brothers, 1956).

Whitehead, R A, *Garrett 200* (Transport Bookman Publications, 1978).

Acknowledgements

As with my previous books about the Second World War, I am grateful to a large number of people for their help in the writing of this volume. Some have asked not to be named, but I do wish to express my debt to three men who have sadly not lived to see its publication: Dennis Wheatley who first told me the story, Jeff Fisher who in part lived it, and W O G Lofts who provided the clues to help finally settle the argument more than sixty years later.

Tom Gondris was again a great help with translating German texts, and Henry Wills, Derek Johnson, Arthur Moore and Kenneth Walker provided invaluable information about the east coast of England during the war. R Douglas Brown was an excellent source of information about the military in East Anglia, as was James Hayward on the story of Shingle Street. I received a great deal of help from the staff of the Imperial War Museum, the National Archive, the British Museum, the British Newspaper Library and the London Library as well as the *Bundesarchiv – Militarchiv* in Freiburg, Germany.

I am also grateful to the following publications for permission to reprint quotes from their pages: *The Times, Daily Telegraph, Daily Mail, East Anglian Daily Times, Illustrated London News* and *Der Landser*. My thanks, finally, to my publisher, Jeremy Robson, and my editors, Jennifer Lansbury and Andrew Armitage, for all their help.

Index